To provide an assured income support to the small and marginal farmers, our Government is launching a historic programme, namely *Pradhan Mantri Kisan Samman Nidhi (PM-KISAN)*. Under this programme, vulnerable landholding farmer families, having cultivable land up to 2 hectares, will be provided direct income support at the rate of ₹ 6,000 per year. This income support will be transferred directly into the bank accounts of beneficiary farmers, in three equal instalments of ₹ 2,000 each. This programme will be funded by Government of India. Around 12 crore small and marginal farmer families are expected to benefit from this. The programme would be made effective from December 1, 2018 and the first instalment for the period up to March 31, 2019 would be paid during this year itself. This programme will entail an annual expenditure of ₹ 75,000 crore.

—Government of India, Ministry of Finance, Interim Budget 2019-20, *Budget Speech of the Minister of Finance*, February 1, 2019.

Agriculture and Economic Development in India

By

Md. Ejaz Anwer
Senior Research Associate,
Indian Council of Agricultural Research-National Institute of Agricultural Economics and Policy Research (ICAR-NIAP),
New Delhi

New Century Publications
New Delhi, India

NEW CENTURY PUBLICATIONS
4800 / 24, Bharat Ram Road,
Ansari Road, Daryaganj,
New Delhi - 110 002 (India)

Tel.: 011-2324 7798, 4358 7398, 4101 7798
E-mail: info@newcenturypublications.com
www.newcenturypublications.com

Editorial office:
LG – 7, Aakarshan Bhawan,
4754-57/23, Ansari Road, Daryaganj,
New Delhi – 110 002

Tel.: 011-4356 0919

First Published: **2019**

ISBN: **978-81-7708-480-1**

Published by New Century Publications and printed at Milan Enterprises, New Delhi.

Designs: Patch Creative Unit, New Delhi.

PRINTED IN INDIA

Dedicated to

My wife Dr. Shagufta Naaz

and

My daughter Naaira Naba

FOREWORD

The present book **Agriculture and Economic Development in India** is a felicitous book highlighting the importance of agricultural diversification and its share in area, production and yield among four major regions, namely western, northern, southern and eastern with special reference to one of the poorest regions viz. eastern region from 1990-91 to 2016-17 by taking various macro and micro economic parameters. It also talks about the future prospects of farm income, food security, and generating employment opportunities through agricultural diversification in favour of high value crops.

The share of agriculture has been continuously shrinking. It contributed only about 12.5 percent to India's total exports during 2015-16. Despite this, agriculture sector still occupies a key position as it provides employment to more than 50 percent of the total workforce and contributes around 17-18 percent to the country's GDP. But studies during the recent past reveal that India has been facing problems of low productivity, low profitability, and low employment in the agriculture sector. This is attributed to drastic fall in real investment in irrigation, poor water management, inadequate infrastructure, low quality of research and extension services, and lack of appropriate policy measures. In recent era, statistics have portrayed a distressing rate of incidents of farmers' suicides in India. This requires immediate attention to alleviate the distress in agriculture.

Given the importance of crop diversification, this book contains deep insights on the growth and pattern of diversification of agriculture, and discerned the issue related to diversification across the states and regions to suggest suitable policy options for further diversification towards the sustainability of agriculture, especially for the least developed region. The study discerns wide gap between area, production and yield of horticulture crops in different regions of India. For bridging these gaps, we need appropriate policies, technology, better institutional options besides adequate inputs and better management practices. However, in this area, region and states-wise studies are rarely seen, whereby this book meets the need of these shortcomings.

This book will be immense useful for researchers in the field of agricultural economics, rural development, geography, and economics. The book reveals the pull and push factors of agriculture diversification besides drawing inferences regarding infrastructure, and growth and pattern of agricultural diversification in India.

My best wishes to Dr. Md. Ejaz Anwer on this endeavour.

Dr. Shiv Kumar

Principal Scientist,

ICAR-National Institute of Agricultural Economics and Policy Research (ICAR-NIAP earlier NCAP)

D.P.S. Marg, Pusa, New Delhi – 110 012

About the Book

Agricultural sector occupies a key position in the Indian economy. Though agriculture has now shrunk as a proportion of gross domestic product (GDP) to around 13 percent, it is a vital sector and provider of livelihood for 2/3rd of India's working population.

Although Indian agriculture is way back compared to the levels in developed countries, some notable developments have occurred since Independence in 1947. Large areas which suffered from repeated failures of rainfall have received irrigational facilities and new crops have come to occupy a significant position in the country's production and trade. Problems of rural indebtedness and the exploitative practices of the village moneylenders are much less.

While there have been farmers-friendly efforts—such as those to promote institutional credit to rural areas, improved access to inputs, subsidies on fertilisers and electricity, minimum support prices etc.—but these have not been fully successful in protecting the interest of the farmers in general, and small/marginal farmers in particular. Marginal and small farmers have borne the brunt of the adverse circumstances in agriculture. The spate of suicides by farmers in many areas is the most disconcerting manifestation of this distress.

Accelerating the rate of growth of agricultural production must be seen as central to a more inclusive growth.

About the Author

Dr. Md. Ejaz Anwer is presently Senior Research Associate, Indian Council of Agricultural Research-National Institute of Agricultural Economics and Policy Research (ICAR-NIAP), New Delhi. He did his M.A. and Ph.D. in Economics from the Department of Economics, Aligarh Muslim University (AMU), Aligarh, Uttar Pradesh. He is a distinguished life member of the Indian Economic Association (IEA), and Indian Political Economy Association (IPEA).

Previously, he worked in the capacity of research associate in the Department of Humanities and Social Sciences, IIT-Roorkee, Uttarakhand and ICAR-NIAP on various Government-sponsored projects under the supervision of eminent agriculture professionals as well as economists of India. He also worked as an Assistant Professor and Convener of Training and Placement Cell in Techwords Engineering and Management Institute, Roorkee, Uttarakhand.

Dr. Ejaz is a regular participant in various national seminars and workshops. He has published several research papers and articles in journals of international and national repute. He also co-authored the technical report on Dubaliya (Jharkhand)—A Village Profile under ICAR-ICRISAT collaborating project sponsored by Bill and Melinda Gates Foundation. His current areas of research interest include food security, market intelligence, farm income and issues related to diversification of agriculture in favour of horticulture and livestock

Contents

Preface

While agriculture no longer dominates the Indian economy in terms of national output, it is still the most important in terms of employment. In other words, declining share of income has not been accompanied by an equivalent decline in employment. It is a classic case of lop-sided structural transformation.

Agricultural sector occupies a key position in the Indian economy. It provides employment to about 65 percent of the working population of India. Agriculture being a State subject, the bulk of public investment in agriculture takes place at the level of States and the Central Government supports the States as a catalyst.

Although Indian agriculture is way back compared to the levels in developed countries, some notable developments have occurred since Independence in 1947. Large areas which suffered from repeated failures of rainfall have received irrigation, new crops have come to occupy a significant position in the country's production and trade, agricultural and the industrial economies now exert a powerful influence on one another, problems of rural indebtedness and the exploitative practices of the village moneylenders are much less, and finally there is visible in the countryside an awakening and a desire for better standard of living.

One of the main reasons for the low levels of yields in Indian agriculture has been the unsatisfactory spread of new technological practices, including the adoption of high yielding varieties (HYVs) of seeds and usage of fertilisers and pesticides, inadequate spread of farm management techniques and other practices such as soil conservation and crop rotation. The adoption of new technology, mainly the HYV seeds requires intensive use of fertilisers and pesticides under adequate and assured water supply.

The consumption of fertilizers has been steadily increasing over the years. A great deal of variability is observed in fertilizer consumption between the States. Amongst States in the plains, per hectare consumption is highest in Punjab, Haryana, Andhra Pradesh and Tamil Nadu. It is the lowest in Madhya Pradesh and Rajasthan. *Kharif* crops account for nearly one-third of the total fertilizer consumption, whereas the *rabi* crops accounted for a much larger share. This has now changed. Consumption is more evenly spread between the two sowing seasons, reflecting perhaps more assured water availability in *kharif* season at all-India level.

Rural indebtedness is noted as a major reason for the spurt in farmer suicides during recent times across a number of states. In most, if not all, such cases, the economic status of the suicide victim was very poor, being small and marginal farmers. After the Green Revolution, agricultural activities have become cash-based individual enterprises requiring high investment in modern inputs and wage labour. This is evident from the list of states with high incidence of farmer suicides, which are not necessarily backward or predominantly agrarian or with low income. Increased liberalization and globalisation have in fact led to a shift in cropping pattern from staple crops to cash crops like oilseeds and cotton, requiring high investment in modern inputs and wage labour, and increasing credit needs but when the prices decline farmers have no means to supplement their incomes.

Marketing is the last link in the chain of production process. An efficient marketing system which ensures reasonable return to the producers is essential to induce them to produce more. Disposal of the produce after harvest and the return obtained have a significant effect on production and on the welfare of the cultivator.

Sale of agricultural produce involves a number of functions such as assembling, storing, grading, standardising, transporting and financing the produce and negotiating sale. Some of these operations may be performed by the farmer, but storage and sale of a commodity and finding finance for purchase, call for specialised knowledge and adequate resources which the individual cultivator does not possess.

In order to facilitate wider market access to farm produce and better price discovery through value addition, the scheme is additionally disseminating information on market requirements in terms of quality, packing, standards, sanitary and phyto-sanitary conditions etc.

Agricultural research is of a continuing nature. New knowledge has to be gained, and fresh problems tackled. The role of universities in promoting agricultural research is a question which needs attention. Although universities are eminently suited for such research, especially of the more fundamental type, they have not taken it up to any significant extent in the past, owing perhaps to lack of funds and other causes. Limitations in the way of the universities to take an appropriate part in agricultural research should be removed and the universities encouraged to make their contribution to research. This will benefit the universities also by bringing their scientific staffs into direct contact with the real problems which are in urgent need of solution for the betterment of the vast majority of rural people.

While there have been efforts—such as those to promote institutional credit to rural areas, improved access to inputs, subsidies on fertilisers and electricity, minimum support price etc.—these have not been fully successful in protecting the interest of the farmers in general, and small/marginal farmers in particular. Small/marginal farmers have inadequate access to: (a) information, (b) agencies promoting technological change, (c) co-operative networks and related organisations, and (d) plethora of governmental interventions. This is significant since, in any case, these farmers are less well placed to take advantage of the markets.

Against the backdrop of the burgeoning demand of population for food grains, degrading natural resource base, emerging concerns of climate change and other challenges, the Government has focused on mobilizing higher investment in agriculture, bridging yield gaps that exist across the states/regions, timely and adequate supply of quality inputs, and providing adequate support services to the farmers to make agriculture a remunerative vocation on a sustainable basis. Increasing agricultural production with limited natural resources in a sustainable manner for ensuring food and nutritional security and providing income security to farmers are the major challenges before the Government.

Accelerating the rate of growth of agricultural production must be seen as central to a more inclusive growth.

Acknowledgments

I take this opportunity to express my gratitude and indebtedness to a host of scholars who each contributed in his/her own way at various stages of the completion of this book.

I express my sincere thanks to my esteemed mentors Dr. Ramesh Chand and Dr. P.S. Birthal, formerly Director, ICAR-NIAP, New Delhi for their incessant encouragement and inspiration.

This endeavour would have remained incomplete without the untiring support from the following scholars: Dr. Raka Saxena, Principal Scientist (PS), ICAR-NIAP, New Delhi; Dr. Anjani Kumar (IFPRI, Delhi), Dr. Shiv Kumar and Dr. Sant Kumar Pandey (PS, ICAR-NIAP), Dr. Rajesh Kumar Rana (PS, ICAR-ATARI, Ludhiana), Dr. Bimal K. Sahoo, Assistant Professor, Department of HSS, IIT-Kharagpur, Dr. Mohd. Rais (PS, CSIR-NISTADS), Dr. P. Shinoj (ICAR-CMFRI), Dr. M.A. Salam, and Dr. S.M. Jawed Akhtar, Department of Economics, AMU, Aligarh.

I express my devotion to my wife Dr. Shagufta Naaz whose immense efforts, valuable sacrifices, care and loving nature gave me strength to bring out this book.

Finally, I am grateful to Mr. Sandeep Sury, Chief Executive, New Century Publications, New Delhi, for his co-operation and deep concern that made the publication of this work possible.

Needless to mention, any errors or omissions are the responsibility of the author.

New Delhi **Md. Ejaz Anwer**

1

Importance and Performance of Agriculture in India

1.1 Introduction

Agriculture has been a lifeline of the rural economy in India. About 58 percent of the rural households in the country rely on agriculture for their principal source of livelihood (IBEF, 2016). [1] It endows with the employment to the workforce, wage goods to the workers, supply of raw materials to the processing industries, and surplus produce to the market. But, after the economic reforms period, particularly since 1995-96, this sector has been largely neglected in terms of policy support by the Government of India. Thus, as a consequence, the agriculture sector of India is inflicted with plethora of problems such as tiny land holdings, poor rural infrastructure, low per capita income, and rising input costs i.e., prices of diesel, fertilizers, power, seeds, wages, agricultural machineries, and other farms inputs which are major hindrances in the development of this sector.

Due to poor agricultural policy, inadequate credit and market access, high production cost, low productivity, depressing prices of agricultural commodities and heavy debt burden have not only made agriculture an unprofitable venture but has also enhanced the distress amongst the farmers. The continuous rising population has adversely affected the average size of land holdings in states vis-à-vis India. The decrease in the net sown area (NSA) and productivity was basically credited to increasing conversion of agricultural land for non-agriculture (industry, houses, services etc.) use that created a major issue related to food security in the country.

Due to crop failures and heavy debt burden, thousands of

farmers have committed suicides in several parts of the country. This is a big challenge before the policy makers and hence they are in a fix over how to increase agriculture productivity in the country under such pathetic circumstances. It is because of the continuous fall in the share of agriculture towards GDP, the vulnerability of Indian agriculture and productivity has severely declined and the cost of production has recorded enormous rise.

This situation calls for substitute/alternative opportunities in the form of agricultural diversification in the country and it has come out as an imperative tool to alleviate farmers' distress. To achieve the objectives of agricultural growth, augmentation in farm income, employment generation opportunities, natural resources' sustainability, poverty alleviation, export promotion, improving food security, and improving environmentally sustainable farming systems through conservation and enhancement of natural resources and conservation of precious soil and water resources is desired (Jha, 1996; [2] Ramesh Chand, 1996; [3] and Joshi et al., 2002). [4]

Diversification of agriculture includes changes in crop-mix, enterprises-mix and activity-mix at the household level. It also considers of a shift of resources from monoculture to a large mix of crops and livestock. Hence, as per the previous studies, agriculture diversification is the only option which acts as a therapy for all the economic maladies among the regions particularly one of the most backward regions such as the eastern region of India. In order to get maximum economic benefits, diversification of agriculture should be in favour of horticulture and livestock which have higher net return per hectare of land in comparison to foodgrains, i.e. cereals and coarse cereals etc.

As per the Agriculture Census, 2010-11, out of the total number of operational holdings, around 85 percent belonged to small and marginal farmers. The diversification in favour of horticulture is likely to contribute more to the well-being of the small and marginal farmers as it entails more labour force and would generate employment opportunities and higher farm incomes than cereals (Joshi et al., 2006). [5]

The dietary pattern of the people in India remarkably shifted from cereals, grams, and cereal substitutes towards vegetables, fruits, milk, edible oils, eggs, meat and fish in both rural and urban areas during the period 1993-94 to 2011-12. The share of expenditure in total food consumption also remarkably declined in both rural and urban areas respectively from 63.2 percent and 54.7 percent during 1993-94 to 48.6 percent and 38.5 percent during 2011-12. In contrast, the share of total non-food grains significantly increased in both rural and urban areas i.e., from 36.8 percent and 45.3 percent in 1993-94 to 51.4 percent and 61.5 percent in 2011-12, respectively (GoI, 2014).

The continuous increase in the demand for non-food grains resulted from the rapid increase in the level of per capita income and fast growing urban population. Hence, to meet the ever increasing demand for high valued crops, diversification in favour of fruits, vegetables etc., is needed at a much faster rate of growth than that of the existing one. The existing rate of growth in the diversification of agriculture (in terms of Simpson Diversification Index) in all the regions is negligible, particularly in eastern and northern region that accounted for negative growth rates during both the period 1990-91 to 1999-00 and 2000-01 to 2013-14.

It is a matter of great concern before the country that the sluggish growth of this sector would have an adverse impact on the supply side which would further lead to hike in the general price level of commodities in the market. Thus, it may be concluded that the performance of agricultural diversification has been sluggish. For bridging the gap between the demand for and supply of fruits and vegetables, spices and other high valued crops, more area is needed to be brought under the cultivation of these crops.

It is also evident from the past studies that higher the growth rate of area under fruits cultivation higher is the returns. This however is more suitable for the big farmers since it entails more capital with a long gestation period, while the cultivation of vegetables including spices generate higher returns with a relatively lesser gestation period entailing more labour and lesser capital which suit the resource endowments of small and marginal farmers in all the regions of India particularly in the eastern states. Thus, we can say that the diversification of agriculture in favour of vegetables and fruits in the eastern region vis-à-vis eastern states is worse since the region is mostly dominated by low value subsistence farming.

1.2 Nature and Importance of Agriculture

Agriculture sector still holds the key position and undeniably provides the largest livelihood source in India. It contributes a major role in the process of growth and development of a predominantly agricultural and over-populated country like India. But, it is evident from the study done by Chand and Parappurathu (2012) [6] after the economic reforms (1990-91) that there were two major structural breaks observed in Indian agriculture: the first was during 1995-96 and second was during the year 2004-05. As per the evidence, after the year 2004-05, agriculture's contribution to GDP of India has been going through a recovery period and in fact has accelerated its growth (Chand, 2014). [7] Despite this recovery period, the growth in agriculture sector is left as a subject of concern as it still engages about 48.9 percent of the workforce in India (The Economic Times, February 28, 2015; GOI, 2016). [8]

In spite of this, due to reasons like, "rise in input cost and the instability in the market due to rising global integration" (Singh, 2007), [9] low returns, poor agricultural infrastructure and price volatility has led to agrarian distress. Consequently, around 22 percent of the Indian farmers are not inclined towards farming (CSDS and Lokniti, 2014). [10] In addition to this, more than 61 percent of people in India prefer to leave farming (28.5 percent absolutely), if they get an employment opportunity for income and livelihood in a city (Ibid). Therefore, enhancing agricultural productivity and sustaining the livelihood of poor and making agriculture an attractive venture are the important challenges before the Indian economy.

Besides, being a highly rural populated country, agricultural sector occupies a key position in the Indian economy. It includes crops and animal husbandry, fisheries, forestry and agro-processing which provide underpinnings for our food and livelihood security. The agriculture sector (including allied activities) in India accounted for 13.94 percent of the GDP (at 2004-05 constant prices) in 2013-14 (GoI, 2014), [11] in comparison to 29.53 percent in 1990-91. It contributed approximately 14.2 percent to India's total exports during 2013-14.

Notwithstanding the fact that the share of agriculture's gross value added (GVA) at new price base (constant at 2011-12 price) has fallen rapidly from 18.5 percent in 2011-12 to 15.4 percent in 2015-16 (GoI, 2017), [12] its role still remains critical as it provides employment to about 48.9 percent of the total workforce in the country (FICCI, 2015; ILO, 2016). [13] [14] Consequently, the percentage of main workers to total workers has declined from 77.8 percent to 75.2 percent. However, in rural areas, it has declined from 73.9 percent to 70.5 percent during the two population censuses viz., 2001 and 2011, respectively.

Out of these, the percentage of main workers among males to the total workers also reported a decline from 87.3 percent in 2001 to 82.3 percent in 2011.

The First Five Year Plan (1951-56) accorded the highest priority to agriculture sector to tide over food scarcity, a problem created by the partition of the country. Agriculture has occupied an important place in every successive Plan. Agricultural products such as cereals (mainly rice), tea, coffee, cashew, spices, and tobacco are important items of India's exports and, hence, potential sources of foreign exchange earnings. Agriculture is also the source of raw material for agro-based industries, including textiles, cigarettes, jute, sugar, paper, processed foodstuffs, and vanaspati.

Moreover, agriculture sector provides market for capital goods (tractors, pump sets and other agricultural machinery), inputs (fertilizers, high yield Varieties (HYVs) seeds, insecticides), and light consumer goods. The nation has deployed huge resources for the development of agriculture under various plans. The development of agricultural sector promotes to a large extent core industries such as power, petroleum, fertilizers and machine tools (Ahuja, 2006). [15]

Agriculture sector plays a strategic role in overall socio-economic development of the country which provides the basic ingredients to mankind and raw materials to industries. Thus, because of the vital roles, agriculture sector occupies an unbeatable place in a developing economy like India. According to Kuznets, the contributions made by agriculture to economic growth are classified under four categories which are as follows:

- **Product Contribution**: Supplying foodstuffs and raw materials to the expanding sectors of the economy.
- **Market Contribution**: Providing an investible surplus of savings and taxes to support investment in other expanding sectors of the economy, i.e., provision of surplus, creation of infrastructure and shift of manpower.
- **Factor Contribution**: Selling for cash a 'marketable surplus' that raises the demand of the rural population for products of other expanding sectors, i.e., create effective demand, contribution to national income, relief from shortage of capital.
- **Foreign Exchange Contribution**: Relaxing the foreign exchange constraint by earning foreign exchange through exports or by saving foreign exchange through import substitution.

As per the above facts, agriculture is also the source of raw material for agro-based industries, including flour mills, rice shellers, oil and pulses (*dal*) mills, bread, chips, biscuits, meat, milk products, sugar factories, jute and textile mills, wineries, processed food stuff, vanaspati and numerous other industries that are directly or indirectly based on this sector. Paucity of agricultural goods has an adverse impact on the industrial production and a consequent increase in general price level. It obstructs the overall growth of the economy. Agricultural innovation is essential for the improvement of sectoral growth, price stability, and supply of raw materials for agro-based industries in the economy.

The advancement of agriculture sector will create surplus agricultural products, such as cereals (mainly rice), tea, coffee, spices, tobacco, cashew, fruits and vegetables which can prove to be important export items for India that will lead to a rise in foreign exchange earnings which is desirable because of the strain in foreign exchange situation considered necessary for financing imports of basic capital goods. Moreover, the agriculture sector absorbs a large number of people, about 49 percent of people were engaged in this sector during 2011-12 which has continuously declined from 263 million (58 percent) in 2005-06 to 228 million (49 percent) in 2011-12 (FICCI, 2015). Due to the continuous rise in population, emphasis should be given on the progression of agriculture sector. Agriculture prosperity will minimize the burden of the country, which is facing shortage of foreign capital. Agricultural growth benefits the poor in rural areas and could well help in reducing the income disparity in the rural economy.

1.3 Performance of Agriculture

Initiated in 1991, economic reforms in India have put the Indian economy on a higher growth trajectory. Annual growth rate in gross domestic product has accelerated from below 5.7 percent during the Ninth Five Year Plan to 8 percent in Eleventh Five Year Plan. The approach paper to Eleventh Five Year Plan found that 8.5 percent growth in GDP will be feasible during the next five years. It now seems more challenging than growth in total GDP which is the sectoral composition of growth, and related to the well-being of a very large segment of population. Since, agriculture is the main source of livelihood for a large section of the population it plays a significant role in the growth composition of the GDP.

Further, the country has been targeting more than 4 percent growth rate in Indian agriculture for Eleventh Five Year Plan, and it has also been kept for the Twelfth Five Year Plan (Chand, 2014; GoI, 2016). Agriculture growth remains key priority for the country, but the actual growth rate has turned out to be even less than this target, i.e. 3.7 percent only (Table 1.1). Against the background of the overall impressive growth rate, the sluggish performance of agriculture has led to serious problems in the economy.

Table 1.1: Plan-wise Growth (Percent) Trend of Total vis-à-vis Agriculture and Allied Sectors to GDP of India @ 2004-05 Prices

Plan	Share of Agriculture	Growth Rate (percent)	
		Agriculture and Allied Sectors	Total Economy
9th Five Year Plan (1997-02)	23.4	2.5	5.7
10th Five Year Plan (2002-07)	19.0	2.4	7.6
11th Five Year Plan (2007-12)	15.2	3.7	8.0

Source: Planning Commission of India, Government of India.

Firstly, it is causing wide disparities between income in agriculture and non-agriculture sectors. The sluggish growth of agriculture would not have caused an increase in disparities, if there was a commensurate decline in population dependent on agriculture. But this is not happening and the population dependent on agriculture is increasing. Secondly, during 2011-12, as about 49 percent of the workforce in the country relies on agriculture for income and livelihood, erratic rainfall, unfavourable weather conditions, price and public policies regarding agriculture have put them in distress. As a result, there has been a net reduction of 30.57 million of workforce from the agricultural sector during 2004-05 and 2011-12 (FICCI, 2015); and recently, there have been a spate of farmer suicides across the states of India.

In order to know the agrarian situation in India, firstly, we have to study the topographical as well as the geographical condition of India. In relation to this, it has been classified into four major zones, namely Northern, Eastern, Western and Southern Zone which are characterized by diversity of climatic, soil and topographical conditions, infrastructure, adequate water resources and fertile soil allowing for cultivation of all varieties of crops (Sidhu, 2008; [16] Singh, 2008). [17] All the states within a region to a large extent are homogeneous in their agro-climatic conditions and crop composition (Birthal et al., 2013). [18] The northern region comprises of states like Haryana, Himachal Pradesh, Jammu and Kashmir, Punjab, Uttar Pradesh, and Uttarakhand; the eastern region includes Assam, Bihar, Jharkhand, Odisha, and West Bengal; the southern region comprises of Andhra Pradesh, Telangana, Karnataka, Kerala, and Tamil Nadu; and the western region consists of Chhattisgarh, Gujarat, Madhya Pradesh, Maharashtra, and Rajasthan.

Further, the northern zone has alluvial soils and a semi-arid to humid climate. Agriculture in this region during 2015-16 contributed about 17.3 percent of the total GVA. The western region is characterized by highly diversified crops towards agriculture and a high urbanization with less dependence on agriculture due to low population density. Agriculture in this region contributed only about 11.2 percent of the total GDP during 2015-16. Thirdly, the southern region is characterized by a low population density, high income level, highly urbanized and developed with homogeneity in the rainfall throughout the region.

Lastly, the eastern region has all the varieties of soil such as alluvial, laterite, and rocky etc. which are found in most of the states in this region. Thus, nature has provided this region with ample opportunities for production of all possible varieties of agricultural crops. There is no dearth of rainfall and bright sunshine in this region. In spite of this, the eastern region is still considered as agriculturally as well as economically, a backward region in India. In most of the states of this region, the dominant crops are cereals, especially, rice (paddy), which is a major cereal food crop of the region. Agriculture sector in this region contributed only about 15.5 percent of GDP during 2015-16.

In the eastern region, natural endowments are favourable for growing all varieties of crops and have enormous potential for agrarian transformation and crop diversification from cereals to non-cereal, foodgrains to non-foodgrains and commercial crops, traditional to horticulture crops like fruits, vegetables and flowers and agriculture to allied activities like animal husbandry and fisheries etc. In spite of this, poverty and unemployment (both open and disguised) as well as tiny land holdings in rural areas in this region are the major consequences of low agricultural production and productivity. Additionally, the predominance of traditional methods of farming used as means for the subsistence by the poor farmers is another factor.

In view of large scale unemployment in rural areas and low labour absorption capacity in the traditional agricultural sector, it has been pointed out by a number of researchers that the rural non-farm sector can absorb a considerable section of the rural labour force (Unni, 1991; [19] Vidyanathan, 1986; [20] Dev, 1990). [21] Even though a number of scholarly studies are available on farm diversification; the issues related to and prospects of agricultural diversification in favour of HVCs i.e., horticulture (fruits, vegetables and flowers etc.) in eastern states particularly Bihar, Assam, West Bengal and Odisha have rarely been discussed. Few studies are also available for north-western states, which address the problems related with crop diversification (Singh and Sidhu, 2004; [22] Singh, 2004; [23] Singh and Singh, 2002; [24] Sidhu, 2002, [25] Jha et al., 2009). [26]

Moreover, it is evident from the past studies that the sluggishness in agriculture in eastern region has taken place after the reforms period. The growth of agriculture in the eastern region has been slower than in rest of the Indian states as well as the country as a whole (GoI, 2001). [27] It is also illustrated by backwardness, in terms of low input use etc., (Bhalla and Singh, 2010). [28] Consequently, deceleration in agricultural growth in eastern states has led to an increase in poverty, unemployment and distress among the rural households.

As a result, only about 67-69 percent of the farmers in north-east India are inclined to farming (CSDS, 2014) as they have no other option than farming. Studies also point out that in terms of development indicators (i.e., literacy, per capita income, poverty and health and sanitation etc.), eastern region has also been treated as the least developed and most backward region in the country. For eliminating these economic constraints and making breakthrough in the development process, issues specific to the region in agriculture and allied sectors need to be addressed.

However, the eastern region holds enormous potential for development of agriculture and allied activities. The substantial gains may accumulate from the increasing demand for horticultural commodities in developed markets. Besides, the wide international border of Nepal, Bangladesh and Bhutan in the north-east regions may offer possible opportunities for cross-boundary trade and exports. The special thrust on growing fruits and vegetables in eastern region can be supportive since it has become a foremost centre for production of varieties of fruits, vegetables and flowers.

On the other hand, through agricultural diversification within crop and livestock sub-sectors, the eastern region may provide not only manifold livelihood opportunities, such as augmentation of farm incomes and employment but also reinforce to achieve all the essential linkages like agriculture credit, road and transportation, market, advancement of farm technologies, inputs etc. 'Tenth Five Year Plan's Working Group, therefore, strongly felt that the eastern and north-eastern regions should focus on agriculture and its allied sectors taking the centre-stage of developmental planning, and the welfare and well-being of the farmers lying at the core of strategies and programmes' (GoI, 2001).

In addition to this, various past studies also suggested that agricultural diversification augments farm income and generate employment opportunities, enhance food security, check soil degradation, avoid risk and uncertainty, and increase exports and overall agricultural development (Barghouti, Kane, Sorby and Ali, 2004; [29] Joshi, et al. 2004; [30] Weinberger, K. and Lumpkin, A.T., 2007; Birthal, Joshi, Roy and Thorat, 2013; [31] Raju and Pandey, 2008; [32] Rao et al., 2006, [33] Chand, 1999, [34] Acharya et al., 2011). [35]

Endnotes

1. Indian Brand Equity Foundation (IBEF) (2016), "Indian Agriculture Industry Analysis", January, available at: http://www.ibef.org/industry/agriculture-presentation.
2. Jha, D. (1996), "Diversification of Agriculture and Food Security in the Context of New Economic Policy", *Indian Journal of Agricultural Economics*, 51 (4), pp. 829-832.
3. Chand, Ramesh (1996), "Diversification through High-Value Crops in Western Himalayan Region: Evidence from Himachal Pradesh", *Indian Journal of Agriculture Economics*, 41(4), pp. 652-663.
4. Joshi, P.K., Ashok Gulati, P.S. Birthal and L. Tewari (2002), "Agricultural Diversification in South Asia", paper presented in a workshop on *Agricultural Diversification in South Asia,* November 21-23, Paro, Bhutan.
5. Joshi, P.K., Laxmi Tewari and P.S. Birthal (2006), "Diversification and Its Impact on Smallholders: Evidence from a Study on Vegetable Production", *Agricultural Economics Research Review,* Vol. 19, No. 2, pp. 219-236.
6. Chand, Ramesh and Parappurathu Shinoj (2012), "Temporal and Spatial Variations in Agricultural Growth and Its Determinants", *Economic and Political Weekly,* Supplement Vol. XLVII, Nos. 26 and 27.
7. Chand, Ramesh (2014), "From Slowdown to Fast Track: Indian Agriculture since 1995," Working Paper 01/2014, ICAR-National Institute (earlier Centre) of Agricultural Economics and Policy Research, New Delhi.

8. Government of India (2016), "Economic Survey, 2016", Ministry of Finance, New Delhi, February.
9. Singh, S.P. (2007), "Corporatization of Agriculture", Alternative Economic Survey, 2006-07, Pampering Corporates Pauperizing Masses, Daanish Books, New Delhi.
10. CSDS (2014), "State of the Indian Farmers Study", A Survey Conducted together with Lokniti and Centre for the Study of Developing Societies (CSDS), December 2013 to January 2014. Report released on March 11, 2014.
11. Government of India (2014), "Economic Survey, 2013-14", key highlights, KPMG, India.
12. Government of India, (2017), "National Accounts Statistics", Ministry of Statistics and Programme Implementation, New Delhi.
13. FICCI (2015), "Labour In Indian Agriculture: A Growing Challenge," available at: http://ficci.in/spdocument/20550/FICCI-agri-Report percent2009-03-2015.pdf.
14. International Labour Organization (2016), "Indian Labour Market Update", ILO Country Office for India, July.
15. Ahuja, Astha (2006), "Agriculture and Rural Development in India: Post Liberalization Initiatives", New Century Publications, New Delhi, p. 6.
16. Sidhu, M.S. (2008), "Diversification of Agriculture in East India-Some Issues", in Thakur, Anil Kumar and K.B. Padmadeo (eds.) 'Growth and Diversification of Agriculture", Deep and Deep Publications, New Delhi, p. 4.
17. Singh, Bikrama (2008), "Agricultural Diversification: A Key to the Development of Agri-Business in East India", in Thakur, Anil Kumar and K.B. Padmadeo (eds.), 'Growth and Diversification of Agriculture', Deep and Deep Publications, New Delhi, p. 357.
18. Birthal P.S., P.K. Joshi, Digvijay S. Negi and Shaily Agarwal (2013), "Changing Sources of Growth in Indian Agriculture: Implications for Regional Priorities for Accelerating Agricultural Growth", IFPRI discussion paper, December.
19. Unnijeemol, K. (1991), "Regional Variation in Rural Non-Agricultural Employment: An Explanatory Analysis", *Economic and Political Weekly*, January 19, Vol. 26, No. 3, pp. 109-122.
20. Vidyanathan, A. (1986), "Labour Use in Rural India: A Case Study of Spatial and Temporal Variation", *Economic and Political*

Weekly, Vol. 21, No. 52, December, pp. A130-A146.

21. Dev, Mahendra, S. (1990), "Non-Agricultural Employment in Rural India: Evidence at Disaggregate Level", *Economic and Political Weekly,* Vol. 25, No. 28, July, pp. 1526-1536.
22. Singh, Joginder and R.S. Sidhu (2004), "Factor in Declining Crop Diversification: Case Study of Punjab", *Economic and Political Weekly*, Vol. 39, No. 52, December, pp. 5607-5610.
23. Singh, Sukhpal (2004), "Crisis and Diversification in Punjab Agriculture: Role of State and Agribusiness", *Economic and Political Weekly*, Vol. 39, No. 52, December 25, pp. 5583-5590.
24. Singh, L. and S. Singh (2002), "Deceleration in Economic Growth in Punjab: Evidence, Explanation and a Way Out", *Economic and Political Weekly*, Vol. 37, No. 6, February 9, pp. 579-586.
25. Sidhu, H.S. (2002), "Crisis in Agrarian Economy in Punjab: Some Urgent Steps", *Economic and Political Weekly*, Vol. 37, No. 30, July 27, pp. 3132-3138.
26. Jha, Brajesh, Amarnath Tripathi and Biswajit Mohanty (2009), "Drivers of Agricultural Diversification in India, Haryana and the Greenbelt Farms of India", Working Paper Series No. E/303/2009, Institute of Economic Growth, University of Delhi, Delhi.
27. Government of India (2001), "Report of the Working Group on Agricultural Development in Eastern and North-Eastern India for the Formulation of the Tenth Five Year Plan", Government of India Planning Commission, August.
28. Bhalla, G.S. and Gurmail Singh (2009), "Economic Liberalization and Indian Agriculture: A State-wise Analysis", *Economic and Political Weekly*, Vol. 44, No. 52, December 26, 2009-January 1, 2010, pp. 34-44.
29. Barghouti, S., Samuel Kane, Kristina Sorby and Mubarik Ali (2004), "Agricultural Diversification for Poor: Guidelines for Practitioners", *Agriculture and Rural Development,* Discussion Paper 1, The World Bank. Washington, D.C.
30. Joshi, P.K., A. Gulati, P.S. Birthal and L. Tewari (2004), "Diversification of Agriculture in South Asia", *Economic and Political Weekly*, Vol. 39(24), pp. 2457-2468.
31. Birthal, Pratap Singh., Pramod Kumar Joshi, Devesh Roy and Amit Thorat (2013), "Diversification in Indian Agriculture toward High-Value Crops: The Role of Small Farmers", *Canadian Journal of Agricultural Economics/Revue canadienne d'agroeconomie*, Canadian Agricultural Economics Society/Societe canadienne

d'agroeconomie," Vol. 61(1), pp. 61-91.

32. Raju, S.S. and L.M. Pandey (2008), "Progress and Potential of Horticulture in India", *Indian Journal of Agriculture Economics*, 63(3), pp. 299-309.
33. Rao, P. Parthasarathy., P.S. Birthal and P.K. Joshi (2006), "Diversification towards High Value Agriculture Role of Urbanization and Infrastructure", *Economic and Political Weekly*, June 30.
34. Chand, Ramesh (1999), "Agriculture Diversification in India", Mittal Publications, New Delhi.
35. Acharya, Saraswati Poudel, H. Basavaraja, L.B. Kunnal, S.B. Mahajanashetti and A.R.S. Bhat (2011), "Crop Diversification in Karnataka: An Economic Analysis", *Agricultural Economics Research Review*, 24, pp. 351-357.

2

Indian Agriculture: Reviews

Before embarking on the study of any area of interest, it is essential to look into the pertinent works previously done on it. It gives a fabulous insight about the topic and provides a way to mend away the lacunae left in the process of exploration of the research study. It also helps in finding out the new horizons in the field of research. Therefore, this section is devoted to the review of various literatures available on different aspects of growth and diversification of agriculture in India.

Saini *et al.* (1996) [1] in their study entitled, "Impact of Diversification on Small Farms Economy in Kangra District of Himachal Pradesh", observed that the diversification of arable farming system with commercial enterprises such as high yielding milk animals, poultry birds, bee-keeping, floriculture etc. resulted in a marked increase in farm income from 6 percent to 138 percent. Since, capital and credit requirements have shown an increasing trend with the extent of diversification, therefore, adequate facilities should be made available by the financial institutions in order to diversify the existing farming system with most systematically remunerative and technically feasible enterprises.

Shah, Anita (1997) [2] in her paper, "Food Security and Access to Natural Resources: A Review of Recent Trends", examined the trends in the production of foodgrains in the country. She reached at the conclusion that the yield-based growth in food production has taken place in most of the states including dry land regions and that diversification is a larger process that had already set in before the liberalization. She also opined that shift from oilseeds to foodgrains production is essential for economic sustainability of dry land farming. She observed that although area under foodgrains crops has reduced marginally during the post-reforms period, the pattern is not uniform across crops and regions. The total production and per capita availability of foodgrains has continued to increase or fluctuate around the level achieved during the period immediately before the reforms. The availability of coarse grains, however, had declined marginally. The main source of growth in production has been the productivity of land; yield of all crops has increased during the post-reforms period.

Shiyani and Pandya (1998) [3] examined the levels of crop diversification in different agro-climatic zones over a period of time. The study observed that the farmers have shifted their cropping pattern from subsistence crops to commercial crops. On an average, relatively higher growth rate of acreage under tur, castor, rapeseed, mustard, sugarcane, maize and wheat were found in different agro-climatic zones of Gujarat, whereas negative compound growth rates of acreage under pearl millet, jowar and cotton were noticed in most of the zones. The study suggested the establishment of agro-processing industries and infrastructural facilities, arrangement for crop protection, construction, maintenance and management of irrigation works, research prioritization, distribution of quality seeds and seed materials of specific crops in the specific zone on the basis of cropping pattern and the needs of the people of the region.

Chand and Haque (1998) [4] in their paper, "Rice-Wheat Crop System in Indo-Gangetic Region-Issues Concerning Sustainability", discussed about the adverse phenomena such as water logging, soil salinity and over exploitation of the natural resource base which have resulted due to rice-wheat rotation crop system in the Indo-Gangetic region during the post-Green Revolution. They observed that the eastern region of Indo-Gangetic plains need human resource development and technological improvement which can solve the problems of low productivity and yield instability in rice-wheat cropping system. There is also lack of managerial expertise which can provide better on-farm research and training to farmers regarding timeliness; improved methods of farm operations; proper use of inputs and by-products and conservation of natural resources. There is need for developing appropriate pest and rust resistant plant varieties for rice-wheat system in various agro-ecological zones, within the Indo-Gangetic plains.

Dev (2002) [5] in his paper, "Bold Initiative Needed on Agriculture and Rural Employment", analyzed various factors affecting the growth of agriculture sector. He also analyzed the slow progress in this sector and its adverse impact on rural employment. He observed that we need to have a viable agriculture and compete with other countries under the WTO scenario, and the growth rate of agricultural credit for small and marginal farmers declined in the 1990s compared with the 1980s. During the same period, there was no decline in credit growth for large farmers. As percentage of agriculture GDP, public investment was between 8 percent in 1990s which was less than that in the 1980s. This decline in public investment is a cause of concern. Agricultural development is an important source of increase in employment. There is a need to shift cropping pattern in favour of non-food and cash crops. Growth in rural non-farm employment (RNFE) can also improve rural wages and employment opportunities.

Desai (2002) [6] in his paper, "Policy Framework for Re-orienting Agricultural Development", states that the six elements namely vision, mission, objectives, strategies, investment, and organization and management should be incorporated in public policy for developing the agriculture sector. According to him, the larger vision recognizes that farming is an entrepreneurial economic activity rather than a way of life. The mission should be to provide higher sectoral growth, narrow regional differences in agricultural productivity and growth. Objectives of agricultural development broadly included its per capita output and real net national product growth and alleviation of poverty. The strategies that can be adopted include extensive farming, intensive agriculture, and scientific knowledge-based technical change.

According to him, we should apply such instruments which will improve barter terms of trade which in turn will have favourable impact on private investment, technical change and growth in agriculture. The multi-agency model is required which will have specializes knowledge and skills that are highly professional in nature.

Joshi *et al.* (2004) [7] in their paper entitled, "Agriculture Diversification in South Asia: Patterns, Determinants and Policy Implications", attempted to examine the extent, nature and speed of agricultural diversification in South Asia and India exclusively. They identified the determinants of agricultural diversification and assessed its implication on food security, employment and sustainable use of natural resources. They applied the generalized least square method (GLS Method) to determine the significance of various variables which affect diversification. It was found in their study that agriculture sector in South Asia is gradually diversifying in favour of high value commodities, namely fruits, vegetables, livestock and fish products. In case of India, markets and roads were the key determinants for diversification. Diversification was more pronounced in rain-fed areas, which were by-passed during the Green Revolution. The rain-fed areas are becoming a hub of non-cereals due to their low water requirement and abundant labour supply. Further, high value crops have substantial potential for generating employment opportunities.

Singh (2004) [8] in his work, "Crisis and Diversification in Punjab Agriculture: Role of State and Agribusiness", analysed farmers' hindrances in getting profitable participation in contract farming. He observed that there is not so much requirement of multinational corporations but the requirement of a variety of enterprises, which can ensure the participation of farmers in agro-industrial development as equal and active partners. Further, since the present system of cooperatives in the state does not work efficiently to cater to the business needs of such farmers, the new generation cooperatives (NGCs) should also be started. This can also help in mobilizing some of the capital surpluses available with these farmers within the cooperative structure. State agencies, farmers' organization and NGOs should intervene in contract farming as intermediaries to protect farmers' interests. The contracting need not be promoted for all crops and the state should play more of a regulatory role rather than a promotional one. Agricultural diversification will work only if current system of procurement based on MSP is in favour of new crops.

Hussain (2004) [9] in his paper opined that the entire North-East has deficit in food production. The Brahamputra valley, the Bark valley in Assam and the small Imphal valley in Manipur, all these three valleys are thickly populated, and the land-man ratio has become increasingly unfavourable. Landlessness among the peasantry has increased substantially, because of concentration of land in few hands. As a result, a large number of landless peasants have become totally unemployed with no alternative means of livelihood. Besides, a large section of people have lost their land and livelihood as a result of environment and conflict-induced displacement—the internally displaced persons (IDPs). The IDPs are most vulnerable people susceptible to food insecurity in the North-East.

Singh and Sidhu (2004) [10] in their work, "Factors in Declining Crop Diversification: Case Study of Punjab", analysed the growth of agricultural output in Punjab and the contribution of crop shift and crop diversification in the growth of agriculture sector. They showed the scale of diversification by calculating the diversification index (DI) for different regions of Punjab in different time period. It was observed that DI for the state as a whole declined from 0.707 in 1970-71 to 0.591 in 2001-02. Rice and wheat continued to grow in area and production at the cost of other crops, and the diversity in the output mix decreased continuously over time. This in turn led to almost a specialization of the wheat-rice system all over the state with the level of specialization varying marginally across regions due to land and water constraints. The future growth in agriculture with the present crop pattern and technology will come largely from the area expansion which is limited due to water constraints. Otherwise, the crop pattern shall have to be changed towards high-value crop like fruits and vegetables.

Rao and Gopaloppa (2004) [11] in their paper, "Agricultural Growth and Farmer Distress: Tentative Prospective from Karnataka", explored the process of agricultural growth in Karnataka and its impact on the livelihood of farmers. They observe that farmers in the state are left without an effective cover against adverse weather effects. This is the reason for the origin of farmers' distress in Karnataka which has accumulated over the years. While the proximate cause is adverse weather, it is the weakness of policy interventions which is the real cause for farmer distress. They suggested that closer ground level monitoring of weather effects and access to crop insurance could avert farmer distress or at least keep it within tolerable limits. The research and extension, and credit and marketing are essential for farmers in a developing country confronted with the powerful forces of modernization and globalization. The quality and dependability of the services provided by the institutions and infrastructure of Karnataka remains poor thereby causing distress and suicides in Karnataka and other states.

Kumar and Chand (2004) [12] estimated a simultaneous equation model to investigate the "Determinants of Capital Formation and Agriculture Growth: Some New Exploration". The result shows that the rate of return on private investment, which in turn depends on the terms of trade and technology, is found to be the most important determinant of private capital formation. The addition of new farm holdings is the second most important determinant of private investment. The institutional support to agriculture was found to be another determinant of private capital formation. The impact of subsidy on private investment is also positive. The increase in farm subsidies and decrease in revenue receipts from agriculture are causing an advert impact on public sector capital formation. The GDP agriculture is affected by both capital formation as well as subsidies, besides terms of trade.

Sidhu and Bhular (2005) [13] observed that the productivity of all the crops except cotton was higher in Indian Punjab than in Pakistani Punjab. Low level and less assured irrigation and low use of modern production inputs were primarily responsible for the low productivity in Pakistani Punjab. Use of fertilizers and pesticides was also higher in Indian Punjab. Rural electrification, high intensity of rural roads and strong input delivery mechanism provided further impetus to growth in Indian Punjab. Intensive agriculture in both the states has led to land and water resources degradation. The increase in area under rice and wheat has put greater pressure on ground water resources leading to a fall in water table depth. Similarly, the nutrients-exhaustive crop patterns have resulted into poor fertility status of soils. The problem of salinity by using brackish water has aggravated in Pakistani Punjab. Consequently, the production patterns are reaching the limits of un-sustainability from both economic and ecological points of view and calls for diversification in both the states.

Chattopadhyay (2005) [14] has made an attempt to explore the distributional impact of agricultural growth on rural West Bengal during the last two decades of the previous century. He classified his analysis with the help of Lorenz Curve and regressing the Gini's Co-efficient through time. He observed that prior to the 1980s, the estimated rate of growth of agricultural output in West Bengal was very poor. It was even less than the ratio of growth of the rural and total population of the state. As a result, a significant portion of rural population lived in abject poverty. The agricultural output started to increase at an unprecedented high rate from beginning of 1980s. As a result, the time profile of the shares of different ordinal groups in total rural consumption expenditure and ratio of the shares between the top 20 percent and bottom 20 percent of the population revealed an improvement in the overall distribution of consumption expenditure in rural West Bengal.

However, during the latter part of 1990s, when rate of growth of agricultural output declined substantially, its impact on rural income distribution was reversed with declaration in average earnings of agricultural labour household.

Mathur *et al.* (2006) [15] analysed the growth trend in agriculture production across the nation and regions. They also analysed the different factors for the growth in agriculture. They used the flexible form of Cobb-Douglas production function to identify the different factors affecting agricultural production. They observed that there has been a decline in the growth of the agricultural sector during the 1990s till the recent past. This is accompanied with the recent decline in yield per hectare for a number of food crops. There are vast inter-state differences in growth rate of agriculture and even more so for foodgrains. The all-India analysis for the period 1990-91 to 2004-05 suggests that government expenditure in agriculture including public investment and subsidy for fertilizer usage and electricity consumption for agriculture are the main factors affecting agricultural production in India. The state-wise analysis shows that the agricultural output at current prices was significantly and positively dependent on government expenditure in agriculture, fertilizer usage, rainfall and population.

Chand (2006) [16] in his paper entitled, "Agricultural Diversification in India: Potential and Prospects in Developed Regions", attempted to explore the potentials and prospects of agricultural diversification in agriculturally advanced Green Revolution regions with focus on the state of Punjab which has attained the highest level of agricultural growth and development in the country. Agricultural diversification acquires special significance in this region because of the emergence of ecological and environmental problems and strain on natural resources associated with the Green Revolution technology which is making it difficult to sustain growth in agricultural output and income. Author considers agricultural diversification as an important alternative to attain the objectives of output growth, employment generation and preserving the natural resources. According to him, states like Punjab and Haryana have attained about 4.0 percent to 4.5 percent growth in net state domestic product in agriculture sector (NSDP Agriculture), during the past two decades by way of diversifying their crop sector in a big way.

The author, on the basis of his analysis, has suggested that the state should follow three types of diversification—first, through items of mass production and consumption which includes the production of milk (dairying), pulses, and oilseeds. The second, through area specific enterprises of moderately high value commodities like vegetables, fruits, potato, onion, cotton, basmati rice and sugarcane etc. and third, through non-conventional high value items of elite consumption which includes production of floriculture, exotic vegetables, mushrooms and alike crops. The demand for these commodities is very narrow and they being highly perishable and sensitive require special arrangements for transportation, packaging and storage etc. Dairying seems to be the best choice for agricultural diversification in the state, on ecological as well as economic grounds. It has vast potential for growth in employment, income and for restoring soil health. Efficient and modern system of marketing and processing is required to give boost to dairy industry in the state.

The author regrets that despite a lot of interest and discussion on diversification, no serious efforts have been made to identify and encourage area specific activities. General type recommendations are being made for the entire state. The research and development (R&D) efforts in the state have focused mainly on wheat and paddy. The research and development efforts should now shift to new and emerging crops and enterprises to benefit other enterprises of future importance.

Thakur (2006) [17] in his paper entitled, "Growth and Diversification of Agriculture in Eastern India", observed that there is a tremendous scope for agricultural diversification in the eastern states of India. This is possible by using scientific practices and inputs appropriate to their local conditions. He argues that crop diversification can be used as a tool to increase the total productivity and farm income in these states. Agriculture can be diversified between crop, livestock, fisheries, horticulture, floriculture, and sericulture etc., for which north-eastern states have ample potential. Finally, the study concludes that floriculture is attractive and has ample future scope of getting revenue by adopting practices like production of scents, rose-water, and oils etc. Herbal farming is another good option because the herbal crops require small holding for their production which suits the eastern states. These crops are used for making ayurvedic medicines and extracting oil for medicinal use. Therefore, diversification of agriculture must be supplemented with small-scale cottage industries.

Ghose (2006) [18] in his paper entitled, "Nature and Pattern of Diversification of Agriculture in Eastern India With Special Reference to Bihar", analyzed the nature and pattern of agriculture diversification in eastern India with especial focus on Bihar. It was observed in the study that there was complete stagnation in agricultural output in eastern India, particularly in Bihar and further deterioration in agricultural performance and occurrence of large scale fluctuation in agricultural production. The natural resource endowment of the state was dominated by land and water, but the lack of opportunities in industries and poor rural-urban growth linkages is hampering the agricultural growth. Since agricultural development will give a big push to overall economic development of eastern India especially Bihar, therefore, the need of the day is diversification of agriculture which will lead to its commercialization and proper integration of local and global market.

What is needed is the creation of awareness among the farmers about the benefits of commercialization and good coordination among them and the government setup. The government on the other hand must be careful in realizing the potentialities of agriculture and must give quick attention for promoting scope of agricultural development. Finally, it can be said that diversification of agriculture is the key for accelerated economic development of eastern India.

Krishnaraj (2006) [19] in his paper, "Food Security, Agrarian Crisis and Rural Livelihood: Implications for Women", highlighted the contribution of agricultural growth in removing poverty and increasing the per capita income of farmers and per capita availability of foodgrains across India. He analyzed that the all-India consumer price index for agricultural and rural labourers, especially for food, indicates a substantial rise in the cost of living. This is the result of policies followed by the government to privilege the growth of rice and wheat through promotion of hybrid variety, accompanied by high input technology and concentration on irrigated areas. Recent data on lower consumption of food and diversion to non-food items is aggregating the financial problems of poor farmers which results in lower incomes due to poor returns from agriculture. The growth rate of average income per worker declined from 0.696 in late 1970s to 0.29 in 2003-04.

Narayanamoorthy (2006) [20] in his paper, "Deceleration in Agriculture Growth: Technology Fatigue or Policy Fatigue?", made a comparison between technological factors and factors related to policy implementation which is really causing a deceleration in the growth of agriculture. According to him, policy fatigue is the main reason for the agrarian crisis and deceleration in agricultural growth. A major policy that confirms fatigue is the faulty agricultural price policy followed for different crops. Nobody would invest money in a venture like agriculture that does not provide reasonable remuneration. The policy makers must keep watch on the movements of both the cost as well as the value of output for fixing of prices for different crops in consonance with the cost of cultivation. The reduction in public investment in agriculture is also one of the reasons for poor performance of agriculture in recent years. There has also been significant reduction in the growth of institutional credit to agriculture during the post-reforms period. Further, the increased dependence on ground water irrigation increases the cost of cultivation.

Birthal and Joshi (2006) [21] in their paper, "Diversification towards High Value Agriculture: Role of Urbanization and Infrastructure", analyzed the diversification process in Indian agriculture towards high value commodities (HVCs) i.e. fruits, vegetables and livestock products. It was found that the share of HVCs in cold agricultural products is high as compared to other food commodities and also the compound annual growth rate of HVCs is also higher as compared to other food commodities thus varying the increased diversification of Indian agriculture towards HVCs. They also found that this diversification was being propelled by increased access to markets and the factors facilitating their transport from production sites to consumption sites. The access to markets is approximated by urbanization and road density. The sample districts with high level of urbanization should then look for greater diversification. Also, with rapid growth in income, the food basket of both rural and urban consumers is changing drastically in favour of high value food commodities. The result suggests that urbanization would remain an important driver for diversification due to increasing population.

Chand *et al.* (2007) [22] discussed about the trends in agricultural growth and factors underlying the slowdown. They also explored ways and means to bring about an acceleration in agricultural growth in India. It was observed that the initial years of reforms were somewhat favourable for agricultural growth but the post-WTO period witnessed a sharp decline in the growth rate of almost all sub-sectors and commodity groups in the agricultural sector. The main reason for deceleration and stagnation in agricultural output after 1995-96 have been a slowdown in the growth of fertilizer use, irrigation and energy (electric power), crop intensity and area under cultivation which have shown either a poor growth or a decline. Diversification towards high value crops has also slowed down. The terms of trade for agriculture has shown deterioration and agricultural incomes have faced an increased instability in the recent years.

Shergill (2007) [23] in his paper, "Sustainability of Wheat-Rice Production in Punjab: A Re-examination", analyzed the sustainability of wheat and rice production at the present scale in Punjab. It was found that the fall in the water table has neither crossed the danger mark nor has the fall been caused by wheat-rice cultivation per sector. The further marketing prospects of Punjab grains are also quite secure. The minimum support price (MSP) of wheat and rice in India has remained quite in line with the world market price of these grains. The contribution of food subsidy in the fiscal deficit of the Central government, and its burden on the economy is rather marginal. He observes that the water table situation in the state is not as serious as is being made out by some experts and newspaper reports. Also, the water use in wheat-rice rotation is not excessive so the economics of wheat-rice cultivation in Punjab is quite sound.

Deshpande *et al.* (2007) [24] in their paper entitled, "Crop Diversification and Agriculture Labour in India", carefully examined the process of crop diversification in agriculture and its impact on agricultural labour. The Herfindal Diversification Index was used for measuring the level of diversification in this study. They recognize that there is a direct connection between the diversification and the welfare of agricultural labour. They prove that diversification in favour of rice and wheat in some states has led to the welfare losses in these regions. This type of diversification leads to thin spreading of resources and misdirecting the engine of growth. They also observe that the share of agriculture sector in the national income has been shrinking at a faster rate than the density of agricultural workers. All these observations unanimously point out to the fact that this type of diversification may have a depressing effect on the welfare of the agricultural labourers.

Jha (2007) [25] in his paper entitled, "Is the Role of Agriculture in Rural Diversification Decreasing?", established the nature and extent of relationship between agriculture and rural non-farm employment in India with the help of log linear regression method. He found that one percent increase in agricultural income would lead to increase in rural non-farm employment by more than 0.70 percent. Determinants of rural diversification were found to be different infrastructural development and various distress-led factors.

Ghosal (2007) [26] in his paper entitled, "Dynamics of Diversification of Rural Employment Structure in India: The Changing Trajectories", attempted to analyze the dynamics of diversification of the rural employment structure and its trajectories during the pre- and post-liberalization period. By adopting the multiple regression models, the author tried to examine the determining factors for the cross-state and cross-time variations scenario in non-farm employment in India. In the study, he observed a continuous process of diversification of rural workforce from agriculture to the non-agriculture sectors, especially to the tertiary non-farm activities. He observed that the rate of diversification of the workforce from farm to non-farm employment is much faster during the post-reforms period as compared to the pre-reforms period.

Further, he identified a high degree of inter-state variations in non-farm employment which are much higher in the case of female workers than male workers. The sharp fall in the growth rate of agriculture during the post-reforms period might have caused a desperate movement of the workforce to non-farm activities. Surprisingly, a tremendous increase in self-employment and regular employment coupled with a fall in the actualization of the workforce irrespective of gender was found between 1999-2000 and 2004-2005.

Singh and Sahoo (2007) [27] in their paper entitled, "Diversification of Agricultural Economy towards Horticulture and Livestock: Regional Variations, Convergence and

Determinants", attempted to examine the inter-state variations in diversification of agricultural economy towards the high value horticulture and livestock products. The study also identified major factors determining diversification and measured the convergences or divergences in diversification among the states. SID (Simpson Index Diversification) tool was used to derive the values of diversification index in this study. The study was based on 13 years panel data for 15 major states of India. The paper found that the share of horticulture and livestock sectors in the total agricultural output significantly increased during the period 1993-94 to 2004-05. In this paper, the analysis revealed that agricultural economy has diversified in all the states except for Punjab, Haryana, Rajasthan and Kerala. The result also testified that the small size of holdings, road, infrastructure, and number of tractors have emerged to have positive and significant influence on the diversification while rural literacy, irrigation, and fertilizer consumption were found to be negatively associated with the Simpson Diversification Index.

Bhaumik (2007) [28] in his paper entitled, "Occupational Diversification among Rural Workers: Results from Field Surveys in West Bengal", made an analytical study in West Bengal to observe the pattern and determinants of occupational diversification by rural workers by using the Probit Regression Model. The study revealed that a majority of the rural workers in both the advanced and backward regions work in the farm sector. There were about 54 percent of the rural workers working in the advanced region and about 62 percent working in the backward region in the farm sector. Apart from this, about one-eighth of the workers have been 'multi-active' as they participate in both farm and non-farm sectors. The study further revealed that in both the advanced and backward regions, nearly three-fourths of all the workers were self-employed while the remaining workers served as agricultural wage labourers.

The paper also found that the non-farm sector having greater intensity of employment generated higher annual earnings for its workers as compared to their counterparts in the farm sector. Therefore, the author suggested that policy efforts should be made to catalyze the process of occupational diversification away from farm to the non-farm sector in rural West Bengal. The development of the non-farm sector seems to be highly significant in ensuring greater employment availability, improving income base of the rural workers, and reducing poverty. Finally, he proved that the workers having lower age, better education, superior caste status, lower land-man ratio and better asset ownership position had a greater probability of obtaining the non-farm sector employments. Besides, more and highly educated workers are likely to prefer non-farm jobs.

Sharma (2007) [29] in his paper entitled, "Crop Diversification in Himachal Pradesh: Extent, Impact, Determinants and Challenges", tried to reveal that the process of crop diversification in the state of Himachal Pradesh was started with the introduction of apple during fifties and sixties and vegetable crops during the eighties. All the categories of households, including small and marginal ones, have adopted the cultivation of high-value cash crops like garlic, ginger, cabbage, cauliflower, peas and tomato. The cultivation of these crops has made a significant impact on the levels of household income and employment. Factor analysis shows that the creation of basic infrastructural facilities, availability of huge market in the neighbouring states, high degree of price responsiveness among farmers and the emergence of self-help institutions triggered the process of crop diversification. The results of regression analysis in the study show that the road length and number of bank branches were important determinants of area under non-food grain crops.

But at the same time, the author has voiced his concern that all is, however, not well with the ongoing process of crop diversification in the state. The so-called 'second generation problems' have started looming large, more ostensibly in regions where the process of crop diversification has reached an advanced stage. The practice of following the same cropping sequence over the years has caused loss of rich crop biodiversity and had an adverse impact on soil fertility. The indiscriminate use of agro-chemicals has also started taking its toll on environment and human health. The process of crop diversification in the state is facing important challenges, which need to be addressed on priority to ensure ecological sustainability and economic viability of high value cash crops in agriculture. Inadequate infrastructure, lack of irrigation facilities, ageing apple plantation, changing climatic conditions and cheaper imports under the post-WTO liberalized regime are important constraints in achieving this goal.

Kumar (2007) [30] in his paper entitled, "Trend in Rural Diversification and its Determinants in Uttar Pradesh", attempted to examine the process of economic transformation of workers from agricultural sector to rural non-farm sector (RNFS) in Uttar Pradesh. He also attempted to estimate the determinants of RNFE (Rural Non-farm Employment) and to assess region specific constraints in the growth of RNFE and draw related policy implications. The author used the statistical techniques of correlation coefficient and multiple regressions to identify the determinants which are closely associated with RNFE. He identified a sharp decline in proportion of agricultural workers during the nineties as compared to the eighties. However, among the agricultural workers, agricultural labourers have sharply declined as compared to cultivators. The study highlights the fact that there has occurred a definite but moderate transformation in favour of non-agricultural rural workers in Uttar Pradesh.

Kumar (2007) [31] in his paper, "Livelihood Diversification: A Case Study in Rural Tamil Nadu", tried to measure the livelihood diversity among the rural households in the rural areas of Tamil Nadu. In this paper, based on survey data, an attempt was made to analyze livelihood diversification among rural households in three villages of K.V. Kuppam Block in Vellore district of Tamil Nadu. The inverse Simpson

Diversity Index was used for analyzing the livelihood diversity. The study highlights the recognition of livelihood diversity and the fact that rural households are no longer generating income from agricultural sources alone. It may be argued that there is a significant difference among different income groups and different landholding groups with respect to livelihood diversity. It was observed that richer households derive a higher proportion of their incomes from non-farm sources than poorer households.

The extent of livelihood diversification in terms of the inverse Simpson Diversification Index was found very small in the study area. The study revealed that the mean diversity index was only 1.9 in the area as against the maximum possible value of 8. The difference in mean diversity index among sample villages was not statistically significant. There was no significant difference in the number of activity involved by the households among sample villages and the mean number of activities undertaken by the sample was 2.42 on 8-point scale. The share of income from agricultural sources constituted 52.90 percent of the total income in the sample villages. Therefore, the share of agricultural income was higher than that of non-agricultural income.

The analysis further revealed that the diversity is high among higher income households and low among the low income households. The higher income group was involved in greater number of activities than the lower income group. The share of non-agricultural income in the total households' income is lesser in the entire income group except in the second highest income group. Richer households derive a higher proportion of their income from non-farm sources than the poorer households. A major portion of income in rich households came from cultivation whereas in the poor households, it came from agricultural labour. The share of non-agricultural income in the total households' income decreased along with an increase in the landholding status.

Vatta and Sidhu (2007) [32] in their paper entitled,

"Income Diversification among Rural Households in Punjab: Dynamics, Impacts and Policy Implication", made an attempt to investigate the patterns of employment and income diversification, determinants of income diversification and impact on income diversification, poverty and income distribution among the rural households. To fulfil the objectives, the authors adopted Herfindal techniques to estimate diversification. OLS technique was used to observe the responsible factors of income diversification, and simple correlation coefficient technique was used to analyze the relationship between income diversification, household income and poverty among the rural households. Going through the OLS (ordinary least square) analysis, they observed that the family size, cast, operational area, indices of rural non-farm employment in the household and worker population ratio in the family significantly influenced the diversification of rural household income.

Further, they observed that rural employment and income in Punjab showed a varied pattern. The income diversification was found to be positively and significantly influenced by the family size and worker population ratio in the family. On the other hand, the impact of caste and operational area was significantly negative. Finally, they concluded the paper with two types of recommendations. In an immediate time horizon, there is need to emphasize on the development of dairying, construction, manufacturing and trade in the rural areas. It is essential to improve access of rural households to more remunerative employment sources i.e. livestock and fisheries, which have traditionally been the stronghold of economically better households, i.e. medium and large farmers in the rural areas.

Toor *et al.* (2007) [33] in their paper entitled, "Agriculture-led Diversification and Labour Use Enhancement in Punjab: Potentials and Constraints", tried to examine the potential of labour absorption and employment generation in agriculture. Authors used the Herfindal Index to measure the index of diversification. The interesting feature that was noticed related to the casualization of agricultural labour in the case of both male and female workforce. The paper identified major reasons behind casualization of farm labour in the state which have been the mechanization of major farm operations, inflow of migrant labour; slow down of agricultural growth, and non-viability of small and marginal holdings. The paper also showed that crop diversification policy of the state government led to better employment opportunities for the agricultural labour, especially women in the rural areas. It was hypothesized that these policy measures will go a long way in generating employment opportunities and improving the economic conditions of the rural economy of the state.

The study revealed that the share of agriculture sector in gross state domestic product has declined. Besides, the capacity of agriculture sector to absorb labour force in adequate numbers has been declining. The study put forward suggestions that a well organized and integrated farming system with crops and other labour-intensive enterprises like dairy, poultry, vegetable, fruits, mushrooms, etc. can significantly increase the employment of farm families particularly small and marginal farmers having surplus family labour. Since agriculture and livestock are the major contributors in state's gross domestic product, emphasis should be given to the proper development of this sector in the coming years to augment the growth of state domestic product.

Singh (2006-07) [34] in his paper entitled, "Pampering Corporates Pauperizing Masses", advocated that the main challenge before the policy makers is how to enhance agricultural productivity, sustainability of the livelihood of marginal and small farmers and to generate productive jobs for the farm workers. In the paper, it was observed that low productivity, high input cost, technology fatigue, unbalanced fertilizer use, low seed replacement rate, degradation of land and water resources, low level of public investment, stagnated net sown area, and inadequate credit and market access to farmers, are the causative factors of unattractive and unprofitable venture in agriculture.

The horticulture sector constituted 10 percent of the gross cropped area and contributed 28 percent to the GDP from agriculture during 2004-05. The policy driven factors, such as input subsidy, reform in tenancy and lease laws, promotion of contract farming, and incentives to food processing sector, attracted corporate investment in hi-tech commercial crops. The demand for fruits is growing due to high income elasticity of demand of affluent urban consumers. It is again a serious issue from the point of view of food security for the masses, as diversion of land towards fruit crops reduces the area under foodgrains. At the national level, the area under fruits has increased from 2.87 million hectares (Mha) in 1991-92 to 4.82 Mha in 2004-05. The area under vegetable crops in India has also increased from 5.59 Mha in 1991-92 to 6.76 Mha in 2004-05. Agriculture business companies have also entered in floriculture. The hi-tech floriculture is highly capital intensive and required high doses of inputs and is ecologically not sustainable. The paper also remarked that while India produces over 162 million tones of fruits and vegetables, the cold storage facilities exist for only for 12 percent of the total produce. It suggested that the diversification of agriculture in favour of hi-tech and high-value horticulture and floriculture is considered by the policy makers as an important strategy to augment farm income and employment.

Shah (2007) [35] in his paper, "Crop per Drop of Diesel? Energy Squeeze on India's Small Holder Irrigation", advocated that three factors are causing adverse effect on the irrigation of small holders in India. They are: (a) deteriorating power supply, (b) embargo on new electricity connections, and (c) an eight-fold increase in diesel prices since 1991. The Government of India's accelerated irrigation benefits programme is investing tens of thousands of crores annually in surface irrigation, which is shrinking. The author observed that promoting fuel-efficient diesel/kerosene pumps of Chinese variety can ease the cost price squeeze. The idea of providing subsidized diesel to farmers as is done for trawler operating fisher folk in some states would help in improving manual irrigation technologies and better management of surface water bodies for gravity flow irrigation that can relieve the stress from the energy squeeze.

Ghose (2007) [36] in his paper, "Sustainable Development in Agriculture", analyzed the sustainability of agricultural development by examining the trends in area under high yielding varieties crops in India and the trend of annual compound growth rate of output and yield of crops in India. His analysis showed that the new technology led growth in agriculture has been associated with growing environmental degradation leading to slowing down of productivity and output growth during the 1990s. The environmental consequences of HYV-technology are important factors imposing limits to growth and sustainable development of agriculture. Sustainable development naturally requires appropriate measures for arresting and reversing the adverse effects of HYV-technology. He noted that National Agricultural Research System (NARS) can play a crucial role in the development of location-specific and environmental friendly technologies.

Raju and Chand (2007) [37] in their work, "Progress and Problems in Agricultural Insurance", analysed the different insurance schemes for agriculture initiated by the government and their impact on the well-being of farmers. According to them, despite various schemes launched from time to time in the country, agricultural insurance has served very little purpose. The coverage in terms of area, number of farmers and value of agricultural output is very small. This requires renewed efforts by the government in terms of designing appropriate mechanism and providing financial support for agricultural insurance. Providing similar help to private sector insurance would help in increasing insurance coverage and in improving the viability of the insurance schemes over time.

Satish (2007) [38] in his paper, "Agricultural Credit in the

Post-reform Era: A Target of Systematic Policy Coarctation", analysed the post-reforms scenario of credit flow to agriculture. He concluded that there has been real squeeze on credit flow to agriculture. He observed from the trends that credit to agriculture as a proportion of total bank credit of commercial banks decreased from 15 percent in 1990-91 to 9.9 percent in 1999-2000 and further to 9.6 percent during 2000-01. The number of small borrowers' account below ₹ 25,000, which can be treated as a proxy for extensiveness of credit flow to priority sectors shrank from 58.8 million in 1991-92 to 39.3 millions in 1999-2000 and further to 36.8 million in 2003-04. The incremental credit-deposit ratio (CDR) which averaged 60.4 percent during 1981-87 drastically reduced to 34.5 percent during 1999-2001. The effects were further reflected in the declining trend in the capital formation in Indian agriculture since early 1990s. The level of capital investment in agriculture that was at 1.88 percent of GDP in 1992-93, declined to 1.27 percent in 2002-03.

Behera and Mishra (2007) [39] in their paper, "Acceleration of Agricultural Growth in India: Suggestive Policy Framework", analysed crisis in Indian agriculture and various types of policies undertaken to solve it. They observed that the absence of institutional control in the input market has not only increased prices of inputs but has also created uncertainty about their availability in the right quantity at the right price and at the right time to small and marginal farmers. This coupled with reduction in subsidies on seeds, fertilizers, pesticides etc. and growing fragmentation of farm land has raised the cost of cultivation. On the other hand, lack of easy proximity to the output market, weak agriculture industry linkage, asymmetric information, and absence of agri-business relations have restricted farmers from getting the right prices for their commodities. All these have resulted in a drastic decline in profitability from agriculture in recent years. This decline in profitability has created disincentives for many farmers to continue cultivation, putting the agriculture sector in a deep crisis.

Singh, *et al.* (2008) [40] in their paper "Indebtedness among Farmers in Punjab" analysed the extent and causes of indebtedness of farmers in Punjab and its repercussion on Punjab farmers' life. They observed from their analysis that 89 percent of farm households in Punjab were indebted and all farm size categories were equally indebted in percentage terms. The amount of indebtedness was the highest in the South-Western region. The smaller farm households on a per hectare basis were more heavily indebted than other farm size categories. The institutional sources accounted for 62 percent of total loans to the farmers. The share of productive loans was 75 percent. The farmers who own tractors were heavily indebted and had the highest share of institutional loans. It was overall observed that Punjab's farmers were severely trapped in the clutches of indebtedness. It warrants multi-pronged strategies and measures for reducing indebtedness in the short-run and increasing the productive income of farmers in the long-run by generating employment.

Raghwan (2008) [41] in his paper, "Changing Pattern of Input Use and Cost of Cultivation", analyzed the trends in the cost of utilization of different inputs in agriculture and so the overall cost of cultivation in different states of India. He observed that the cost of cultivation have soared to unprecedented heights coinciding with the economic reforms. The analysis showed that all items of costs have not increased at the same pace. While fixed costs seemed to exhibit a gradual deceleration, operational costs have continued their relentless acceleration. Further, during the post-reforms period, there has been a decline in the labour hours applied in cultivation. So, the agrarian crisis in the post-reforms period afflicted not only the cultivating households but also the entire agriculture dependent population. During this period, there has been a deceleration in the rate of growth of fertilizers applied in cultivation. Nonetheless, the corresponding rate of growth of fertilizers charges was three times higher than that of its physical application.

Reddy and Mishra (2008)[42] in their paper "Crisis in Agriculture and Rural Distress in Post-reform India", observed that the incidence of suicide had been higher among small and marginal farmers moving from subsistence agriculture to high value crops with a strong motivation to improve their social and economic status. They are indeed risk-taking small agricultural entrepreneurs whose success would be the basic premise for the transformation of rural India towards better and equitable income and livelihood. Hence, farmers' distress is not due to enterprising qualities of farmers who peruse growth and even achieve it in good measure, but due to drought-prone environment and non-caring policy regime. There is an increasing evidence that there cannot be rural development, even in relatively prosperous regions like Andhra Pradesh and Punjab without high agricultural growth.

Patil (2008) [43] in his paper "Agricultural Indebtedness-Crisis and Revival", observed that there is no doubt that agriculture has suffered due to long neglect and inadequate allocation of resources. Inclusive growth would require a major shift in our planning strategies and a much higher allocation of development and plan resources. High growth rate of Indian economy may be sustained but a 2 percent growth of agriculture would continue to be a major obstacle in reducing rural poverty and easing social tensions. The high indebtedness of the Indian farmers is a manifestation of the neglect and inadequate investment in agriculture. The small and marginal farmers who form the overwhelming percentage of Indian farmer's are the worst sufferers. Most of them are continuing in agriculture because of the complete absence of alternatives. The growing unrest in large parts of rural India is a serious issue but has not attracted adequate attention of the authorities.

Acharya *et al.* (2011) [44] in their work "Crop Diversification in Karnataka: An Economic Analysis", analysed the nature and extent of crop diversification in Karnataka for the period 1982-83 to 2007-08 by using Composite Entropy Index

(CEI). The results revealed that except vegetables and oilseeds, almost all the crops accounted a higher diversification index during the post-WTO (1995-96 to 2007-08) period as compared to the pre-WTO (1982-83 to 1994-95) period due to technological and infrastructural factors. Apart from these, in order to find the factors which affected agriculture diversification, they applied multiple regression model for the entire period under study. The results revealed that out of the eight variables, irrigation ratio, market density, fertilizer consumption, and road and transportation were the key determinants of agricultural diversification in the study area.

Birthal *et al.* (2015), [45] in their paper titled "Agricultural Diversification and Poverty in India", tried to examine the poor performance of agriculture in India and attributed it to climate change and fragmentation of land holdings due to continuous rise in population in rural areas and constrained employment opportunities. The study also suggested that agricultural diversification in favour of high valued crops (HVCs) can eliminate the above stated economic maladies and it can be an instrument to improve the livelihood of the people. The study also tried to identify the relationship between the degree of diversification and economic benefit of the farmers.

The above examined studies reveal that change in technology, urbanization, increase in per capita income, consumption patterns and globalization have been the main driving forces for diversification of agriculture and allied sectors in India and other Asian countries. Agriculture and allied sectors have been diversified in favour of high value crops, livestock and fisheries. Within India, the speed of diversification widely varies across the states. The poor and backward regions, particularly eastern region have shown a slow rate of diversification which has resulted in slow growth rate in agriculture and allied sectors and hence a slow rate of income and employment generation in these states. Proper agricultural policies together with availability of infrastructural facilities is the need of the hour for promoting and speeding up agriculture diversification, enhancing income and employment of the people engaged in these sectors, and raising their living standards.

Given the importance of crop diversification under the changing scenario, this study is undertaken to examine agricultural diversification in India with special reference to one of the least developed regions of the country i.e. the eastern region and suggest suitable policy options for further diversification towards the sustainability of agriculture in the region and states including Bihar, West Bengal, Odisha, Jharkhand and Assam. There are wide gaps between area, production and yield in foodgrains and non-foodgrains in different agro-climatic zones of India. For bridging the gaps between area, production and yield of these crops in different agro-zones of India, we need appropriate policy measures, better technology, adequate inputs and better management practices. These issues have been highlighted in this book.

Endnotes

1. Saini, A.S., K.D. Sharma and B.K. Singh (1996), "Impact of Diversification on Small Farms Economy in Himachal Pradesh", *Indian Journal of Agricultural Economics*, Vol. 51, No. 4, pp. 697-698.
2. Shah, Anita (1997), "Food Security and Access to Natural Resources: A Review of Recent Trends", *Economic and Political Weekly*, Vol. XXXII, No. 26, June 28, pp. A46-A54.
3. Shiyani, R.L, and N. Pandya (1998), "Diversification of Agriculture in Gujarat: A Spatio-Temporal Analysis", *Indian Journal of Agricultural Economics*, Vol. 53, No. 4, pp. 627-639.
4. Chand, R. and T. Haque (1998), "Rice-Wheat Crop System in Indo-Gangetic Region-Issues Concerning Sustainability", *Economic and Political Weekly*, Vol. XXXIII, No. 26, June 7, pp. A108-A112.
5. Dev, S. Mahendra (2002), "Bold Initiative Needed on Agriculture and Rural Employment", *Economic and Political Weekly*, Vol. XXXVII, No. 12, March 23, pp. 1088-1091.
6. Desai, M. Bhupati (2002), "Policy Framework for Re-orienting Agricultural Development", *Indian Journal of Agricultural*

Economics, Vol. 57, No. 1, January-March, pp. 1-21.

7. Joshi, P.K., A. Gulati, P.S. Birthal and L. Tiwari (2004), "Agriculture Diversification in South Asia: Pattern, Determinants and Policy Implications", *Economic and Political Weekly*, June 12, Vol. 39 (24), pp. 2457-2467.
8. Singh, S. (2004), "Crisis and Diversification in Punjab Agriculture-Role of State and Agribusiness", *Economic and Political Weekly,* Vol. XXXIX, No. 52, December 25, pp. 5583-5590.
9. Hussain, Monirul (2004), "Food Security and the North-East" *Economic and Political Weekly*, Vol. XXXIX, No. 41, October 9, pp. 4515-4516.
10. Singh J., and R.S. Sidhu (2004), "Factors in Declining Crop Diversification-Case Study of Punjab", *Economic and Political Weekly,* Vol. XXXIX, No. 52, December 25, pp. 5607-5610.
11. Rao, V.M. and D.V. Gopaloppa (2004), "Agricultural Growth and Farmer Distress-Tentative Prospective from Karnataka", *Economic and Political Weekly,* Vol. XXXIX, No. 52, December 25, pp. 5607-5610.
12. Kumar, P. and Ramesh Chand (2004), "Determinants of Capital Formation and Agriculture Growth Some New Exploration", *Economic and Political Weekly,* Vol. XXXIX, No. 52, December 25, pp. 5611-5616.
13. Sidhu, R.S. and A.S. Bhular (2005), "Patterns and Determinants of Agricultural Growth in the Two Punjabs" *Economic and Political Weekly*, Vol. XL, No. 53, December 31, pp. 5620-5627.
14. Chattopadhyay, A.R. (2005), "Distributive Impact of Agricultural Growth in Rural West Bengal", *Economic and Political Weekly,* Vol. XL No. 53, December 31, pp. 5601-5610.
15. Mathur A.S., S. Das and S. Sircar (2006), "Status of Agriculture in India-Trends & Prospects", *Economic and Political Weekly,* Vol. XLI, December 30, pp. 5327-5336.
16. Chand, Ramesh (2006), "Agricultural Diversification in India: Potentials and Prospects in Developed Region", Mittal Publications, New Delhi.
17. Thakur, N.K. (2006), "Growth and Diversification of Agriculture in Eastern India", seminar volume organized by Economic Association of Bihar, March 26-28.
18. Ghose, Rinku (2006), "Growth and Diversification of

Agriculture in Eastern States with Special Reference to Bihar", seminar volume organized by Economic Association of Bihar, March 26-28.

19. Krishnaraj, M. (2006), "Food Security, Agrarian Crisis and Rural Livelihood-Implications of Women", *Economic and Political Weekly,* Vol. XLI, December 30, pp. 5376-5386.
20. Narayanamoorthy, A. (2006), "Deceleration in Agricultural Growth: Technology Fatigue or Policy Fatigue?", *Economic and Political Weekly*, Vol. XLII, No. 25, June23, pp. 2375-2379.
21. Birthal, S. and P.K. Joshi (2006), "Diversification towards High Value Agriculture-Role of Urbanization and Infrastructure", *Economic and Political Weekly,* Vol. XLI, June 30, pp. 2747-2753
22. Chand, R., S.S. Raju, and L.M. Pandey (2007), "Growth Crisis in Agriculture-Severity and Options of National and State Levels", *Economic and Political Weekly*, Vol. XLII, No. 26, June 30, pp. 2528-2533.
23. Shergill, H.S. (2007), "Sustainability of Wheat-Rice Production in Punjab: A Re-examination", *Economic and Political Weekly*, Vol. XLII, No. 52, December 29, pp. 81-85.
24. Deshpande, R.S., Pradeep Mehta, Khalil Shah (2007), "Crop Diversification and Agriculture Labour in India", *The Indian Journal of Labour Economics*, Conference Issue, October-December, Vol. 50(4), pp. 597-610.
25. Jha, Brajesh (2007), "Is the Role of Agriculture in Rural Diversification Decreasing?", *The Indian Journal of Labour Economics*, Conference Issue, October-December, Vol. 50(4), pp. 633-642.
26. Ghosal, Ratan Kumar (2007), "Dynamics of Diversification of Rural Employment Structure in India: The Changing Trajectories", *The Indian Journal of Labour Economics,* Conference Issue, October-December, Vol. 50(4), pp. 643-656.
27. Singh, S.P. and Bimal Kishore Sahoo (2007), "Diversification of Agricultural Economy toward Horticulture and Livestock: Regional Variations, Convergence, and Determinants", *The Indian Journal of Labour Economics*, Conference Issue, October-December, Vol. 50(4), pp. 657-672.
28. Bhaumik, S.K. (2007), "Occupational Diversification among Rural Workers: Results from Field Surveys in West Bengal", *The Indian Journal of Labour Economics*, Conference Issue,

October-December, Vol. 50(4), pp. 673-688.

29. Sharma, H.R. (2007), "Crop diversification in Himachal Pradesh: Extent, Impact, Determinants and Challenges", *The Indian Journal of Labour Economics*, Conference Issue, October-December, Vol. 50(4), pp. 689-703.
30. Kumar, Nomita P. (2007), "Trend in Rural Diversification and its Determinants in Uttar Pradesh", *The Indian Journal of Labour Economics*, Conference Issue, October-December, Vol. 50(4), pp. 703-714.
31. Surjeet Kumar, P.S. (2007), "Livelihood Diversification: A Case Study in Rural Tamil Nadu", *The Indian Journal of Labour Economics*, Conference Issue, October-December, Vol. 50(4), pp. 715-722.
32. Vatta, Kamal and R.S. Sidhu (2007), "Income Diversification among Rural Households in Punjab: Dynamics, Impacts and Policy Implication", *The Indian Journal of Labour Economics,* Conference Issue, October-December, Vol. 50(4), pp. 723-736.
33. Toor, M.S, A.S. Bhullar and Inderpreet Kaur (2007), "Agriculture-led Diversification and Labour Use Enhancement in Punjab: Potentials and Constraints", *The Indian Journal of Labour Economics*, Conference Issue, October December, Vol. 50(4), pp. 737-748.
34. Singh, S.P. (2007), "Corporatization of Agriculture: Alternative Economic Survey, India, 2006-07: Pampering Corporates, Pauperizing Masses, Daanish Books, New Delhi, pp. 81-98.
35. Tushar, Shah (2007) "Crop per Drop of Diesel? Energy Squeeze on India's Small Holder Irrigation", *Economic and Political Weekly*, Vol. XLII, No. 39, September 29, pp. 4002-4009.
36. Ghosh, M. (2007), "Sustainable Development in Agriculture", in 'Economic Reforms and Indian Economic Development', Bookwell, New Delhi, pp. 65-85.
37. Raju, S.S. and Ramesh Chand (2007), "Progress and Problems in Agricultural Insurance", *Economic and Political Weekly*, Vol. XLII, No. 21, May 26, pp. 1905-1908.
38. Satish, P. (2007), "Agricultural Credit in the Post Reform Era: A Target of Systematic Policy Coarctation", *Economic and Political Weekly*, Vol. XLII, No. 26, June30, pp. 2567-2575.
39. Behera, Bhagirath and Pulak Mishra (2007), "Acceleration of Agricultural Growth in India: Suggestive Policy Framework", *Economic and Political Weekly*, Vol. XLI, No. 42, October, pp.

4268-4271.

40. Singh, S., H.S. Kingra, and M. Kaur (2008), "Indebtedness among Farmers in Punjab", *Economic and Political Weekly*, Vol. XLIII, No. 26, June28, pp. 130-136.
41. Raghvan, M. (2008), "Changing Pattern of Input Use and Cost of Cultivation", *Economic and Political Weekly*, Vol. XLIII, No. 26 and 27, June 28, pp. 123-129.
42. Reddy, D.N. and S. Mishra (2008) "Crisis in Agriculture and Rural Distress in Post Reform India", in 'India Development Report, 2008', Indira Gandhi Institute of Development Research; Oxford University Press, New Delhi, pp. 41-52.
43. Pati, B.V. (2008), "Agricultural Indebtedness, Crisis and Revival", *Economic and Political Weekly*, Vol. XLIII, No. 5, February 2, pp. 47-52.
44. Acharya, Saraswati Poudel., H. Basavaraja., L.B. Kunnal., S.B. Mahajanashetti and A.R.S. Bhat (2011), "Crop Diversification in Karnataka: An Economic Analysis", *Agricultural Economics Research Review,* Vol. 24, July-December, pp. 351-357.
45. Birthal, Pratap S., Devesh Roy and Digvijay S. Negi (2015), "Agriculture Diversification and Poverty in India", The International Food Policy Research Institute (IFPRI) Discussion Paper 01446, June, New Delhi.

3

Agriculture and Farm Diversification: Methodological Aspects

3.1 Objectives of the Study

The following are the formulated objectives of the study:

1. To examine the growth pattern and diversification of agriculture amongst the regions, namely eastern, western, northern and southern region vis-à-vis at all-India level.
2. To analysis the share of horticulture crops under agricultural diversification in eastern region vis-à-vis northern, southern and western regions of India.
3. To examine the growth pattern and performance of livestock across the regions of India.
4. To identify problems and prospects of growth and diversification of agriculture in India.
5. To suggest measures for strengthening agriculture and allied sectors in India especially in eastern region of India.

3.2 Hypotheses of the Study

The study aims to test the following hypotheses:

1. The average share of agriculture and allied sector in GSDP/GSVA of India is less than that of the share of agriculture and allied sector in GSDP/GSVA of northern region.
2. The average share of agriculture and allied sector in GSDP/GSVA of northern region is greater than the share of agriculture and allied sector in GSDP/GSVA of eastern region.
3. There has been no significant difference in the annual growth rate of Simpson Diversification Index (SID) between eastern and southern region.

3.3 Importance of the Study

In order to analyse the growth and diversification of agriculture in favour of high valued crops, on the basis of geographical and topographical propinquity, all the Indian states have been classified into four major regions viz. eastern, northern, western and southern. As per the data related to population, density, and geographical area for the year 2011 and average per capita income for the year 2016-17, have been computed and compiled from Census 2011 and Statistical Year Book India, 2017, respectively. The northern region is characterized as the third most populated region (282 million) in the country having the second largest geographical area (667 thousand square kilometre) and population density (i.e. 423 people per square kilometre) with average per capita income of ₹ 55,569 and this region comprises of states Haryana, Himachal Pradesh, Jammu and Kashmir, Punjab, Uttar Pradesh, and Uttarakhand; the western region is classified as a highly populated region (340 million) in India having the largest geographical area, i.e. 1,290 thousand square kilometre, lowest population density (263 person per square kilometre) including the second largest urban population (35.2 percent) and third largest average per capita income of ₹ 53,701. This region comprises of Gujarat, Madhya Pradesh, Maharashtra, Rajasthan and Chhattisgarh. However, as per the Census 2011, the southern region is the least populated (251 million), with second lowest population density (395 person per square kilometre) and is highly urbanized (40.9 percent) having the highest level of average per capita income ₹ 61,901 and includes states of Andhra Pradesh, Karnataka, Kerala, and Tamil Nadu.

The eastern region includes Assam, Bihar, Odisha, West Bengal and Jharkhand. This region is considered as the least developed and is socially and economically a backward region in the country. This region is characterized by the second largest population (302 million) having a high level of population density (607 persons/square kilometre) with lowest levels of geographical area (497 thousand square kilometre), and a per capita income

₹ 30,104 and urban population amounting to 20 percent. Agriculture and allied sectors are backbone in this region and a majority of the population is dependent on agriculture. Hence, a sustained agricultural growth in eastern region will have a positive impact on the conditions of the workers and would help in alleviation of poverty, since a majority of people living below poverty line in this region are agricultural labourers. Unfortunately, the performance of agriculture sector in this region has been constantly poor in comparison to the remaining regions of India. The region not been able to exploit its potential of agricultural growth and resources remain untapped due to poor planning and lacklustre agricultural policies.

Thus, the present work analyzes the growth and trends of diversification in the region vis-à-vis India. Further, as per various studies, agriculture diversification of small farms is often suggested as a means for rapid rural development in India. As per the Agricultural Census 2011, small and marginal holdings accounted for about 85 percent of the total operational holdings in the country, operating more than 44 percent of the total area. Majority of small and marginal farmers cultivate mainly low value subsistence crops. In the absence of adequate farm and non-farm employment opportunities, they are also forced to live below poverty line. The situation is likely to worsen because of the growing pressure of population on land and the limited scope of increasing additional production. Through subsistence farming, commercialization and diversification of small farms within and outside agriculture and their proper integration with local and global markets can be achieved. This is intended not only to liberate the small and marginal farmers from poverty trap, but also to meet the country's growing demands for fruits, vegetables, milk and milk products, meat, fish, eggs etc. which generally show rising trends with increasing levels of per capita income in the economy.

However, the moot question today is how we can achieve the goal of diversification of small farms by overcoming various technological, infrastructural, institutional and policy constraints. The present study intends to analyze the problems and prospects of diversification of small farms in India mainly by keeping in view some of the above mentioned constraints.

3.4 Database and Methodology

The present study is mainly based on time-series data. The statistics is collected from different official documents of Government of India and states published by different Government bodies and official websites. Only four major regions of India have been included in the study and among them the main focus is on eastern region vis-à-vis northern, southern and western regions. Data on production of major food grains and non-food grains was compiled from Centre for Monitoring Indian Economy (CMIE) database, Agricultural Statistics at a Glance, Directorate of Statistics, Ministry of Agriculture and Farmers' Welfare, Government of India and Handbook of Statistics on Indian Economy, 2016-17, Reserve Bank of India. Data on area, production and yield of horticultural crops was collected from National Horticulture Board, Ministry of Agriculture and Farmers' Welfare, Government of India, and EPW Research Foundation India Time Series Online Database.

The time-series data on gross state domestic product and its components was compiled from the official website of the Ministry of Statistics and Programme Implementation, Government of India and Reserve Bank of India, respectively. Statistics related to consumption of fertilizers, gross and net cropped area, gross and net irrigated area and proportion of total holdings, agriculture credits, road lengths and consumption of pesticides was gathered from Centre for Monitoring Indian Economy (CMIE), and Agricultural Statistics at a Glance (various issues). Information on rural and urban literacy, agriculture workforce, and region and gender-wise population was gathered from Census of India, Office of the Registrar General and Census Commissioner, Government of India. Data on poverty ratio has been taken from Planning Commission, Government of India.

The significance of a study to a great extent depends on the methods followed in the study area viz., collection of data and the methods implemented for its analysis. For this purpose, we used simple and easy to comprehend statistical and econometric tools in the light of the objectives and nature of the data. The methods of analysis adopted in the study are explained below.

Compound annual growth rate (CAGR) was computed by showing trends with respect to agriculture GSDP, agricultural exports and imports, agricultural inputs like agricultural credit, road and transportation, consumption of fertilizers, consumption of pesticides and area under irrigation. The CAGR based on the dummy techniques was computed to show trends in outputs like area, production and yield of major agricultural crops. Further, the CAGR with dummy techniques was also computed for area, production and yield of traditional and horticultural crops (fruits, vegetables) in order to know the degree of diversification in favour of high valued commodities.

We also estimated the region-wise compound annual growth rate of GSDP and area, production and yield of major food grains and non-food grains in order to know the disparities among the regions of India. As the number of observation was less than thirty and population parameter not known, we used paired t-test to know the significance of difference in the share of agricultural GSDP for India versus regions over the period. Besides, descriptive statistics like means and coefficient of variations were also used for the purpose of analysis.

Simpson Diversity Index (SID) was calculated to know the nature of diversification for horticulture, livestock, pulses, oilseeds in the eastern states vis-à-vis India and Bihar vis-à-vis India during 1990-91 to 2012-13.

3.4.1 Compound Annual Growth Rate (CAGR): CAGR measures an annual average growth rate over a period of time. This measure is a constant percentage rate at which a variable grows or declines from year to year to reach its current value.

If a variable y is growing at a constant proportionate rate of growth 'r', the value (*Yt*) at time period 't' will be:

$$Y_t = Y_o(1 + r)^t + e^{u_t} \text{ ------------------------------------ } \textit{Equation (1)}$$

Where *Yt* and *Yo* are values of the variable of time period t and initial value respectively. By taking logarithm in both sides of equation (1)

$\ln Y_t = \ln Y_o + t\ln(1+r) + u_t$ --------------------------*Equation (2)*

$\ln Y_t = b_o + b_1 t + u_t$ ------------------------------------*Equation (3)*

Where 'ln' refers to natural log

Where, *Yt* is the value of the variable in *t*th year whose annual compound growth rate is to be found out, and t is the number of years. Numbers 1, 2, 3 etc. are used for the consecutive years. And resultantly the following formula w is used for getting compound growth rate (r):

Where: $b_o = \ln y_o$

$b_1 = \ln(1+r)$

$r = [anti\ \ln(\hat{b}_1) - 1] \times 100$ ------------------------*Equation (4)*

Where, r = compound annual growth rate (percent).

3.4.2 Compound Annual Growth Rate (CAGR) by Using Dummy Variable Technique: The number of observations available for estimation of rate of growth should be fairly large. This is essential so as to provide sufficient degree of freedom (≥12) for precise estimation and statistical testing of the unknowns. This point needs to be critically kept in mind while computing rates of growth over different sub-periods from an available time series (Sethi, 2008). [1] However, sub-periodization may result in a severe loss of degrees of freedom available for estimation/testing of the rates of growth (Sethi and Raikhy, 2001). [2]

Thus, for testing of null hypotheses regarding constancy, acceleration or deceleration in rate of growth, we may estimate an exponential equation of the type:

$X_t = b_o b_1^{(1-D)t} b_2^{Dt} . e^{u_t}$ ----------------------------------*Equation (1)*

Where, D stands for dummy variable, assuming values of 0 and 1 during pre- and post-periods respectively. During the first and second period, equation (1) would be equivalent respectively to:

Pre-Period; $X_t = b_o b_1{}^t e^{u_t}$

$r_1 = (b_1 - 1) \times 100$

Post-Period; $X_t = b_o b_2^t e^{u_t}$

$r_2 = (b_2 - 1) \times 100$

Taking logarithm of equation (1) we get:

$\ln x_t = \ln b_0 + (1 - D)t \ln b_1 + Dt \ln b_2 + u_t$ -----------*Equation (2)*

$\ln x_t = \hat{b}_0 + \hat{b}_1(1 - D)t + \hat{b}_2 Dt + u_t$ -----------------*Equation (3)*

Where: $\ln b_o = \hat{b}_0$ and $\ln b_1 = \hat{b}_1$, Where: Star (^) means estimated and '$\ln$' refers to natural log

Providing rate of growth in the corresponding periods as:

Pre-Period: $r_1 = [anti\ \ln(\hat{b}_1) - 1] \times 100$

Post-Period: $r_2 = [anti\ \ln(\hat{b}_2) - 1] \times 100$

Nevertheless, as could be easily seen, the two rates could be obtained in a single stroke by estimating equation (3) involving the entire series.

3.4.3 t-Test (one-tail): The one-tailed test is a directional hypothesis test which refers to a test in which one mean would be greater or less than another mean, but not both. A statistical hypothesis test, wherein the alternative hypothesis (H_a) has only one ending direction, i.e., either left or right. Therefore, one direction i.e. left or right should be chosen even before testing the t-test. However, if the alternative hypothesis does not appear in a directional manner, then we call it a two-tail test.

On the other hand, one-tailed test is a significance test, in which at the end of the sampling distribution, the area of a rejection appears on either right or left side which exhibits that the estimated test parameter is greater or less than the critical value. If the sample that is being tested falls into the rejection region i.e., one-sided critical area, either left or right side, we reject the null hypothesis in favour of the alternative.

Furthermore, the level of significance also indicates that if the resulting p-value is less than 5 percent which means that the differences between both the observations (i.e., the average share of agriculture and allied sector in GSDP/GSVA of India is less than that of share of agriculture and allied sector in

GSDP/GSVA of northern region and the average share of agriculture and allied sector in GSDP/GSVA of eastern region is less than the share of agriculture and allied sector in GSDP/GSVA of northern region) is statistically significant and the null hypothesis is rejected.

$$t = \frac{\bar{x}_1 - \bar{x}_2}{S.E.(\bar{x}_1 - \bar{x}_2)}$$

Where; t = t-statistics S.E. = standard error of difference between the sample mean $(\bar{x}_1 - \bar{x}_2)$

3.4.4 Average Annual Growth Rate (AAGR): The study also uses AAGR in cases where estimating CAGR will consume degree of freedom as the period is short.

$$AAGR = \frac{1}{n}\sum\left[\frac{Y_t - Y_{t-1}}{Y_{t-1}}\right] \times 100$$

Where, AAGR = average annual growth rate (percent)

Yt = value in the final year of the period

Yt-1 = value in the initial year of the period

n = number of years contained in the period.

3.4.5 Coefficient of Variation (C.V):

$$C.V. = \frac{\sigma}{Mean} \times 100$$

Where, 'σ' is the Standard deviation.

3.4.6 Simpson Index of Diversification (SID): We use Simpson Index to estimate agriculture diversification index. The index presents a clear dispersion of commodities in a geographical region. It is given by:

$$SID = 1 - \sum_{i=1}^{n} P_i^2$$

Where, SID is the Simpson Index of Diversification, and *Pi* is the proportionate value (or area) of the *i*th crop in the total value (area) of output. In this study, *'i'* varies for crops other than livestock and horticulture. Hence, the interpretation of when SID for a region increases, will imply that the value of livestock and horticulture output is going up. This indicates that in the region, resources used for production of traditional crops shift towards production of horticulture and livestock products. The SID has been established for the entire agricultural sector as well as within the crops sector, dividing it into broad sub-sectors like cereals, pulses, oilseeds, fruits, vegetables, spices and condiments, and the other crops.

Endnotes

1. Sethi, Amarjit Singh (2008), "Some Methodological Aspects of Rates of Growth Computations: Limitations and Alternatives", *South Asian Economic Journal*, 9:1, Sage Publications, p. 199.
2. Sethi, A.S. and P.S. Raikhy (2001), 'Changing Sources of Economic Growth in India: Implications for Second Generation Reforms', in Rudar Datt (ed.) Second Generation Economic Reforms in India, Deep and Deep Publications, New Delhi, pp. 120-37.

4

Growth and Employment Generation in Agriculture

4.1 Growth and Share of Agriculture in Gross State Domestic Product (GSDP)

In 1991, the country initiated economic reforms aimed at far-reaching changes in regulations, fiscal policy, trade policy, exchange rate, role of market forces, and private sector participation in economic activities. The agricultural sector was not targeted directly by the reforms for a couple of years, but it was affected indirectly by export liberalization and terms of trade resulting from deportation to industry.

4.1.1 Region and State-wise Growth Rate of Agriculture in GSDP: The gross domestic product (GDP) statistics provide a wide view of the overall performance of an economy and reveal the basic changes in the economy in the past and indicate the trends for the future.

GDP is measured either in terms of current market price or constant market price or in terms of factor cost. The GDP at current market price will not reveal the real changes in the nation's income if there are changes in general prices. Similarly, GDP at constant market price will not indicate real changes in the national income if there is greater level of government indirect business taxes and transfers, even though it overcomes the price effect inherent in the GDP at current market price.

GDP at factor cost can only measure the real national income of the economy. For a comparative analysis, composition of gross state domestic product (GSDP) was estimated in terms of gross value added (GVA) at 2004-05 prices of all the major states within the regions during pre-period (1990-91 to 1999-00), post-period (2000-01 to 2015-16) and overall period (1990-91 to 2015-16) that have been presented in Table 4.1.

It reveals that the annual growth rate in agriculture and allied sector in India stood at about 3.1 percent during the overall period which marginally grew from 3.3 percent during the pre-period to 3.5 percent per annum during the post-period.

Table 4.1: Region and State-wise CAGR (percent) of Agriculture, Industry, and Services Sector vis-à-vis Total GSDP @ 2004-05 Prices from 1990-91 to 2015-16

State/ Region	Agriculture and Allied			Industry		
	Pre	Post	Overall	Pre	Post	Overall
Assam	0.8	2.9	1.5	2.5	4.1	3.9
Bihar	-0.2	3.1	2.7	4.2	11.9	8.9
Odisha	1.8	3.6	2.3	4.9	8.8	7.3
West Bengal	5.2	2.2	2.9	6.0	5.8	6.3
Jharkhand	3.8	6.7	5.4	5.8	5.1	3.5
Eastern Region	2.7	3.1	2.7	5.2	5.9	5.5
Haryana	1.9	3.3	2.7	6.1	7.6	7.5
Himachal Pradesh	0.7	3.3	3.4	11.1	8.2	8.4
Jammu & Kashmir	4.5	2.1	3.0	2.7	4.3	3.7
Punjab	2.5	1.7	2.0	7.0	8.1	7.1
Uttar Pradesh	2.6	2.4	2.4	5.7	6.6	5.8
Uttarakhand	2.6	2.3	2.3	4.5	15.9	12.4
Northern Region	2.5	2.4	2.4	6.1	7.7	6.8
Gujarat	4.4	6.0	4.1	9.9	10.8	8.9
Madhya Pradesh	3.7	6.3	3.5	8.3	6.9	7.0
Maharashtra	4.4	3.5	3.5	6.7	8.0	6.3
Rajasthan	3.4	5.7	3.8	9.7	7.8	7.8
Chhattisgarh	-1.4	5.2	1.9	7.7	9.3	7.9
Western Region	3.5	5.2	3.5	8.0	8.7	7.4
Andhra Pradesh	2.6	4.5	4.0	6.8	6.9	6.9
Karnataka	4.4	3.1	2.1	8.0	6.7	7.2
Kerala	2.2	-0.4	0.6	6.9	7.2	6.8
Tamil Nadu	3.0	4.0	2.4	6.0	8.0	6.6
Southern Region	3.1	3.3	2.9	6.8	7.3	6.9
All-India	3.3	3.5	3.1	6.2	8.2	7.2

contd...

State/ Region	Services			GSDP		
	Pre	Post	Overall	Pre	Post	Overall
Assam	3.9	7.2	6.0	2.5	5.3	4.2
Bihar	4.8	8.2	7.1	2.8	7.4	6.0
Odisha	6.4	9.3	8.1	4.4	7.9	6.3
West Bengal	8.4	8.4	8.2	6.9	6.6	6.5
Jharkhand	5.9	9.9	7.6	5.5	7.2	5.3
Eastern Region	6.6	6.9	7.1	5.0	6.9	5.9
Haryana	7.6	11.7	10.9	5.1	8.6	7.7
Himachal Pradesh	6.9	9.8	8.5	6.3	7.8	7.1
Jammu & Kashmir	7.0	7.6	6.8	4.9	5.4	5.0
Punjab	5.9	8.0	7.0	4.8	6.2	5.4
Uttar Pradesh	4.5	8.1	6.4	4.1	6.1	5.1
Uttarakhand	7.2	12.4	10.0	5.1	11.7	9.0
Northern Region	5.5	9.0	7.5	4.5	6.9	5.9
Gujarat	8.8	10.3	9.3	8.3	9.8	8.2
Madhya Pradesh	5.9	7.7	6.3	5.6	7.1	5.6
Maharashtra	8.6	9.6	8.7	7.3	8.4	7.3
Rajasthan	7.7	8.6	7.4	6.8	7.6	6.5
Chhattisgarh	6.3	8.5	7.3	4.0	8.1	6.0
Western Region	8.0	9.3	8.3	7.0	8.4	7.1
Andhra Pradesh	6.4	2.3	4.8	5.3	7.8	6.9
Karnataka	9.1	9.1	9.0	7.3	7.4	6.9
Kerala	7.4	9.0	8.5	5.9	7.2	6.7
Tamil Nadu	8.9	9.8	8.9	6.9	8.5	7.3
Southern Region	7.9	7.8	7.9	6.4	7.8	7.0
All-India	7.8	9.8	8.8	6.2	8.2	7.2

Sources: Based on data computed and compiled from Ministry of Statistics and Programme Implementation, Government of India, and EPW Research Foundation India Time Series Online Database.

Note: Old Series 1980-81, 1993-94, 1999-00 and new series i.e., 2011-12 data were spliced into 2004-05 prices. Star '*' refers that the state of Telangana's data is merged with Andhra Pradesh. Pre: 1990-91 to 1999-00; Post: 2000-01 to 2015-16 and Overall: 1990-91 to 2015-16.

Among the regions, in terms of annual growth rate, the western region achieved the highest growth rate in agriculture and allied sector i.e., about 3.5 percent per annum followed by southern region (2.9 per cent), and eastern region (2.7 percent), while northern region laddered at the bottom level i.e., 2.4 percent per annum over the period of time (1990-91 to 2015-16). It is noticeable that, besides agriculture sector, western region also accounted for higher growth rates than that of the national average during the overall period. The main reason for this was that the region recovered significantly in its agricultural performance during the post-period (5.2 percent per annum) as compared to pre-period (3.5 percent per annum) with a major contribution by Madhya Pradesh (6.3 percent per annum) followed by Gujarat (6 percent per annum), Rajasthan (5.7 percent per annum) and Chhattisgarh (5.2 percent per annum). However, agriculture growth in Maharashtra declined sharply from 4.4 percent per annum in pre-period to 3.5 percent per annum in post-period which is why it listed at the bottom. In the present analysis, the appreciable dynamics of agriculture growth were observed that except Maharashtra, remaining all the states of western region, namely Madhya Pradesh, Gujarat, Rajasthan and Chhattisgarh accounted for faster agricultural growth rates than the national average (3.5 percent per annum) during the post-period.

Table 4.1 also highlights that after the western region, the second highest growth rate in agriculture and allied sector was witnessed in the southern region during the post-period with major contribution from Andhra Pradesh (including Telangana) (4.5 percent per annum) followed by Tamil Nadu (4 percent per annum), and Karnataka (3.1 percent per annum). Contrary to the western region, barring Jharkhand and Odisha, annual growth of agriculture in eastern states such as Bihar, Assam and West Bengal was comparatively below the national average, despite a notable increase in its growth rates during the later period as compared to earlier period.

In relation to achieving agricultural growth, states within the northern region were rated as the lowest amongst all the regions of the country. It was due to poor performance of agriculturally-dominated states viz. Punjab, Uttar Pradesh, including Uttarakhand and Jammu and Kashmir as their agriculture growth rates were found below the national average during the post-period.

Contrastingly, even after achieving impressive growth rates in agriculture and allied sector GSDP by two northern states viz. Himachal Pradesh and Haryana, the northern region registered the least annual growth rate in this sector during the post-period as against the pre-period. It was mainly caused by deceleration in agriculture growth by agriculturally-dominated states of Punjab and Uttar Pradesh, along with J&K, and Uttarakhand during the same period of time. Despite the sluggish growth rates coupled with continuous decline in its share, northern region still occupies the largest share in agriculture to total GDP in the country.

It can be summarized from the above evidence that the agriculture sector recorded miserable growth rates in both the regions namely northern and eastern regions and its values lay between 2.4 percent and 3.1 percent, respectively.

The western region registered an impressive growth in agriculture and allied sector (5.2 percent) and its growth rate accounted above the national average and consequently it stood at the first place. After western region, the southern region accounted for a substantial growth rate (3.3 percent) in agriculture and allied sector. Following this, it was marked as the second largest agriculture growing region in India during the post as well as overall period of study.

It is notable that, besides agriculture, western region also stood as the highest industrially growing region in India during the post-period. During the same period, its growth rate was reported above the all-India (8.2 percent) level.

After the western region, industrial sector of the northern region achieved the second highest growth rate of by 7.7 percent per annum followed by southern region (7.3 percent) for the same period. However, similar to agriculture, eastern region also achieved the lowest growth rate (5.9 percent) in industrial sector during the same period.

State-wise analysis reveals that states such as Gujarat, Chhattisgarh, Maharashtra, Rajasthan, and Madhya Pradesh registered impressive growth rates in industrial sector in western region. In southern region, Tamil Nadu, Kerala, Andhra Pradesh, and Karnataka accounted for the highest growth rates i.e., more than 6.7 percent per annum; in northern states, Uttarakhand, Himachal Pradesh, Punjab, Haryana, and Uttar Pradesh recorded the highest growth of 15.9 percent, 8.2 percent, 8.1 percent and 7.6 percent per annum, respectively, during the post-period.

On the other hand, among eastern states, Bihar recorded the highest rate of growth in industrial sector i.e., 11.9 percent per annum followed by Odisha, West Bengal, Jharkhand and Assam with 8.8 percent, 5.8 percent, 5.1 percent, and 4.1 percent per annum respectively during the post-period.

While analyzing the growth of GSDP at factor cost in services sector, the highest contribution was made by the western region (9.3 percent) followed by northern region (9 percent), southern region (7.8 percent), and eastern region (6.9 percent) during the post-period. The highest progress in services sector in western region was mainly due to major contribution of Gujarat, Maharashtra, Rajasthan, Chhattisgarh, and Madhya Pradesh during the post-period.

The northern region was found as the second largest contributor to the services sector during the same period with major contributions of Uttarakhand, Haryana, Himachal Pradesh, Uttar Pradesh, and Punjab. Simultaneously, southern region achieved the third largest growth rate in services sector, with its main source points being Tamil Nadu, Karnataka, and Kerala, while, Andhra Pradesh stood at the bottom.

As expected, similar to the industrial sector, eastern region also reported the least growth rates in services sector in all the regions, due to deterioration of services growth rate in West Bengal from 8.44 percent during earlier period to 8.36 percent during the later period. On the other hand, except West Bengal, the remaining states of eastern region showed increasing growth rates during the same period. Thus, it may be concluded that the growth rate in services sector in states of eastern India was abysmally lower than that of the national average.

4.1.2 Region and State-wise Share of Agriculture and Allied Sector in GSDP (at 2004-05 Prices): Available evidence indicates that at all-India level, the share of agriculture continuously declined from 29.5 percent in 1990-91 to 11.6 percent in 2015-16, i.e., its share declined by 18 percent between the two comparable periods (Table 4.2). Moreover, it is surprising to witness from Table 4.2 that in all the states as well as regions, there was a general decline in the share of agriculture and allied sector during 2015-16 as against 1990-91. This was mainly because agriculture sector appears to be oriented in favour of non-farm sector. However, despite the continuous decline, agriculture and allied sector of the country still continued to be the major source of livelihood for people especially the rural people and played a significant role in country's economic development. This is so because the agriculture sector still provides about 62.7 percent of India's employment and more than 58 percent of households depend on agriculture for their principal means of livelihood [Indian Labour Organization (ILO), July, 2016] [1].

According to region-wise analysis, the highest share in agriculture and allied sector was observed in the northern region which stood at 17.3 percent followed by the eastern region (15.5 percent). These two regions registered growth rates above the national level (11.6 percent) during 2015-16. However, the state-wise analysis reveals that the highest contribution in agriculture was obtained by the northern region following major contributions by Uttar Pradesh (20.2 percent), followed by J&K (19.7 percent), Punjab (19.4 percent), Himachal Pradesh (15 percent), Haryana (13 percent) and Uttarakhand (8.2 percent) during the same period. Similarly, in the eastern region, Assam (20.9 percent), Bihar (19.4 percent), West Bengal (14.8 percent), Odisha (14.1 percent) and Jharkhand (13.4 percent) were the major contributors in agriculture sector during 2015-16. Alternatively, the southern region (11.5 percent) and western region (11.2 percent) were identified as the least contributors to the agriculture sector, and their share was slightly below the national average during the same period of time.

A comparative estimation of the share of agriculture is presented in Table 4.2. In terms of percentage change between 1990-91 and 2015-16, the highest deceleration was seen in the northern region i.e., by 20.7 percent, and this deceleration was largely curbed by services (18.3 percent) and industrial (4 percent) sector during the same period. Similar to northern region, eastern region accounted for second highest decline in its agriculture share by 18.8 percent, followed by southern (17.3 percent) and western (16.2 percent) regions during the same period.

Following the analysis, it is surprising to note that the eastern region is a region whose contribution in all the sectors, such as agriculture, industry and services has fallen rapidly between the two comparable periods i.e. 1990-91 to 2015-16. To sum up, it can be inferred that despite a decrease in the overall share of agriculture, still about 62.7 percent of India's labour force relies on this sector and the situation continues to be a major challenge before the policy makers.

Table 4.2 also reveals that in western states, Chhattisgarh recorded the highest decline in their share in agriculture by 27 percent followed by Rajasthan (18.8 percent), Gujarat (17.1 percent), Madhya Pradesh (14.1 percent) and Maharashtra (11.3 percent) during 2015-16. However, during the same period, in southern states, the highest share of agriculture declined in Karnataka and Kerala by 21.8 percent individually, followed by Andhra Pradesh (17.2 percent), and Tamil Nadu (11.8 percent).

Finally, it can be observed that the share of agriculture and allied sector in GSDP was found lower while gauging on all-India basis i.e., about 29.5 percent and 11.6 percent as compared to the northern region's (38 percent and 17.3 percent respectively) during 1990-91 and 2015-16. The statistical result also depicts that amongst the regions, northern region registered the highest average share of agriculture as against all-India vis-à-vis the eastern region during the post as well as the overall period.

In addition to the data presented in Table 4.2, the estimated 't' values can make it easier to understand our results for finding the significance of difference between these samples (the mean value of share of agriculture and allied sector in GSDP during the period 1990-91 to 2015-16) as shown in Table 4.3.

Table 4.2: Region and State-wise Changes in the Share of Agriculture and Non-Agriculture Sector to Total Gross State Domestic Product in India @ 2004-05 Prices

Year	Agriculture and Allied Sector		Change between two periods	Industry		Change between two periods
	1990-91	2015-16		1990-91	2015-16	
(1)	(2)	(3)	(3-2)	(4)	(5)	(5-4)
Assam	37.9	20.9	-17.0	24.2	21.6	-2.6
Bihar	45.9	19.4	-26.5	11.6	21.5	9.9
Odisha	36.7	14.1	-22.6	29.6	34.0	4.4
West Bengal	32.4	14.8	-17.6	20.9	18.5	-2.4
Jharkhand	15.6	13.4	-2.3	56.7	38.5	-18.2
Eastern Region	34.4	15.5	-18.8	25.6	16.3	-9.3
Haryana	39.2	13.0	-26.2	30.2	28.3	-2.0
Himachal Pradesh	39.2	15.0	-24.2	28.0	40.8	12.8
J&K	30.1	19.7	-10.4	33.1	23.1	-10.0
Punjab	42.1	19.4	-22.7	20.9	29.2	8.3
Uttar Pradesh	37.0	20.2	-16.8	19.7	21.6	1.9
Uttarakhand	38.1	8.2	-29.9	19.1	37.6	18.5
Northern Region	38.0	17.3	-20.7	22.4	26.4	4.0
Gujarat	26.9	9.8	-17.1	35.5	46.0	10.5
Madhya Pradesh	38.3	24.1	-14.1	20.7	25.3	4.6
Maharashtra	17.4	6.1	-11.3	36.2	28.2	-7.9
Rajasthan	38.3	19.4	-18.8	22.3	29.8	7.5
Chhattisgarh	43.4	16.4	-27.0	29.2	45.6	16.5
Western Region	27.4	11.2	-16.2	31.0	33.5	2.5
Andhra Pradesh*	34.8	17.6	-17.2	21.8	20.1	-1.7
Karnataka	32.8	11.0	-21.8	27.8	26.7	-1.1
Kerala	29.3	7.6	-21.8	19.7	21.0	1.3
Tamil Nadu	19.6	7.8	-11.8	35.3	28.6	-6.7
Southern Region	28.8	11.5	-17.3	26.9	24.5	-2.4
All-India	29.5	11.6	-18.0	27.6	26.6	-1.0

contd...

Year	Services Sector		Change between two periods
	1990-91	2015-16	
(1)	(6)	(7)	(7-6)
Assam	37.9	58.5	20.5
Bihar	42.6	59.7	17.1
Odisha	33.7	53.0	19.3
West Bengal	46.7	66.7	20.0
Jharkhand	27.6	48.8	21.1
Eastern Region	40.1	31.1	-9.0
Haryana	30.6	61.6	31.0
Himachal Pradesh	32.8	44.3	11.5
J&K	36.7	56.9	20.2
Punjab	37.0	53.1	16.0
Uttar Pradesh	43.4	60.0	16.6
Uttarakhand	42.8	55.6	12.8
Northern Region	39.6	57.9	18.3
Gujarat	37.6	44.9	7.3
Madhya Pradesh	41.0	51.3	10.3
Maharashtra	46.4	68.3	21.8
Rajasthan	39.4	52.3	13.0
Chhattisgarh	27.5	37.7	10.3
Western Region	41.6	56.8	15.2
Andhra Pradesh*	43.4	24.6	18.8
Karnataka	39.5	61.7	22.2
Kerala	51.0	73.8	22.8
Tamil Nadu	45.1	65.0	19.9
Southern Region	44.3	53.1	8.8
All-India	42.5	61.9	19.3

Sources: Same as for Table 4.1.

Table 4.3: Average Share of Agriculture in GSDP and GDP @ 2004-05 Price, by using Paired t-test Statistics (1990-91 to 2015-16)

Variable	Result-I		Result-II	
	All-India <	Northern	Northern >	Eastern
Mean	20.48	25.76	25.76	20.00
Std. Err.	1.1493	0.2848	0.2848	0.1646
Std. Dev.	5.8601	1.4521	1.4521	0.8391
t-statistics#	*-5.6907**		*-28.0865**	

Source: Estimated by the author.

* We find that the means are statistically different from each other at any level greater than 1 percent level of significance; # refers one-tailed t-test.

The result reveals that the average share of agriculture and allied sector in terms of GSDP @ 2004-05 prices is significantly high for northern region as compared to all-India (Result-I). Similarly, the average share of agriculture and allied sector in terms of GSDP is low for eastern region as compared to the northern region.

Moreover, one more aspect is also seen from the result that the average share of agriculture and allied sector in eastern region is not only significantly lower than that of the northern region; but it is also lower than that of all-India level over the reference period of study.

4.1.3 Region and State-wise Trend in Growth of Agricultural Output and Yield (TE-1993 to TE-2008): The total value of output from agriculture and allied sectors, yield in rupees per hectare of gross cropped area (₹/Ha of GCA) and its annual growth rates have been presented in Table 4.4., for period-I and period-II for analysing the growth and performance of agriculture and allied sectors across the regions vis-à-vis the country.

At the national level, the agricultural output growth and the yield growth rate accelerated by 2.10 percent and 1.77 percent per annum respectively during the period-II (i.e. TE-1993 to TE-2008). In the eastern region, the growth rate of agricultural output grew at 0.78 percent and 1.09 percent per annum during the same period which was much below the national average.

Table 4.4: Growth of Value of Output and Crop Yield across Regions of India from TE-1993 to TE-2008

Region	Value of Output				
	in ₹ '000 million			CAGR (percent)	
	TE-1983	TE-1993	TE-2008	Period-I	Period-II
Northern	249.3	353.4	444.4	3.55	1.54
Eastern	140.5	200.3	224.9	3.61	0.78
Western	227.2	313.6	504.9	3.27	3.23
Southern	214.8	300.5	403.3	3.41	1.98
All-India	843.5	1,174.5	1,605.1	3.37	2.10

contd...

Regions	Yield				
	₹/Ha of GCA			CAGR (percent)	
	TE-1983	TE-1993	TE-2008	Period-I	Period-II
Northern	6,423	9,244	11,191	3.71	1.28
Eastern	4,944	6,894	8,115	3.38	1.09
Western	3,464	4,551	6,649	2.77	2.56
Southern	6,848	9,178	1,21,682	2.97	2.18
All-India	5,090	6,957	9,050	3.17	1.77

Sources: Bhalla and Singh (2010) and Bhalla and Singh (2012) [2]
Period: I (TE-1983 to TE-1993) and Period-II (TE-1993 to TE-2008).
Note: Data for output and yield includes 44 crops for both the periods.

Table 4.4 also reveals that the eastern region as a whole recorded a significant growth in yield from ₹ 6,894 in TE-1993 to ₹ 8,115 in TE-2008 per hectare of gross cropped area, and growth rate achieved was 1.09 percent per annum during the given period. In spite of the significant growth in yields, eastern region has been found at the bottom of all the regions as well at all-India level during the same period. Similarly, the western region accounted for the highest growth rate in yields at about 2.56 percent followed by the southern region (2.18 percent). The northern region at 1.28 percent and eastern region at 1.09 percent were placed at the bottom during period-II.

Therefore, based on the above mentioned data and analysis, we can conclude that in terms of yield growth rate, the eastern region was at the bottom rung among all the regions in the country during period-II. Since yield growth rate is a pre-dominant source of growth of agricultural output, a slow growth in both output and yield in eastern states of India should be a matter of great concern for the policy makers. It is also important to underline that the disparity among the eastern states continues to be very high, coupled with severe climatic, structural and institutional factors like erratic rainfall and irrigation, gamble of monsoon and the level of infrastructural and technological investments in this region.

4.1.4 Region and State-wise Change in the Cropping Pattern: Cropping pattern refers to the allocation of cultivated land among the diverse crops, grown in a country.

In addition to this, cropping pattern also deals with the nature of agricultural operations e.g., the importance of food crops vis-à-vis other high value crops (HVCs) like fruits, vegetables, and flowers etc. Table 4.5 depicts that at the national level, the share of food grains in gross cropped area (GCA) declined from 68.9 percent in TE-1993 to 63.8 percent in TE-2008.

The decline in the total area under food grains adversely affects the growth of food grains output and its share in total value of agricultural output decelerated from 52.7 percent to 48.2 percent during the same period (Bhalla and Singh, 2012). Data further reveals that in the western and the eastern region, the share of area under food grains declined by 6.1 percent and 4.2 percent respectively between the two periods (i.e., TE-1993 and TE-2008) from 64.0 percent and 76.5 percent in TE-1993 to 57.9 percent and 72.3 percent in TE-2008.

At the national level, the share of remaining crops (including fruits and vegetables) in GCA increased sharply from 9.6 percent to 13.6 percent; however the share of oilseeds, cardamom and spices, plantation and fibre crops remained almost constant during the same period.

Table 4.5: Region-wise Share of various Crops in Total Gross Cropped Area during TE-1990-93 to TE-2003-08

Region	Year	Rice	Wheat	C.C.	Pulses
North	1990-93	20.9	35.2	11.8	8.9
	2005-08	23.0	37.3	9.6	7.2
Eastern	1990-93	54.9	7.3	4.5	9.8
	2005-08	54.3	8.0	3.7	6.2
Western	1990-93	9.9	9.3	28.4	16.4
	2005-08	9.5	9.6	22.3	16.4
Southern	1990-93	21.9	0.6	20.1	11.7
	2005-08	21.2	0.8	18.5	13.5
All-India	1990-93	23.0	13.0	18.6	14.4
	2005-08	22.4	13.9	15.5	12.0

contd...

Region	Year	FG	Oilseeds	C and Spices	Remaining Crops*
North	1990-3	76.9	6.3	0.1	8.4
	2005-8	77.1	4.6	0.2	9.8
Eastern	1990-3	76.5	6.3	0.8	11.9
	2005-8	72.3	4.5	1.0	16.1
Western	1990-3	64.0	17.6	0.6	10.6
	2005-8	57.9	20.7	0.8	12.7
Southern	1990-3	54.4	20.7	2.5	13.4
	2005-8	53.9	18.4	2.6	15.2
All-India	1990-3	68.9	13.3	0.9	9.6
	2005-8	63.8	13.8	1.0	13.6

Sources: Same as Table 4.4.

* remaining crops includes fruits and vegetables etc.

However, in the eastern region, the share of remaining crops (i.e., fruits and vegetables) in total cropped area increased moderately from 11.9 percent to 16.1 percent, while cardamom and spices crops remained almost constant during TE-1993 and TE-2008.

In terms of value of output, the share of horticultural crops such as fruits and vegetables etc., increased sharply from 18.3 percent in TE-1993 to 23.9 percent in TE-2008, while cardamom and spices crops showed almost a constant growth i.e., 2.7 percent during both the periods (Bhalla and Gulati, 2010 and 2012).

In short, there has been a significant change in cropping pattern during TE-1993 and TE-2008, both in terms of area allocation and share in total value of output.

The most important change that can be seen is the significant decline in the share of area under coarse cereals and increase in the share of area under high value crops (HVCs) which brought about changes in relative prices and productivity.

There exists significant growth in area from LVCs like cereals and coarse cereals, pulses etc., towards HVCs like fruits and vegetables, spices and oilseeds.

4.2 Agriculture and Employment Generation

Since inception, it is well known that the pressure of population on Indian agriculture has continually increased, as a majority of Indian population is largely dependent on Indian agriculture for their livelihood. But, Indian agriculture is not growing at the speed, at which Indian population is increasing, and hence, the average size per capita land holdings have been declining continuously. Thus, we can say that the Indian agriculture is associated with the plethora of problems such as an ever declining land-man ratio, small and fragmented holdings, highly unfair land distribution structures, etc. In continuation, the traditional pattern of agriculture cannot provide a doable solution to the problem of rural unemployment and under-employment. Therefore, diversification of agriculture in favour of high valued crops and livestock in rural employment has gained significant importance over a period of time. During the last two decades, several scholars have studied on the growth and speed of employment diversification in rural India (Visaria, 1995; Chaddha and Sahu, 2002; Mukhopadhyay and Rajaraman, 2007). Majority of them have found that the contribution of non-agricultural sector has been increasing over a period of time and the ability to generate additional employment in agriculture has reached its peak. In this situation, agriculture diversification should in favour of high valued crops i.e., horticulture which has emerged as a tool to generate additional employment opportunities and augment farm incomes in India (Joshi et al., 2006). In view of the above predicament, in this section of the study, an effort has been made to estimate and analyze rural employment in India especially in eastern India across the various sub-sectors of agriculture.

4.2.1 Share of Employment in Agriculture: Table 4.6 presents growth and pattern of rural employment in agriculture and non-agriculture sectors in India for the period 1993-94 to 2011-12 (i.e., 50th, 61st and 66th NSSO rounds). The data reveals that at the national level the share of rural employment in agricultural and allied sectors decelerated from 64.8 percent in 1993-94 to 58.5 percent in 2004-05, which further decelerated to 48.9 percent during 2011-12. However, the corresponding figures at the national level highlight that in non-agricultural sector, rural employment accelerated from 35.2 percent to 41.5 percent in 1993-94 and 2004-05, respectively and also increased by 51.1 percent during 2011-12. Alternatively, the total share of employment in non-agricultural sector increased by more than 45 percent i.e., from 35.2 percent in 1993-94 to 51.1 percent in 2011-12, while in agriculture and allied sector it decelerated by 24 percent during the same period i.e., from 64.8 percent in 1993-94 to 48.9 percent in 2011-12.

Table 4.6: Changes in the Employment (UPSS) Structure of India: 1993-94 to 2011-12

Sector/Industry	1993-94	2004-05	2011-12
Agricultural and Allied-Activities	64.8	58.5	48.9
Mining and quarrying	0.7	0.6	0.5
Secondary Sector	14.7	18.1	24.4
Tertiary Sector	20.5	23.4	26.7
Non-agriculture	35.2	41.5	51.1
Total	100.0	100.0	100.0

Sources: Papola, T.S. (1994), "Structural Adjustment, Labour Market Flexibility and Employment", *The Indian Journal of Labour Economics*, 37(1):3-16; Papola, T.S. (2013), "Employment Growth during the Post-Reform Period", *The Indian Journal of Labour Economics*, 56(1):1-13.

Table 4.7 also depicts that the share of rural employment in non-agricultural sector in almost all the states of India showed an increasing trend during 2009-10 as compared to 1993-94. However, eastern states such as Bihar, Jharkhand and Odisha; western states like Madhya Pradesh and Rajasthan; northern states like Jammu & Kashmir, Uttarakhand, Himachal Pradesh, Uttar Pradesh and Haryana; and southern states, namely Andhra Pradesh and Kerala have shown higher growth rates in rural employment in non-agricultural sector during 2009-10.

Thus, it can be summarized that the growth rate of agricultural employment in rural areas declined over the period.

This is due to decline in the share of agriculture coupled with the decline in the farm wages and purchasing power of the wage earners.

Table 4.7: State-Wise Share and Growth Rates of Non-Farm Sector in Rural Employment (percent)

Region	State	Percent of Non-Agriculture		CAGR (Percent)
		1993-94	2009-10	1993-94 to 2009-10
Eastern	Assam	21.3	29.5	3.2
	Bihar	16.9	33.1	7.1
	Jharkhand	23.9	45.2	5.9
	Odisha	21.9	32.4	3.5
	West Bengal	26.9	43.7	2.0
Northern	Himachal Pradesh	22.8	37.1	4.8
	Haryana	28.6	40.2	3.9
	Jammu & Kashmir	28	40.3	10.6
	Punjab	22.7	38.2	3.3
	Uttar Pradesh	20.7	33.1	4.2
	Uttarakhand	34.9	30.5	5.4
Western	Gujarat	20.7	21.7	0.9
	Madhya Pradesh	13.8	17.6	4.6
	Maharashtra	20.3	20.6	1.8
	Rajasthan	19.2	36.7	5.6
	Chhattisgarh	9.4	15.1	3.6
Southern	Andhra Pradesh	22.7	31.3	2.8
	Karnataka	18.3	24.3	1.9
	Kerala	42.3	64.3	3.9
	Tamil Nadu	31.3	36.3	0.5
	All-India	21.7	32.1	3.2

Source: Kumar, Anjani, Sant Kumar, Dhiraj. K. Singh and Shivjee (2011), "Rural Employment Diversification in India: Trends, Determinants and Implications on Poverty", *Agricultural Economics Research Review*, Vol. 24, pp. 361-372.

Endnotes

1. Indian Labour Organization (ILO) (2016), "India Labour Market Update", ILO Country Office for India, July.
2. Bhalla, G.S. and Gurmail Singh (2012), "Economic Liberalisation and Indian Agricult ıre: A District Level Study", Sage Publications, New Delhi.

5

Growth and Share of Agriculture in India's Exports

Though India has been importing food grains for quite some time since Independence, it has also been exporting agriculture products thereby helping the country not only to pay for food imports but for other imports which include capital goods. The data on India's total exports and imports during 1990-91 to 2016-17 has been presented in Figure 5.1 and Table 5.1.

It is noted from Table 5.1 that total exports of the country during the year 1990-91 was to the extent of ₹ 32.56 thousand crores which noticeably increased to ₹ 1,854.1 thousand crores in 2016-17, i.e. more than 57 times greater than base year (i.e., 1990-91), registering a significant annual growth rate of about 17.4 percent per annum over the period 1990-91 to 2016-17. Simultaneously, agricultural exports from India also increased from ₹ 6 thousand crores in 1990-91 to ₹ 217 thousand crores in 2016 17, registering a significant annual growth rate at about 14.9 percent per annum during the same period (Table 5.1). Though, over the years, agricultural exports have increased manifold, yet after various ups and downs, the share of agricultural exports in total national exports decelerated from 18.49 percent in 1990-91 to 11.70 percent in 2016-17 (Figure 5.2).

On the other hand, it can also be noticed from Figure 5.2 that agricultural imports increased remarkably from ₹ 1.21 thousand crores in 1990-91 to ₹ 143.0 thousand crores in 2016-17 (Figure 5.1). Although, the percentage share of agriculture imports for India significantly increased from 2.79 percent to 5.57 percent during 1990-91 to 2016-17 respectively (Figure 5.2), registering a statistically significant annual growth rate of 18 percent per annum, yet the total national imports increased remarkably by 19 percent per annum (Table 5.2).

Figure 5.1: Trends of India's Imports and Exports of Agricultural Commodities vis-à-vis Total National Imports/Exports: 1990-91 to 2016-17 (₹ thousand crore)

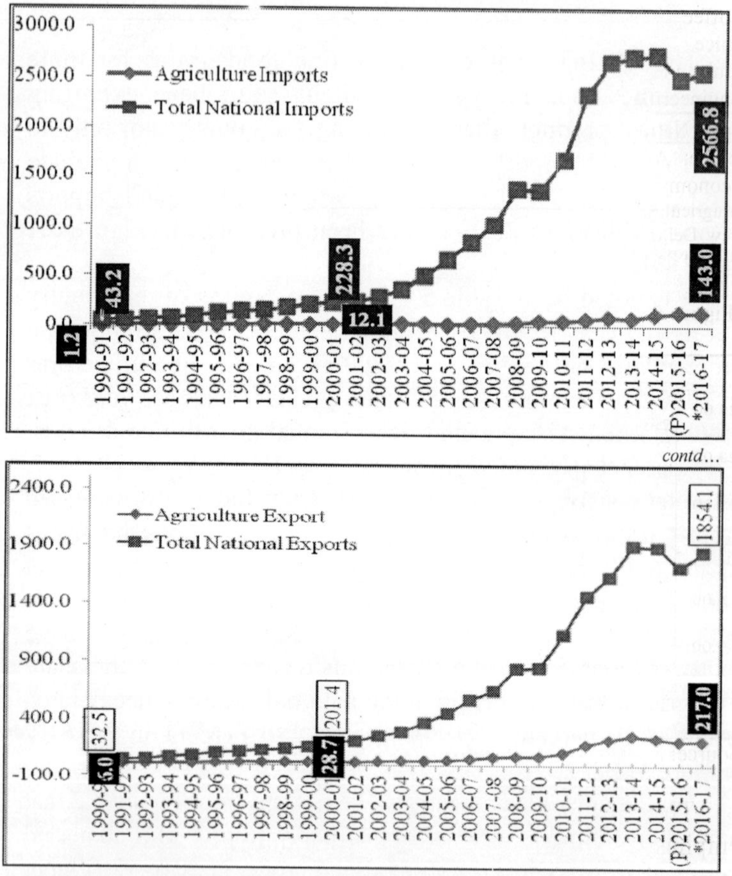

contd...

Source: Author's estimates based on Agriculture Statistics at a Glance, 2017, and Handbook of Statistics on Indian Economy, 2017, RBI, GoI. Note: For the year 2016-17, data related to agricultural exports were compiled from Economic Times (Online), Aug 9, 2017, New Delhi; and data related to agricultural imports were computed based on the information collected from Annual Report, 2016-17, Ministry of Commerce and Industry, Department of Commerce, GoI.

Table 5.1: Exports of Principal Commodities in India

(₹ in thousand crore)

Commodity	1990-91	2000-01	2016-17#	CAGR (percent)		
				Pre	Post	Overall
Agriculture Export	6.0	28.7	217.0	19.0	17.0	14.9
Rice	0.5	2.9	38.7	29.2	20.0	16.9
Tea	1.1	1.8	4.9	7.8	8.7	6.6
Coffee	0.3	1.2	5.7	25.9	13.2	10.0
Spice	0.2	1.6	19.4	25.5	20.9	17.4
Fruits and Vegetables	0.2	0.8	16.4	11.1	23.4	17.8
Engineering Good	4.0	31.2	450.3	20.8	19.5	20.7
Total National Exports	32.5	201.4	1854.1	19.0	17.2	17.4

Source: Author's estimates based on Handbook of Statistics on Indian Economy, 2016-17, Reserve Bank of India, GoI. # For the year 2016-17, data related to agricultural exports were compiled from Economic Times (Online), Aug 9, 2017, New Delhi; Pre-Period: 1990-91 to 1999-00; Post Period: 2000-01 to 2016-17 and Overall Period: 1990-91 to 2016-17.

Figure 5.2: Percentage Share of Agriculture in Total Import and Export of India: 1990-91 to 2016-17

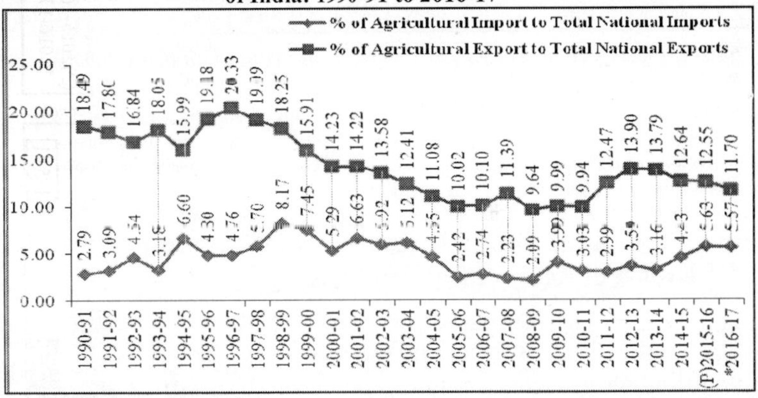

Source: Estimated by author.

The new agriculture policy under the liberalized regime emphasized diversification of agriculture and promotion of farm exports. The globalization scenario offers enough opportunities for deriving large benefits through substantial increase in agricultural exports. India exported agricultural commodities worth of ₹ 6 thousand crores during the 1990-91 while during the same year imports were worth of ₹ 1.21

thousand crores, showing a positive balance of trade and the same continued over the years. However, during the recent past, i.e. during 2016-17, India exported agricultural commodities worth ₹ 217 thousand crores and the total agricultural imports were worth ₹ 143 thousand crores. This analysis reveals a trade balance indicating an increasing surplus balance of trade in the country.

Table 5.2: Compound Annual Growth Rate and Coefficient of Variation of Export and Import of India since 1990-91 to 2016-17

(₹ in thousand crore)

Year	1990-91	2000-01	2016-17	CAGR (percent)			CoV **
				Pre	Post	Overall	
Agriculture Imports	1.2	12.1	143.0*	33.8	17.5	18.0	115.9
Total National Imports	43.2	228.3	2566.8	20.2	19.1	19.0	107.5
Agriculture Exports	6.0	28.7	217.0**	19.0	17.0	14.9	105.5
Total National Exports	32.5	201.4	1854.1	19.0	17.2	17.4	104.4

Source: Author's estimates based on Handbook of Statistics on Indian Economy-2016-17, Reserve Bank of India; for the year 2016-17, data related to agricultural exports were compiled from Economic Times (Online), Aug 9, 2017, New Delhi; and data related to agricultural imports were computed based on the information collected from Annual Report, 2016-17, Ministry of Commerce and Industry, Department of Commerce, GoI. **Figure in parentheses is coefficient of variation (CoV) for overall period (1990-91 to 2016-17).

5.1 Export of Agricultural Products

As stated earlier, agriculture sector continues to occupy an important place in the Indian economy in terms of its contribution to GDP, foreign trade and in terms of its share in work force. India's share in total world trade was about 2.7 percent (GoI, 2014) [1] out of which agricultural exports accounted for 11.70 percent during 2016-17. During the post-WTO period, agricultural exports showed an increase in absolute terms, but it had been falling steadily as a proportion of the total exports till 2005-06. Thereafter, the share increased dramatically up to 2007-08, but since 2008-09 onwards again, it has increased rapidly and reached to the level of 12.64

percent during 2014-15 (Figure 5.2).

The plummeting in the relative share of agricultural exports was due to the relatively faster growth of India's total exports. Besides, it may be due to structural breakthrough as well as the foremost target of agricultural policy which is related to achieving self-sufficiency in agriculture thereby limiting the scope of trade. In contrast, increase in absolute value of agricultural exports was mainly due to significant increase in export of cereals, sugar, oil meals, processed foods, fruits and vegetables, poultry and dairy products.

5.2 Export of Rice

Rice has been considered as a staple food in many countries including India. Apart from this, rice along with wheat is also considered as major food grains in India. Therefore, as a major source of food grains, rice exports from India increased in absolute terms but its annual growth declined in the post-period as compared to pre-period. The total export of rice rose from ₹ 0.5 thousand crores in 1990-91 to ₹ 2.9 thousand crore in 2000-01; thereafter it remarkably increased to ₹ 38.7 thousand crore, registering a compounded annual growth rate of about 16.9 percent per annum over the period 1990-91 to 2016-17. But, in comparison with both the pre- and post-periods, it was found that the annual growth rate in the export of rice declined from 29.2 percent per annum in pre-period to 20 percent per annum in post-period (Table 5.1).

5.3 Export of Horticulture and Commercial Crops

India is known for its wealth in spices, producing more than 50 varieties including black pepper, cardamom, ginger, turmeric, chilies etc., and at least one or more spices is grown in almost all states of India and occupy an important place among the agro products exported. Out of the total production of spices, around 10 percent is exported as raw and value added product and rest is consumed for domestic purposes. In India, North-Eastern region has become a spice growing region, especially for ginger, chillies, garlic and coriander as compared to other states (GoI, 2001). India exported spices worth ₹ 0.23 thousand crores in the year 1990-91 which increased to ₹ 1.62 thousand crores in 2000-01 and thereafter increased sharply to ₹ 19.40 thousand crores in 2016-17. Thus, the total export of spices grew at a fast pace i.e., by 17.4 percent per annum during the last 27 years i.e., from 1990-91 to 2016-17.

Similar to spices, vegetables and fruits are also being considered as one of the most potential commodities for exports. Recently, the contribution of horticulture which comprises of fruits, vegetables, and flowers including livestock products, to the agricultural GDP, has increased significantly. It is worth noting that 8.5 percent of the gross cropped area (GCA) was shared by horticulture sector and it contributed about 30 percent of the GDP from agriculture during 2004-05 (Singh, 2015). [2]

It is also evident from Table 5.1 that export earnings from fruits and vegetables rose from ₹ 0.21 thousand crores in 1990-91 to ₹ 0.8 thousand crores in 2000-01 and thereafter increased to ₹ 16.4 thousand crore in 2016-17, registering a remarkable annual growth rate of 17.8 percent per annum over the period of study, i.e. from 1990-91 to 2016-17. Moreover, during the post-period, it is observed from the Table 5.1 that the highest CAGR was observed in the total export of fruits and vegetables and spices which was higher than that of the total export of rice, which led us to conclude that the growth of fruits and vegetables export in India's overall export basket increased rapidly by 17.8 percent per annum during the overall period, i.e. from 11.1 percent per annum during pre-period to 23.4 percent per annum during the post-period. This is expected to continue in future also, mainly because of the increase in per capita income, urbanization etc., which would lead to an increase in demand for these products. In contrast, other agricultural products viz. rice and coffee are observing a significant decline in their growth rates during the same period.

Hence, as per the above analysis, it can be concluded that there may be a paradigm shift in agricultural exports from rice and coffee to high remunerative crops including fruits and vegetables, spices, and tea. This remarkable shift may be due to the efforts which have been taken to promote the horticulture exports though the National Horticulture Mission launched in 2005-06 by the Government of India.

Endnotes

1. Government of India (2007), "Economic Survey: 2006-07", Ministry of Finance, New Delhi.
2. Singh, Arundhati (2015), "Horticultural Statistics", Department of Agriculture and Cooperation, Government of India, available at: www.nhm.nic.in/conf-ppt/3-horticulture-statistics.ppt.

6

Agriculture and Food Security

For the past several decades, the term 'food security' for alleviating poverty as well as malnutrition is still one of the major hindrances, because, it is a key constituent for the growth and development of any economy especially the developing economies in the world. Due to complexity in nature, so far, more than 200 definitions and 450 indicators (FAO, 2002) [1]; IFPRI (1999) [2] have been generated for addressing the issues related to poverty and its elements in the world. But the final report of The World Food Summit, 1996 defined the term 'food security' which has been globally acceptable as, *"when all people at all times have access to sufficient, safe, nutritious food to maintain a healthy and active life"*. Generally, the term food security includes ensuring physical and economical access to balanced diet, safe drinking water, environmental sanitation, basic health care, and education which they need for the purpose of livelihood security at the level of each household and all members within. Therefore, to meet the levels of attaining food security and hence overcoming poverty, enhancing food security, and spurring growth, agriculture comes forward as a strong option, because, food is one of the most important necessities of human beings and people have been working since ages to fulfil it. The dependence on food grains and alarming increase in human population has made the problem of availability of food grains more complicated.

Malthus was probably the first person who cautioned the world about the food crisis that human beings may face in future due to growing population on the one hand and the limited capacity of land to produce food on the other hand. He predicted starvation at mass level which will bring population back at the subsistence level. This pessimistic view of Malthus has been proven false by the fact that malnutrition at mass level has been successfully ignored globally, despite the continuously increasing population. However, intermittent food crises in the form of rising food prices and resulting incidence of hunger and malnutrition among the poor have been general phenomena in developing countries. Food and nutritional security is a serious global concern. Three international studies/reports have addressed this problem. These are: (i) World Agriculture: Towards 2020: An FAO Study, (ii) Population and Food in Early Twenty-first Century by the International Food Policy Research Institute and (iii) full house by the World Watch Institute.

The problems of meeting the growing demand for food will be greatest in the most densely populated countries. India is one of the most densely populated countries of the world where a very high proportion of land is cultivated. It is estimated that the requirement of food stock to feed India's projected population of 1.4 billion in 2030 will be 114 million tonnes of rice, 83 million tonnes of wheat, 13 million tonnes of maize, 104 million tonnes of fruits and 193 million tonnes of vegetables (TERI, 2005). [3] According to a study by ICAR (2011), [4] it has been estimated that there is a strong need of increasing production of food grains at the rate of 5.5 percent per annum, so that the projected demand of food grains from 192 million tonnes in 2000 to 345 million tonnes in 2030 can be fulfilled accordingly.

Further, Swaminathan (2013) [5] also proposed and suggested that the population of India is likely to increase up to 1.8 billion by 2050 and therefore it would be needing 460 million tonnes of cereals to meet the needs of the projected population as well as to meet the needs of the livestock and poultry too. This is really a big challenge while having limited availability of natural resources viz., land and water. Besides, various studies reveal that a large part of the land area is uncultivated. It is also hypothesized that the augmentation and amplification of agriculture in this area will be highly expensive, so, there is a need to be focused on the extensive work for soil renovation, water conservation, and irrigation etc. The use of fertilizers has been an important factor contributing to the growth in yields of agricultural crops during the last two and half decades. Application of judicious doses of fertilizers in agricultural production is induced by expansion of area under irrigation as the latter further increases the yields and reduces the risk of investment in fertilizers. Therefore, production and yield of food grains can be increased by increasing the irrigated area.

Food demand in India is continuously rising due to growing population. In the Report of the Technical Group on Population Projection constituted by the National Commission on Population, India's population is projected to be 1400 million by 2026 which will result in further intensive use of agricultural land to meet the rising demand for food. A recent study also advocated that the projected population growth of India was observed at about 1.4 percent per annum, however, the annual growth rate of food grains production was estimated at about 2.5 percent per annum during 2020 respectively (Anwer et al., 2015) [6] which reveals that India will produce surplus food grains with their growing population during 2020.

However, the declining land-man ratio will result in strong exploitation of agricultural resources. A single-minded focus on increasing yields of agricultural crops without paying any heed to its probable side effects in the long-run will lead agriculture towards non-sustainability and would prove disastrous. Therefore, it is vital to ensure that all the valuable non-renewable agricultural resources are protected from damages whatsoever.

Moreover, the gap between population and land-based agricultural production is still persisting in many parts of the country despite modernization and technological improvements that had been brought about in raising agricultural productivity. The belief that food from land resources will be able to support the ever increasing population is relatively becoming paradoxical and Malthusian pessimism still pervades in many parts of the world.

6.1 Changing Patterns of Production and Composition of Food Grains

As per table 6.1, at the national level, the production of food grains increased by more than 57 percent during 1990-91 to 2016-17 from 176.4 million metric tonnes (MT) in 1990-91 to 275.7 MT in 2016-17. However, among the food grains, there has been a tremendous increase in the production of wheat which was the main crop associated with the Green Revolution. The production of wheat increased by about 78 percent from 55.13 MT to 98.4 MT during the reference period. However, except wheat, a decreasing trend was observed in the production of coarse cereals and pulses in the total food grain production during the pre-period and thereafter, i.e. during the post-period, the production of these commodities registered an increasing trend.

Table 6.1: Region-Wise Production of Food grains
(million tonnes)

Region	Year	Rice	Wheat	Coarse cereals	Pulses	Food grains
Eastern	1990-91	25.5	4.3	1.9	2.2	33.9
	2000-01	28.1	5.7	2.0	1.2	37.0
	2016-17	39.7	6.5	4.3	2.0	52.5
Northern	1990-91	19.3	38.1	6.4	3.5	67.3
	2000-01	24.7	51.5	6.7	2.4	85.3
	2016-17	29.8	60.1	7.2	2.4	99.5
Western	1990-91	9.0	12.5	17.6	6.9	46.0
	2000-01	5.9	12.1	12.7	5.1	35.8
	2016-17	18.0	31.5	20.5	14.7	84.7
Southern	1990-91	18.9	0.1	6.6	1.6	27.3
	2000-01	24.4	0.3	9.4	2.3	36.4
	2016-17	14.5	0.2	8.9	3.1	26.7
All-India	1990-91	74.3	55.1	32.7	14.3	176.4
	2000-01	85.0	69.7	31.1	11.1	196.8
	2016-17	110.2	98.4	44.2	23.0	275.7

Source: Author's estimates based on Handbook of Statistics on Indian Economy, 2016-17, Reserve Bank of India.

According to region-wise analysis, the total production of food grains in northern region was observed to be high at 99.5 MT followed by the western region (84.7 MT) during 2016-17, while the eastern region (52.5 MT) and southern region (26.7 MT) remained at the bottom during the same period.

In absolute terms, the most prosperous and major contributing region in the production of food grains was the northern region with major contributions of wheat (60.1 MMT), rice (29.8 MMT), and somehow coarse cereals (7.2 MMT) followed by western, eastern, and southern region in the country during the overall period. But in terms of absolute increase or decrease, the northern region lowered in their position due to stagnation in the production of pulses and coarse cereals. As a result, it increased second highest margin in the total food grains production by 32.3 MMT as compared to the western region (38.7 MMT) during 2016-17 over the period 1990-91.

Table 6.1 reveals that despite decline in its production with a huge margin, northern region was still the largest producer of food grains in India during 1990-91 to 2016-17. Similar to the northern region, western region was also the second largest producer of food grains (84.7 MMT) in the country with major contributions in terms of wheat (31.5 MMT), coarse cereals (20.5 MMT), rice (18 MMT) and pulses (14.7 MMT) during the same period of time.

The eastern region was the third largest producer of food grains in India and rice being the major staple food of the residents of this region, eastern region is known as a big producer of rice in the country. Thus, the production of rice in this region rose by 14 MMT during 2016-17 in comparison to 1990-91. The southern region witnessed a deceleration in the production of food grains (-0.6 MMT) during the same period due to a surprising decline in the production of rice (-4.5 MMT), and the stagnation in the production of wheat (0.0 MMT) during the same period.

Finally, as regards the progress in food grains production in India, it witnessed an increase of more than 99 MMT with major contribution by wheat (43.2 MMT), rice (35.9 MMT), coarse cereals (11.5 MMT) and pulses (8.7 MMT) between the two comparable periods i.e., 1990-91 and 2016-17 (Table 6.2).

Table 6.2: Differences in Production of Food grains across the Regions between Pre, Post and Overall Period

(million tonne)

Region	Period*	Rice	Wheat	Coarse cereals	Pulses	Food grains
Eastern	1999-00 over 1990-91	2.6	1.4	0.1	-1.0	3.1
	2016-17 over 2000-01	11.6	0.8	2.3	0.8	15.5
	2016-17 over 1990-91	14.2	2.2	2.4	-0.2	18.6
Northern	1999-00 over 1990-91	5.4	13.4	0.3	-1.1	18.0
	2016-17 over 2000-01	5.2	8.6	0.4	0.1	14.2
	2016-17 over 1990-91	10.5	22.0	0.8	-1.0	32.3
Western	1999-00 over 1990-91	-3.1	-0.4	-4.9	-1.8	-10.2
	2016-17 over 2000-01	12.1	19.4	7.8	9.6	48.9
	2016-17 over 1990-91	9.0	19.0	2.9	7.8	38.7
Southern	1999-00 over 1990-91	5.5	0.1	2.8	0.7	9.1
	2016-17 over 2000-01	-10.0	-0.1	-0.5	0.8	-9.7
	2016-17 over 1990-91	-4.5	0.0	2.3	1.5	-0.6
All-India	1999-00 over 1990-91	10.7	14.5	-1.6	-3.2	20.4
	2016-17 over 2000-01	25.2	28.7	13.1	11.9	78.9
	2016-17 over 1990-91	35.9	43.2	11.5	8.7	99.3

Source: Same as for Table 6.1.

* Pre: 1999-00 over 1990-91, Post: 2016-17 over 2000-01 and Overall: 2016-17 over 1990-91.

Crop-wise analysis of the absolute increase or decrease in the percentage share of the production of rice, wheat, coarse cereals, and pulses to the total food grain production is presented in Table 6.3. The total increase in the share of rice was more profound in the western region (1.71 per cent) followed by northern region (1.3 percent), and the eastern region (0.32). However, among the regions, southern region had a highly negative (-15.18 percent) rate of change in production share of rice between the two comparable periods i.e., 1990-91 and 2016-17. It shows that rate of change of rice production in southern region deteriorated by 15.18 percent during 2016-17 in comparison to 1990-91. Similarly, the rate of change in wheat production was more prominent among the western region i.e. 10 percent followed by northern (3.73 per cent) and southern (0.14 per cent) region, but the eastern region accounted for a negative performance by (-)

0.21 percent during the same period of time.

Contrary to the rice production in southern region, the region displayed a better progress in the share of coarse cereals production (9.23 percent) during 2016-17 as against 1990-91, followed by the eastern region (2.62 percent). But among the remaining regions, western and northern region showed a negative progress in the share of coarse cereals production i.e. (-) 14 percent and (-) 2.33 percent respectively, during the same period.

The major component of the food grains is pulses which showed their highest progress among the southern region by 5.81 percent followed by western region (2.31 percent) during the same period. But the remaining two regions, namely eastern and northern registered a negative performance in the share of pulses by (-) 2.73 percent and (-) 2.71 percent respectively during the same period.

Table 6.3: Differences in the Production Share to Total Food grains across the Regions during the Period 1990-91 to 2016-17

Region	Period of difference	Rice	Wheat	Coarse cereals	Pulses
Eastern	1999-00 over 1990-91	0.63	2.85	-0.14	-3.34
	2016-17 over 2000-01	-0.31	-3.06	2.75	0.61
	2016-17 over 1990-91	0.32	-0.21	2.62	-2.73
Northern	1999-00 over 1990-91	0.27	3.75	-1.64	-2.38
	2016-17 over 2000-01	1.04	-0.02	-0.69	-0.33
	2016-17 over 1990-91	1.30	3.73	-2.33	-2.71
Western	1999-00 over 1990-91	-3.04	6.57	-2.78	-0.75
	2016-17 over 2000-01	4.75	3.42	-11.23	3.05
	2016-17 over 1990-91	1.71	10.00	-14.01	2.31
Southern	1999-00 over 1990-91	-2.33	0.20	1.63	0.50
	2016-17 over 2000-01	-12.85	-0.06	7.60	5.31
	2016-17 over 1990-91	-15.18	0.14	9.23	5.81
All-India	1999-00 over 1990-91	1.06	4.15	-2.75	-2.46
	2016-17 over 2000-01	-3.22	0.28	0.24	2.70
	2016-17 over 1990-91	-2.16	4.43	-2.51	0.24

Source: Same as for Table 6.1.

While summing up, it can be inferred that the progress in the share of production of rice and wheat was more prominent in western and northern region, coarse cereals were cultivated in larger quantities in southern and eastern regions, while the pulses were grown more in southern and western states during the two comparable periods i.e., from 1990-91 till 2016-17. It is evident from the present analysis that, except the southern region, the eastern region was found as one of the second less progressive regions, in terms of share of almost of all the crops including rice, wheat, coarse cereals and pulses in the total food grains production over a span of 27 years i.e., from 1990-91 to 2016-17. However, despite the laggard performance in the share of production in agriculture, the eastern region is still known as the largest rice producing region in the country.

Hence, as per the present analysis of food grains production, we can infer that the Engel's law seems to be operative in India during the post-reforms period which supports the fact that people of the country are spending more on superior varieties of food grains and horticulture produce. As a result, production of wheat, coarse cereals, pulses and horticulture crops such as fruits, vegetables and flower etc., has been increasing at a fast rate as compared to rice, especially during the post-period i.e., from 2000-01 to 2016-17. It is further to be analyzed that the sharp increase in wheat and pulses production may be due to the effective implementation of the government sponsored scheme of "National Food Security Mission" that was launched in 2007-08 and facilitated by high yielding variety (HYV) of seeds, mechanization of agriculture, use of modern technologies, large scale public investment in irrigation and minimum support price policy.

Thus, the scheme of National Food Security Mission (NFSM), launched in 2007-08 encompassing an increase in annual production of rice by 10 million tonnes, wheat by 8 million tonnes and pulses by 2 million tonne by the end of the Eleventh Five Year Plan, met with an overwhelming success and achieved the targeted additional production of rice, wheat and pulses (GoI, 2009). [6] Further, the mission continued till the end of the Twelfth Five Year Plan with new targets and objectives of additional production of rice by 10 million tonnes, wheat by 8 million tonnes, pulses by 4 million tonnes and coarse cereals by 3 million tonnes (GoI, 2012). [7] Besides, the increase in the share of area devoted to wheat production has also been facilitated by the growth in area brought under irrigation. The study done by Pal (2009) [8] also supported that the area under wheat increased at the rate of 0.7 percent per annum and area under jowar and bajra declined at the rate of 2.96 percent and 0.6 percent per annum respectively during 1990-91 to 2007-08.

Figure 6.1 also supports Engel's law that the average annual growth rates (AAGRs) of horticulture crops (4.9 percent) such as fruits (4.9 percent) and vegetables (5.1 percent) seems to be very high in comparison to food grains (2 percent) which confirms diversity in the dietary pattern from low valued crops to high valued crops over the period of study. Moreover, the AAGR of fruits and vegetables registered a high growth rate i.e., 4.9 percent and 5.1 percent per annum respectively over the period 1990-91 to 2016-17.

Figure 6.1: AAGR of Food grains and Non-Food grains Production vis-à-vis Total Population: 1990-91 to 2016-17

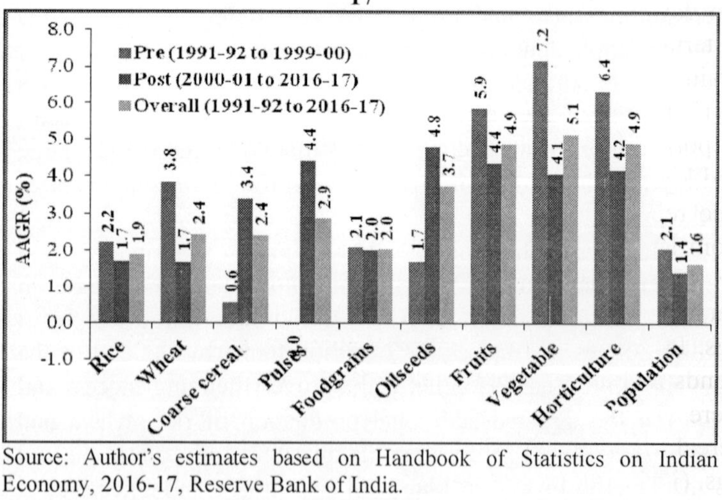

Source: Author's estimates based on Handbook of Statistics on Indian Economy, 2016-17, Reserve Bank of India.

On the other hand, during the same period, the total

population of the country rose by 1.6 percent per annum which was much lesser than that of the growth rates achieved by horticulture crops (4.9 percent per annum). Thus, there is a view that by reducing food grains intake in rural India, and indeed in the country as a whole, the people of the country are going to a voluntary shift in dietary habits towards high valued crops such as fruits, vegetables etc., owing to higher disposable incomes. The significant decline in cereals consumption is attributed to changes in consumer tastes and preferences towards superior food items as the income of the households increase (Radhakrishna and Ravi, 1991; [9] Business Standard, 2015, [10] GoI, 2015). [11] This is partly due to the diversification of agriculture in favour of superior non-cereal foods, particularly vegetables and fruits, milk and milk products, etc.

6.2 Availability of Food Grains

The per capita availability of food grains in 2017 remained remarkably lower than that for the year 1991. At all-India level, per capita availability of food grains fell to 485.4 gram per capita per day (PCPD) in 2017 from 510.1 gram per capita per day (PCPD) in 1991. Similarly, availability of food grains in terms of kilogram per annum, per capita availability of food grains fell down to 177.17 kg. per capita per annum (PCPA) in 2017 from 186.2 kg. PCPA during 1991 (Economic Survey Report, 2017). Apart from this, in terms of both gram/per day and kgs./per annum, per capita availability of cereals and rice also reportedly declined in India over the period of time i.e., from 1991 to 2017.

However, cereal consumption in India fell from 171 kgs. per capita per annum (468.5 grams PCPD) in 1991 to 157.5 kgs. PCPA (431.6 grams PCPD) in 2017. Thus, the declining trends in total cereal consumption with various ups and downs were visible in most of the years since 1990. The decline of cereal was very prominent in 2001 when it declined to 149 kgs. (i.e., 386.2 grams PCPD) per capita per annum (Ibid).

6.3 Consumption Expenditure on Food Grains

Table 6.4 shows a gradual decline in average monthly per capita expenditure b tween the two NSSO rounds (i.e., 66th and 68th rounds). The data indicates that the average monthly per capita consumption expenditure (MMRP) of India sharply increased by 36 percent from ₹ 1,053.04 to ₹ 1,429.96 in rural areas during 2009-10 and 2011-12 respectively. Similar to rural areas, average monthly per capita expenditure in urban areas increased by 33 percent per annum from ₹ 1,984.46 to ₹ 2,629.65 during the same period.

Thus, according to the above analysis, it may be concluded that the percentage increase in the average MPCE (monthly per capita consumption expenditure) in rural areas seems to be comparatively high (36 percent per annum) than that of urban areas (33 percent per annum) during the two NSSO rounds.

Table 6.4: Average MPCE in India

(in ₹)

MPCE	Rural		Urban	
	2009-10*	2011-12**	2009-10*	2011-12**
MPCE (URP)	927.7	1,278.94	1,785.81	2,399.24
MPCE (MRP)	953.05	1,287.17	1,856.01	2,477.02
MPCE (MMRP)	1,053.04	1,429.96	1,984.46	2,629.65

Source: NSSO (2013), "Key Indicators of Household Consumer Expenditure in India, 2011-12", Ministry of Statistics and Programme Implementation, Government of India, *66th **68th NSS Rounds.

Figure 6.2 reveals the extent of under nourished population across the states of India between the two National Sample Survey (NSS) Rounds data i.e., 1983 and 2011-12. At the national level, the percentage of under nourished population declined from 30.3 percent to 20.8 percent between the two comparable NSSO rounds. Thus, it can be said that the under nourished population and poverty gradually declined which can be testified through the percentage increase in the average MPCE in rural and urban areas by 36 and 33 percent respectively during 2009-10 and 2011-12. The present results from this study were also evident from the Global Hunger Index (GHI), 2014; in terms of hunger, India improved its ranking from at 55th during 2014, to 63rd. Despite this, it could not exit from the alarming situation and its hunger is classified as "serious" (Anwer, et al., 2015). Undoubtedly, increase in literacy levels, urbanization, shift in the dietary pattern toward high value crops and a constant increase in per capita income has enabled people in India to improve their standard of living. Besides this, during the same time, poverty in the country is still persisting which presents an alarming situation. Because of this, India's rank in the Global Hunger Index slipped by 3 positions from 97 in 2016 to 100 in 2017 (GHI, 2017). Thus, a continuous increase of GHI score in this way is quite frustrating for India and that is great concern for the policy makers.

Figure 6.2: State-wise Percentage of Under Nourished Population in India during the NSSO Rounds (1983 and 2011-12)

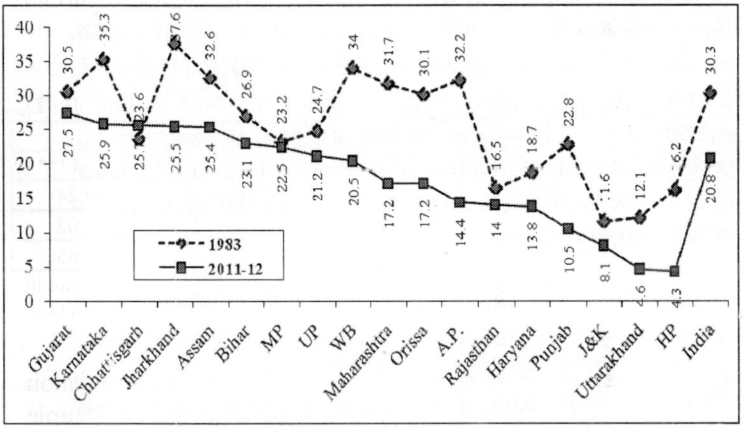

Source: Anwer, Md. Ejaz, Rajesh Kumar Rana a d Prem Narayan (2015), "Present Status of Food Security in India", *ICAR-Kheti*, A Hindi Journal, October, 67(7):3-7.

Moreover, India achieved success in fighting short-term food insecurity caused by supply side fatigue including droughts or flood; however, it miserably failed to make much dent in chronic food insecurity as reflected in the low energy intake and high incidences of malnutrition. The overall improvement in nutritional status has also been very slow. There is chronic under nourishment in about half of the population (Figure 6.2).

Curiously, the proportion of consumption expenditure spent on food is slowly going down even in the households with chronic malnutrition.

6.4 Summary

Food grains production of India has increased by more than 57 percent during 1990-91 to 2016-17 from 176.4 million tonnes (MT) in 1990-91 to 275.7 MT in 2016-17. According to region-wise analysis, the total production of food grains in northern region was observed to be high at 99.5 MT followed by western region (84.7 MT) during 2016-17.

The progress in the share of production of rice and wheat was more prominent in western and northern regions; coarse cereals were more dominant in southern and eastern regions, while the pulses were grown more in southern and western states during the two comparable periods from 1990-91 to 2016-17. It is evident from the present analysis that, except for the southern region, the eastern region has been found as one of the second less progressive region, in terms of share of almost all the crops like rice, wheat, coarse cereals and pulses in the total food grains production over a span of 27 years from 1990-91 to 2016-17.

The per capita availability of food grains in 2017 remained remarkably lower than that in 1991. At all-India level, per capita availability of food grains fell to 485.4 gram per capita per day (PCPD) in 2017 from 510.1 gram per capita per day (PCPD) in 1991. Apart from this, in terms of gram/per day, per capita availability of cereals and rice also reportedly declined in India during 1991 to 2017.

Endnotes

1. The Food and agriculture Organization (FAO) (2002), "Trade and Food Security: Conceptualizing the Linkages Expert Consultation", Rome, July 11-12, available at: http://www.fao.org/ locrep/005/y4671e/y4671e03.htm#TopOfPage.
2. IFPRI (1999), "Technical Guides for Operational Zing Household Food Security in Development Projects", Food Consumption and Nutrition Division, Washington.

3. TERI (2005), "Energy Data Directory and Yearbook", The Energy and Resources Institute, TERI Press, New Delhi.
4. ICAR (2011), "Vision 2030", Indian Council of Agricultural Research, New Delhi.
5. Swaminathan, M.S. and R.V. Bhavani (2013), "Food Production and Availability: Essential Pre-requisites for Sustainable Food Security", Indian Journal of Medicinal Research, September, 138(3): 383-391.
6. Anwer, Md. Ejaz, Rajesh Kumar Rana and Prem Narayan (2015), "Present Status of Food Security in India", *ICAR-Kheti,* October, 67(7): 3-7.
7. Government of India (2012), "National Food Security Mission: Operational Guidelines", Ministry of Agriculture and Farmers Welfare, New Delhi.
8. Pal, Prankrishna (2009), "Growth and Instability of Agricultural Production in India during the Reform Periods: A Decomposition Analysis", *The Indian Economic Association,* Conference Volume, Shri Ram Printers, Visakhapatnam, Part-II, 21.
9. Radhakrishna, P. and C. Ravi (1990), "Food Demand Projections for India," Centre for Economic and Social Studies, Hyderabad.
10. Business Standard (2015), "India's Per Capita Income up 10 Percent", July 4, New Delhi.
11. Government of India (2015), "Central Statistical Organization, 2015: Gross and Net State Domestic Product at 2004-05 Series", Ministry of Statistics and Program Implementation, New Delhi.

7

Reasons, Nature and Pattern of Agricultural Diversification

7.1 Growth and Trend of Agricultural Diversification

Agriculture sector has been continuously declining as regards its share in GDP and has been losing its importance in India's economic growth in the recent years. However, the continuous growth in agriculture sector in India since 2004-05 (GoI, 2015) [1] is not a sign of prosperity for the Indian farming. It is a fact that this sector has been experiencing a continuous decline in its share (at 2004-05 prices), from 29.53 percent in 1990-91 to 22.6 percent in 2000-01 which further declined to 13.94 percent in 2013-14 (GoI, 2014) [2].

However, at constant prices (2011-12), the share of agriculture and allied sector accounted about 15.16 percent during 2016-17 which actually decelerated from 18.53 percent in 2011-12. The persistent decline in the share of agriculture and allied sector (GoI, 2017) is a matter of great concern before the policy makers of the country. The first sign of slowdown in agriculture was observed in the mid-1990s mainly due to decline in public investment in agriculture sector.

The total production of food grains decreased from 259.3 million tonnes in 2011-12 to 257.1 million tonnes during 2014-15 which is estimated lesser than by 2.2 million tonnes as compared to the production of the previous year 2011-12 caused by lower production of rice, coarse cereals and pulses due to erratic rainfall during the monsoon season in 2014 (GoI, Economic Survey, 2014-15, Volume II).

Moreover, the growth rate of agriculture and allied sector in total GDP (at 2011-12 constant prices) increased from 1.2 percent per annum in 2012-13 to 43.7 percent per annum in 2013-14 but declined to 21.1 percent per annum during 2015-

16 (Economic Survey, 2015-16). National income statistics reveal that India registered a significant GDP growth rate of 7.4 percent due to impressive growth in service (10.6 percent) as well as industrial sector (5.9 percent) during the period 2014-15, despite facing a deceleration in the growth of agriculture and allied sector.

Farming is the back-bone of the Indian economy encompassing about 90.2 million agricultural households, including an estimated 58 percent of the rural households in the country which directly or indirectly depend upon agriculture for their livelihood (NSSO, 2015). [3] In spite of this, agriculture sector of the country is not only facing a deceleration in its share in GDP but is also facing the menace of natural disasters like floods, erratic rainfall, unprecedented rainfall, drought, and water logging every year.

The farmers of today are not only experiencing a slowdown in agricultural productivity vis-à-vis high input costs, increase in wage rates of labour and other marginal costs (Narayanamoorthy, 2007) [4] but also the technological fatigue, low seed replacement rate, inadequate credit supply, inefficient market access facilities, unbalanced use of fertilizers, low level of public investment, degradation of land and water resources, and stagnated net sown area (Singh, 2007). [5]

Moreover, the agriculture sector is also facing a number of constraints like declining total factor productivity (Shivay et al., 2010), [6] rural indebtedness (Dwarkanath, 2010), [7] fragmentation of land holdings, erratic rainfall, unprecedented and uncertain weather conditions, weak agro-based industry, illiteracy, lack of training, host of pest diseases, and decrease in investment in agriculture sector (Hazra, 2001), [8] lack of infrastructure like poor road network, transport, cold storage and processing infrastructure (Birthal et al., 2006), [9] deterioration of soil health, depletion of water table, inefficiency in transfer of technology, lack of investment in post-harvest technologies, decline in the gross capital formation in agriculture sector (Birthal et al., 2008), [10] poor power supply, dismal rural credit scenario (Patel, 2010) [11] and volatility of markets caused by the increasing global integration.

In addition to this, many arguments emerged contributing to the cause of stagnation in agricultural growth including technology and policy fatigue, incomplete agricultural transformation and higher level of specialization (high dependence on wheat and rice cultivation) and declining public support (Deshpandey, 2007) [12] making agriculture an uninviting and loss-making venture.

This situation necessitates for alternate opportunities where agriculture diversification has emerged as an important tool to alleviate farmers' distress. Diversification should be used as a means of not only getting the process of commercialization by increasing the markets for agricultural items on account of stability and change in the comparative advantages of crops over time (Deshpandey, 2007) but also to achieve the objectives of output growth, to augment farm income, employment generation opportunities (Bharghouti *et al*, 2004) [13] and natural resources' sustainability (Chand, 1999), [14] alleviate poverty, export promotion, improving food security, improving productivity of scarce resources (e.g., water) and improving environmentally sustainable farming systems through conservation and enhancement of natural resources (Jha, 1996; [15] Ramesh Chand, 1996; [16] Vyas, 1996; [17] and Joshi et al., 2002) [18] and conserve precious soil and water resources (Joshi et al., 2004). [19]

Agriculture diversification in favour of horticulture and livestock products is desirable to increase farm employment and income, reduce disparities across space and time, check degradation of natural resources and enhance export (Chand, 1999; Joshi et al., 2006; [20] Lumpkin, 2007). [21] Moreover, "diversification of agriculture will minimize the adverse effects of the current system of crop specialization and monoculture or sole cropping for better resource use, nutrient recycling, reduction of risk uncertainty and better soil conditions and also it can be an efficient mechanism for diminishing the impact of risk on farmers' welfare (Jorge and Valdes, 1995). [22] It will also insulate better economic viability with value added products and also improvement of ecology" (Jana, 2006). [23]

The country is now in the phase of agricultural development where it needs paying more attention to agricultural diversification and productivity enhancement. Union Budget 2010-11 proclaimed with reinforced vigour that "the agriculture sector occupies centre stage to promote inclusive growth, enhance rural incomes and sustain food security and nutritional security. To spur growth in this sector, the Government of India intends to follow with a four-pronged strategy covering: (i) agriculture production; (ii) reduction in wastage in produce; (iii) credit support to farmers and (iv) thrust to the food processing sector" (Srinivasan, 2010; [24] Shivay and Rahul, 2010). [25]

The approach paper to the Eleventh Five Year Plan envisaged a growth target of 8 percent of GDP, the agriculture and horticulture sector has to grow by 4 percent and more than 7 percent respectively with the contribution of 18.8 percent share in total agricultural production and 52 percent in total agricultural export (Yadav et al., 2003) [26] The Union Budget 2010-11 also announced that the farm sector has expanded Green Revolution to the eastern region of the country comprising of states like Bihar, Chhattisgarh, Jharkhand, Eastern U.P., West Bengal and Odisha with the energetic participation of *gram sabhas* and the farming families (Srinivasan, 2010).

Therefore, the policy makers in India have been focusing on the need for crop diversification in favour of high valued crops as a major strategy of agricultural development. This is the reason, that with an increase in per capita income, the demand for food grains is likely to grow at a slow rate as compared to high valued crops like oilseeds, fibers, sugarcane, livestock and horticultural commodities i.e., fruits and vegetables. And it compels the policy makers of the country for thinking that agriculture diversification not only provides opportunities for increasing farm incomes significantly but is also likely to put less pressure on natural resources which leads towards sustainable development of agriculture.

Hence, a road map is needed for agricultural sustainability which may focus on agricultural diversification in favour of horticultural crops including dairy, fisheries, poultry, oilseeds and many other subsidiaries. Horticulture and allied activities have emerged as a prominent sector which offers a wide scope in foreign exchange earnings and employment generation, and process of diversification is likely to resolve the problems of low productivity and thereby play an important role in removing poverty (Basu, 2008). [27]

With respect to the national economy, diversification generally conveys an inter-sectoral movement of resources, production, and income in an economy (agriculture, industry, services, etc.). Many economists advocate that diversification is a tool which helps in mitigating price risks and production risks of falling output. It is a strategy that involves doing more than one activity at any given time.

However, within the agriculture sector, diversification is a shift, in terms of area, production, income, uses, and transfer of resources from one crop (or livestock) to a large mix of crops and livestock, or from one enterprise to another, and it also involves moving away from farm to non-farm production like agro-processing, keeping in view the varying nature of risks and expected returns from each crop/livestock activity, and adjusting it in such a way that it leads to optimum portfolio of income. Agricultural diversification infers the transformation in crop-mix, enterprises-mix and activity-mix at the household level and it is considered as shift of resources from monoculture to a large mix of crops and livestock (Chand, 1999). On the other hand, the concept of crop diversification in agriculture refers to a "paradigm shift from one crop to another crop, bringing out a desirable change in the existing cropping pattern towards a more balanced cropping system to meet the ever increasing demand for cereals, pulses, oilseeds, fibers, fodders and grasses, fuel etc.". (Jana, 2006) [28]

This definition of diversification needs to be distinguished as movement of production-portfolio or resources from low-value commodity mix (crop and/or livestock) to high-value commodity mix (crop and/or livestock). "And it is precisely the movement to high value crops that indicates yet another way to augment income, besides the traditional ways of increasing yield, area or cropping intensity. Crop diversification is a strategy for ensuring food and nutritional security, alleviation of poverty, natural resource management for sustainable agricultural development and proper agricultural planning for different regions with varied resource bases" (Joshi et al., 2004).

Thus, based on these definitions, the nature of diversification can be broadly described as:

1. A shift from less profitable crops, i.e. food grains, coarse cereals etc., to high valued crops, i.e. fruits and vegetable etc.
2. Diversification from cereals to non-cereal food crops.
3. A shift of resource from farm to non-farm activities, like animal husbandry, fishing, poultry etc.
4. Use of resources in larger mix of diverse and complementary activities within the agriculture sector.
5. Diversification from low productivity to high productivity crops.

7.2 Reasons for Agricultural Diversification

The need for agriculture diversification in India arises due to various factors. Agricultural output, nearly 52.38 percent of un-irrigated area to total cropped area during 2012-13 (GoI, 2015) [29] depends upon erratic rainfall due to the gamble of monsoon. Apart from this, a majority of the Indian farmers belong to small and marginal farmers' category and cultivate low value subsistence crops like wheat and paddy. This subsistence farming system has led to severe economic, social and ecological problems, such as deceleration in productivity growth, decrease in agricultural self-employment, over exploitation of groundwater resources and decline in soil productiveness (Chand, 1999).

Moreover, Indian farmers experience low productivity, low per capita income, low purchasing power, low capital formation and low investment, low prices, high production cost, poor infrastructure and dramatic occurrence of two sets of natural disasters like floods and droughts which adversely affect the gross cropped area resulting in farmer distress which leads to a higher number of farmers suicides in many states of the country.

On the other hand, India is the second largest populated country in the world after China (PRB, 2015). [30] Therefore, the continuous rise in population with limited availability of land is a major challenge before India—how this limited land can be used for feeding the rapidly growing population. Hence, agriculture diversification is needed for proper land use planning for food security, risk coverage, mono-cropping, rural employment opportunities, sustainability of production system etc. (Punam, 2008). [31]

Agricultural diversification in favour of high value crops, such as fruits, vegetables and livestock products is desirable for farm employment generation, increase in farm incomes, reduction in disparities across space and time, check on soil degradation and enhancement of exports (Chand, 1999; [32] Joshi, et al. 2006; Weinberger, K. and Lumpkin, A.T., 2007).

In fact, horticulture crops including fruits and vegetables have been shown to earn more foreign exchange per unit of area as compared to low value crops like cereals. Alternatively, globalization of agriculture under the WTO regime also permits the Indian farmers to produce high value horticulture and livestock products for growing prosperous domestic and foreign consumers. Chand (1999) finds that in Punjab, horticulture and livestock engage more workforce than the traditional crops.

Therefore, in these circumstances, agriculture diversification is often suggested as a means to resolve these problems, and also it can be an efficient mechanism for reducing the impact of risk on farmers' welfare (Jorge et al., 1995). The Government also recognized that agriculture diversification in favour of horticulture and livestock is a tool to augment farm income and employment besides also as a mean for making agriculture a more attractive venture through efficient land use and optimal utilization of natural resources (Salve, 2008). [33]

7.3 Nature and Pattern of Agricultural Diversification

In today's economic order, agricultural diversification has assumed major importance from micro as well as macro point of view. However, India's existing liberalized regime is basically different from that during the Green Revolution period. During that period, agricultural growth was mostly accomplished by supply driven policy instruments like public investment in irrigation, power, agricultural R&D, extension services, price support, input subsidies, reform in tenancy and lease laws etc., (Singh, 2005), [34] while after the reforms period, agriculture growth and diversification towards high value crops in the country is mostly a demand-induced phenomenon.

Growing population, increasing urbanization, rising per capita income, increasing participation of women in job market, liberalized trade and convergence of food habits have largely shifted the consumption demand from cereals and starchy food commodities towards high value commodities, livestock and horticulture products.

As far as the horticulture commodities are concerned, it is a big challenge before the country as the farmers cannot store them for a long or even for stipulated time due to their highly perishable nature, and it is thus a threat, especially in case the market price depresses. Definitely, it seems like a challenging and undertaking task for establishing a remunerative price for the farmers as well as reducing the post-harvest losses that are estimated to be over ₹ 50 thousand crore per annum, that is nearly 30 percent of the country's production (GoI, 2008). [35]

7.3.1 Trends of Consumption Expenditure in India: In general, as the income of people rises their food baskets change. People replace inferior food items by superior ones in their food consumption baskets. This substitution of inferior food items by more qualitative one in consumption bowls of people is known as the Engel's law which states that as the income increases, the expenditure on food items decline.

Table 7.1 reveals that the share of all food items, such as cereals, grams and coarse cereals etc., in total consumption expenditure showed a declining trend both in rural and urban areas of India from 1993-94 to 2011-12.

While the share of rich calorie diets like pulses, milk, edible oil, eggs, meat and fish, and high valued crops i.e., vegetables and fruits in total food consumption expenditure in both the rural and urban area has been rising, the share in urban areas has been increasing at a very small rate i.e., by about 4 percent while in rural areas, it has accounted for a remarkable increase i.e., by 19.2 percent between 1993-94 and 2011-12.

Table 7.1: Trends in Percentage Composition of Consumer Expenditure in India

Item Groups	Rural		Urban	
	1993-94	2011-12	1993-94	2011-12
Share of cereals, gram and cereal subs in food total	38.8	25.3	26.1	19.5
Share of pulses, milk, edible oil, eggs, meat and fish, vegetables and fruits in food total	45.4	54.1	52.7	54.8
Share of food in total consumption	63.2	48.6	54.7	38.5
Share of non-food in total consumption	36.8	51.4	45.3	61.5

Source: Planning Commission of India (2014), "Report of the Expert Group to Review the Methodology for Measurement of Poverty", pp. 1-79.

Thus, it can be stated that the dietary patterns of Indians have been reclining over the years and has shifted towards fruits, vegetables and rich calorie diets.

Hence, the present results could be related with the results of the previous studies that the demand for HVCs food products, such as fruits, vegetables, milk, meat and fish has been increasing rapidly in domestic as well as global markets (Kumar et al., 2003; [36] Aksoy, 2005, [37] Kumar et al., 2012. [38]

Accordingly, the share of pulses, milk, edible oil, eggs, meat and fish, vegetables and fruits in total food consumption in India grew up by 54.1 percent in rural and 54.8 percent in urban areas from 45.4 percent in rural and 52.7 percent in urban areas during 1993-94 and 2011-12, respectively. Similarly, the share of food in the total consumption decelerated by 48.6 percent and 38.5 percent from 63.20 percent and 54.7 percent in rural and urban areas, respectively, during the same period.

Thus, the present trend clearly depicts that the share of non-food grains remarkably grew up by 51.4 percent from 36.8 percent in rural areas and from 45.3 percent to 61.5 percent in urban areas during the same period. To sum up, the share of non-food grains, especially horticulture products, in total consumption expenditure in India was comparatively higher than that of the food grains during the two NSSO rounds.

In the recent past, the contribution of horticulture and livestock products to the agricultural GDP has increased significantly. The horticulture sector constituted more than 12 percent of the total cropped area, and it contributed about 30.4 percent to the total agricultural GDP during 2012-13 (GoI, 2013-14). [39]

Recently, it has also been estimated that the area under horticulture crops voluminously grew up by 18 percent, while the expansion of area under food grains grew only by 5 percent during the period 2010-11 to 2014-15 (GoI, 2016). [40]

Furthermore, the area under horticulture crops substantially increased from 116.20 lakh hectares in 1990-91 to 156.90 lakh hectares in 2000-01 which further increased to 249.3 lakh hectares in 2016-17. During the above period, the total production of horticulture went up from 863.90 lakh tonnes to 1,502 lakh tonnes.

7.3.2 Trends in Area, Production and Yield of Horticulture Crops: In this section, we analyse the trends in area, production and yield of horticulture crop (fruits, vegetables and flower) among the major regions vis-à-vis all-India and examine the disparities among the selected regions of India, i.e. northern, eastern, western, and southern region (Table 7.2).

It is evident from Table 7.2 that the area under fruits in India significantly increased from 25.10 lakh hectares (Lha) in 1990-91 to 38.70 Lha in 2000-01 and further increased to 64.8 Lha in 2016-17.

It registered a statistically significant annual growth rate of 4.43 percent with 31.13 percent coefficient of variation.

Similarly, the production of fruits also increased from 275.20 lakh tonnes in 1990-91 to 431.40 lakh tonnes in 2000-01 and further to 928.5 lakh tonnes in 2016-17, recording a significant compound annual growth rate (CAGR) of 4.63 percent (CoV 36.0 percent) during the above mentioned period.

It is important to highlight that during the same period, although the area and production of fruits in India recorded a positive and significant growth rate, during the same time period, the annual growth per hectare in yield of fruits was almost constant.

Similar to fruits, Table 7.2 also shows that the area under vegetable crops incrεased significantly from 45 lakh hectares in 1990-91 to 102.9 lakh hectares in 2016-17. During the last 27 years, area under vegetables significantly grew by 3.1 percent per annum with 25.0 percent of coefficient of variation.

However, during the same period, production of vegetables increased at a faster rate than that of area i.e., from 496.30 lakh tonnes to 1750.1 lakh tonnes, registering a statistically significant growth rate of 4.79 percent (37.0 percent CoV) per annum.

Table 7.2: Area, Production and Yield and CAGR of Horticulture in India

(area in lakh hectare and production in lakh metric tonnes)

Crop	APY	1990-91	2000-01	2016-17	Average		
					Pre	Post	Overall
Fruits	Area	25.1	38.7	64.8	33.2	56.9	48.1
	Prod.	275.2	431.4	928.5	379.7	670.5	562.8
	Yield	11.0	11.1	14.3	11.4	11.7	11.6
Vegetables	Area	45.0	62.5	102.9	53.3	80.0	70.1
	Prod.	496.3	938.5	1750.1	702.8	1303.6	1081
	Yield	11.0	15.0	17.0	13.1	16.1	15.0
Flowers and Aromatic	Area	0.5	1.0	9.4	0.7	3.8	2.9
	Prod #	2.3	5.6	32.8	3.6	15.4	11.9
	Yield	4.4	5.7	3.5	4.9	5.1	5.0
Horticulture	Area	116.2	156.9	249.3	136.6	207.0	180.9
	Prod.	863.9	1502	2951.6	1201.4	2171.0	1811.9
	Yield	7.4	9.6	11.8	8.7	10.3	9.8

contd...

Crop	APY	CAGR (percent) ¥			CoV (percent) Overall
		Pre	Post	Overall	
Fruits	Area	4.1*	3.89*	3.9*	30.0
	Prod.	6.9*	5.0*	4.6*	36.0
	Yield	2.7*	1.0*	0.6*	10.3
Vegetables	Area	3.2*	3.1*	3.1*	25.0
	Prod.	5.6*	4.9*	4.7*	37.0
	Yield	2.4*	1.7*	1.6*	13.2
Flowers and Aromatic @	Area	22.1*	15.1*	13.8*	112.0
	Prod #	17.1*	12.9*	12.2*	90.0
	Yield	-4.1	-1.9**	-1.5***	29.6
Horticulture	Area	2.9*	3.0*	3.0	23.4
	Prod.	6.1*	4.9*	4.6	35.8
	Yield	3.1*	1.8*	1.5	13.5

Source: Author's estimation based on Indian Horticulture Database, 2017, Ministry of Agriculture and Farmers Welfare, Government of India, New Delhi and EPW Research Foundation, India Time Series Online Database (www.epwrfits.in).

* indicates at 1 percent, ** at 5 percent and *** at 10 percent level of significance; figures in parenthesis are coefficient of variations (percent of CoV), ¥ indicates CAGR (percent) estimated based on dummy variable; # Production of loose flower; @ data related to floriculture were gathered from 1993-94 to 2016-17.

Annual growth rate of yield of vegetables was found at a comparatively low level as compared to area under production of vegetables. It was because of the significant decline in growth rates of both the area and production of vegetables during the post-period (2000-01 to 2016-17) against the pre-period.

In horticulture crops, cultivation of floriculture gained prominence. Consequently, it has achieved remarkable growth rates in recent years. Corporate sector has aggressively entered in this sector in different activities, such as R&D, extension, production, processing, storage, marketing, export, etc. If we look at the data given in Table 7.2, we observe that the area under flower crops increased from 0.5 lakh hectares in 1993-94 to 9.4 lakh hectares in 2016-17, achieving a significant annual growth rate of about 13.8 percent with 112.0 percent coefficient of variation during the reference period. Similarly, the production of cut flowers (including aromatic plants) also grew by 17.1 percent per annum, while loose flower production grew by 12.9 percent per annum which is less than that of the area growth (13.8 percent).

However, on an average, area and production of horticulture crops achieved figures of 173.2 lakh hectares and 1640.4 lakh metric tonnes respectively during the period 1990-91 to 2013-14. If we analyze on the basis of major horticultural crops, we find that the highest land area was used under vegetable cultivation and then fruits, while the lowest area was found in the cultivation of flower during all the pre-, post- and overall periods under this study.

However, in absolute terms, average area and production of total horticulture crops of India accounted for 136.6 lakh hectare (Lha) and 1201.4 lakh metric tonne (LMT) during the pre-period that increased to 207 Lha and 2,171 LMT, respectively, during the post-period. But, if we look at the growth rates, we find that the growth rate of both the area and production declined in the post-period compared to the pre-period at a 1 percent level of significance.

Thus, based on the above analysis, we can summarize that, especially after 2000-01, the area, production and yield of almost all major horticulture crops such as fruits, vegetables and flowers and aromatic plants declined steadily. The main reason for this decline is that during the last five years especially after 2012-13, various ups and downs have been shown in the area and production of these crops (Horticulture Statistics at a Glance, 2017).

Among the horticulture crops, at the national level, the highest area was recorded under vegetables (66.05 lakh hectares), followed by fruits (46.2 lakh hectares), and flowers (1.3 lakh hectares) with corresponding units in the production standing at 1005.3 lakh MT, 518.9 lakh MT and 31.4 lakh MT respectively over the period of time. However, in terms of yield, vegetables registered a higher yield at 14.7 tonne/hectare (t/ha) followed by fruits (11.2 t/ha) and then flowers (5.8 lakh t/ha of flower) during the reference period.

7.3.3 Region and State-wise Share of Area, Production and Yield of Horticulture Crops

Region and state-wise share of area and production of fruits, vegetables and flowers is shown in Table 7.3. However, the data reveals that increase in the area under fruits and vegetables is not uniformly distributed across the regions as well as states of India.

Among the regions, southern region and the western region had major contributions to the area under fruit cultivation. In case of production of fruits too, similar to the area, southern region occupied the first place with a share of about 34 percent followed by western region (30.1 percent), northern region (17.8 percent) and eastern region (14.9 percent) region during 2016-17.

The present analysis leads us to conclude that among the regions, eastern region was found as the least fruit growing region in the country. It is lagging behind not only in having the least share in area under fruit cultivation but also having the least share in the total fruit production in the country during the above period. Following a state-wise analysis during this period, the western region was found as the major fruit growing region in the country with major contributing states of this region including Maharashtra, Gujarat, Chhattisgarh and Madhya Pradesh.

Hence, it may be concluded that during the study period, in terms of both the share of area and production of fruits, southern region was found as the major fruit growing region in the country with major contributing states being Andhra Pradesh, Karnataka, Tamil Nadu and Kerala. Alternatively, during the same period, the eastern region was found as the least fruit growing region in India.

Table 7.3: Region and State-wise Share of Area and Production of Total Fruits and Vegetables

(percent)

States/Region	Fruits					
	Area			Production		
	1991-92	2001-02	2016-17	1991-92	2001-02	2016-17
Assam	2.5	2.8	2.5	3.1	3.1	2.6
Bihar	9.3	6.8	4.8	9.8	6.7	4.6
Jharkhand	0.0	0.8	1.5		0.7	1.1
Odisha	4.7	5.6	5.3	3.4	3.2	2.6
West Bengal	3.9	3.7	3.9	4.0	4.6	4.0
Eastern Region	20.4	19.6	18.0	20.2	18.3	14.9
Haryana	0.5	0.8	1.0	0.4	0.5	1.0
Himachal Pradesh	5.5	5.6	3.5	1.2	0.6	0.7
Jammu and Kashmir	4.1	3.5	4.4	2.4	2.3	2.3
Punjab	2.5	0.9	1.4	2.3	1.2	2.0
Uttar Pradesh	10.5	7.2	7.3	8.6	5.3	11.2
Uttarakhand	5.2	4.9	2.7	1.5	0.9	0.7
Northern Region	28.4	22.9	20.2	16.4	10.9	17.8
Gujarat	2.9	3.7	6.1	6.4	5.5	9.1
Madhya Pradesh	2.3	1.2	5.1	4.3	2.7	6.4
Maharashtra	8.9	14.5	11.8	12.3	20.6	11.2
Rajasthan	0.8	0.6	0.7	0.4	0.5	0.8
Chhattisgarh		0.4	3.3		0.5	2.6
Western Region	14.9	20.3	27.0	23.4	29.6	30.1
Andhra Pradesh*	10.9	14.4	13.7	14.0	14.3	16.813
Karnataka	7.3	6.4	6.8	11.1	9.4	8.0
Kerala	8.2	5.8	3.8	3.8	4.1	2.7
Tamil Nadu	4.7	5.7	4.8	8.1	10.1	6.5
Southern Region	31.1	32.3	29.1	37.1	37.9	34.0
All-India	100.0	100.0	100.0	100.0	100.0	100.0

contd...

Vegetables						
States/Regions	Area			Production		
	1991-92	2001-02	2016-17	1991-92	2001-02	2016-17
Assam	4.0	3.9	3.0	3.6	3.3	2.2
Bihar	15.1	9.4	8.2	14.8	9.1	8.1
Jharkhand	0.0	2.6	2.8		2.0	2.1
Odisha	12.7	10.5	6.2	12.4	8.4	5.0
West Bengal	8.2	18.5	13.5	8.0	20.4	14.6
Eastern Region	39.9	44.8	33.7	38.8	43.1	32.0
Haryana	1.1	2.4	4.2	1.5	2.4	4.0
Himachal Pradesh	0.7	0.6	0.8	0.8	0.7	1.0
Jammu and Kashmir	3.2	0.8	0.6	1.3	0.8	0.8
Punjab	1.5	2.2	2.2	2.5	2.6	2.7
Uttar Pradesh	10.3	12.6	13.6	16.4	17.0	15.1
Uttarakhand	1.0	1.5	0.9	1.1	0.8	0.5
Northern Region	17.8	20.2	22.4	23.6	24.3	24.0
Gujarat	2.0	3.8	6.8	2.8	3.7	7.7
Madhya Pradesh	3.2	2.2	8.6	3.8	2.1	9.5
Maharashtra	4.3	6.5	6.7	7.1	5.8	5.9
Rajasthan	1.1	1.6	1.9	0.5	0.5	1.1
Chhattisgarh		1.7	4.8		1.5	3.8
Western Region	10.6	15.8	28.8	14.3	13.6	28.0
Andhra Pradesh*	2.8	3.6	3.7	2.5	2.9	4.8
Karnataka	6.3	5.8	4.7	6.3	4.7	4.7
Kerala	3.6	1.9	1.3	5.5	2.9	1.1
Tamil Nadu	15.9	3.5	2.5	6.5	6.1	3.6
Southern Region	28.6	14.8	12.3	20.8	16.6	14.2
All-India	100.0	100.0	100.0	100.0	100.0	100.0

Source: Author's estimation based on Indian Horticulture Database, 2017, Ministry of Agriculture and Farmers Welfare, Government of India, New Delhi and EPW Research Foundation India Time Series Online Database (www.epwrfits.in). *Andhra Pradesh includes Telangana also.

The third major fruit growing region of the country was the northern region with contribution by prominent states like Uttar Pradesh followed by Jammu and Kashmir, Himachal Pradesh and Uttarakhand.

Among the regions, eastern region is lagging behind all the remaining regions and has the least share to the total area under production of fruits in the country during the study period. And there were three states, namely Odisha, Bihar and West Bengal which had major contributions but their share in both area and produc ion dramatically decelerated compared to the country's total area under fruits over the period. Despite this, in 1991-92, Bihar was the only state which constituted about 9.3 percent of the total area under fruits cultivation followed by Odisha at 4.74 percent and West Bengal at 3.9 percent. But, it is surprising to note that these states have experienced either deceleration or stagnation in their percentage share of the total area under production of fruits during 2013-14 as compared to 1991-92. Although, in case of production of fruits, too, Bihar occupied the first place with a share of over 4.5 percent followed by West Bengal (3.3 percent) and Odisha (2.4 percent) in 2013-14.

On the other hand, area under vegetable crops in India increased from 45 lakh hectares in 1990-91 to 96.10 lakh hectares in 2013-14. During this period, in terms of the share of area under production of vegetables, eastern region was the major contributor, constituting about 33.7 percent followed by western region at 28.8 percent, northern region at 22.4 percent and southern region at 12.3 percent during 2016-17. The main reason for the highest share in area under production of vegetables in eastern region was the major participation of states like West Bengal, Bihar and Odisha.

However, during 1991-92, among the eastern region, Bihar was the only state in the eastern region that was a major contributor and had about 15.1 percent of the total area under vegetables cultivation. After Bihar, Odisha was found as the second major contributor that constituted about 12.7 percent of the total area under vegetables cultivation, followed by West Bengal and Assam with their shares at 8.2 percent and 4.0 percent respectively. However, during 2016-17, Bihar's share slackened and slowed down from its position and stuck at the second place due to a sharp decline in the area under vegetables (8.2 percent). During 2016-17, West Bengal emerged as the major contributor constituting about 13.5 percent of the total area under vegetables cultivation. Further, besides Bihar, the percentage share of Odisha and Assam also reported declined during 2016-17. Among all the states in the eastern region, only West Bengal reflected a noticeable improvement in its area share compared to country's total area under vegetables. On the other hand, the share of area under vegetable cultivation for Odisha, Bihar and Assam declined sharply between 1991-92 and 2016-17.

Table 7.4: Region and State-wise Percentage Share of Area and Production of Flowers in India

(percent)

Regions/States	Area			Production		
	1993-94	2003-04	2016-17	1993-94	2003-04	2016-17
Assam	0.7	--	1.7	0.0	--	4.1
Bihar	0.2	0.1	0.2	0.6	0.3	0.4
Jharkhand	--	--	0.1	--	--	0.7
Odisha	0.2	0.3	2.1	0.2	0.0	3.2
West Bengal	30.8	17.1	8.4	4.0	7.5	12.1
Eastern Region	31.9	17.5	12.5	4.9	7.8	20.6
Haryana	2.9	4.2	2.0	10.0	10.1	3.2
Himachal Pradesh	0.1	0.3	0.2	0.0	0.3	1.5
Jammu Kashmir	--	0.1	16.7	--	0.0	1.3
Punjab	0.8	0.6	0.7	0.2	0.5	0.6
Uttar Pradesh	0.0	6.3	7.0	--	1.7	5.3
Uttarakhand	--	0.1	0.4	--	0.1	0.6
Northern Region	3.8	11.6	27.1	10.3	12.7	12.5
Gujarat	--	4.9	6.4	--	5.2	8.3
Madhya Pradesh	2.2	--	6.0	0.4	--	9.6
Maharashtra	5.6	8.3	4.0	8.1	8.4	4.8
Rajasthan	2.9	1.9	1.1	--	0.4	0.3
Chhattisgarh	--	0.0	3.7	--	0.0	4.7
Western Region	10.7	15.1	21.0	8.5	14.0	27.6
Andhra Pradesh	14.1	12.8	7.3	7.7	8.5	7.3
Karnataka	37.2	18.0	10.6	39.2	24.7	12.5
Kerala	0.0	0.0	8.6	0.0	0.0	0.0
Tamil Nadu	0.0	20.0	10.4	27.5	27.9	18.5
Southern Region	51.3	50.8	37.0	74.4	61.1	38.4
All-India	100.0	100.0	100.0	100.0	100.0	100.0

Source: Author's estimation based on Indian Horticulture Database, 2017, Ministry of Agriculture and Farmers Welfare, Government of India, New Delhi and EPW Research Foundation India Time Series Online Database (www.epwrfits.in).

Moreover, in case of vegetable production too, West Bengal topped the list by having about 14.6 percent share in the total production during 2016-17. It was distantly followed by Bihar (8.1 percent) and Odisha (5.0 percent). These three states from eastern India together accounted for more than 29 percent of the vegetable production of the country in 2016-17.

The floriculture has been witnessing significant growth in recent years. It has been getting acceptability in world markets, but it is limited to only a few states in India.

Table 7.4 illustrates that during 2016-17, southern region (37 percent) was found having the largest flower growing area in the country followed by northern region (27.1 percent), western region (21.0 percent), and eastern region (12.5 percent). However, similar to the area share, the southern region was also the largest flower producing region in India during the same period. It is pertinent to highlight that in terms of both the share of production and area under floriculture, eastern region was found as one of the least diversified region in the country during the period 2016-17.

It is further noticed that the area under floriculture in northern region increased dramatically from 3.8 percent in 1993-94 to 27.1 percent during the period 1993-94 to 2016-17. Hence, as per the statistical figures available, northern region displayed a commendable performance in favour of flower cultivation.

However, the share of eastern region in flower cultivation declined sharply from 31.9 percent to 12.5 percent during 1993-94 to 2016-17, a sharp reduction of almost 19 percent. A reason responsible for this declining trend was the shift in the area under cultivation from floriculture towards vegetable cultivation. In case of production too, the share of loose flowers increased by 15.7 percent despite a decline in the area under this crop by more than 19 percent during 2016-17.

Further, among the eastern states, the share of area under floriculture in West Bengal declined by more than 73 percent over the period 1993-94 to 2016-17. But, interestingly it can be observed that the share of production of cut flower increased sharply by more than 26 percent during the same period. To sum up, across the regions, northern and eastern region was found as being the least diversified regions in favour of floriculture during 2016-17.

7.3.4 Region-wise Share of Livestock and Horticulture to Total Value of Agricultural Output: It is discernible from Table 7.5 that in 2014-15, the contribution of livestock sector in the total value of agricultural (agriculture and allied sector) output was found highest in the northern region (31.1 percent) followed by southern region (29.9 percent), and western region (26.4 percent). The least share was reported by the eastern region, accounting for only 23.2 percent during the same period.

Table 7.5: Region-wise Share of Horticulture and Livestock to Total Value of Agriculture and Allied Sector Output @ 2004-05 Prices: 2004-05 to 2014-15

(percent)

Region	Livestock		Change in Share	Horticulture and Livestock		Change in Share
	2004-05	2014-15	(3-2)	2004-05	2014-15	(6-5)
(1)	(2)	(3)	(4)	(5)	(6)	(7)
Eastern	20.8	23.2	2.4	47.7	51.3	3.6
Northern	26.4	31.1	4.8	37.8	49.7	11.9
Western	24.0	26.4	2.4	35.2	39.7	4.6
Southern	24.8	29.9	5.1	39.9	46.9	7.1
All India	24.2	27.6	3.4	39.5	45.7	6.3

Source: Author's estimation based on the Central Statistical Organization (various years), Ministry of Statistics and Program Implementation, New Delhi (www.mospi.in).
Note: For comparative analysis, new series @ 2011-12 prices data of total value of agriculture and allied activities were spliced with old series @ 2004-05 prices. Due to lack of the common year in both the series, linking factors of GSDP as well as GDP were used for this splicing, and some of the missing data for the year 2011-12 of 2004-05 series were also projected on the basis of the existing pattern of the data.

If we look at the combined share of horticulture and livestock sector in the total value of agricultural output during 2014-15, we find that the total percentage share ranges from 39.7 percent in the western region to 51.3 percent in the eastern region. Thus, the eastern region recorded the highest combined share of horticulture and livestock in the total value of agricultural output during 2014-15. This may be due to the shifting of area under cultivation towards vegetable cultivation. Besides this, it is important to highlight that among the eastern states, only in Bihar, the share of these two sectors i.e. horticulture and livestock was approximately 38.9 percent to the total value of agricultural and allied sector's output. Because of the recurrence of floods, most of the gross cropped area (GCA) was ruined during the *kharif* season. For the compensation of these losses, people of the eastern region, particularly Bihar, utilized livestock for their livelihood. However, Assam, Odisha and West Bengal observed relatively lower share of these sectors in the total agricultural output.

However, it can be observed that the eastern states of Bihar and Odisha recorded a remarkable increase in the contribution of livestock to the total agriculture output.

Endnotes

1. Government of India (2015), "Economic Survey, 2015", Ministry of Finance, New Delhi, Vol. 2, p. 77.
2. Government of India (2014), "Data Book for Use of Deputy Chairman, Planning Commission, New Delhi", March 10,available at: http://planningcommission.nic.in/data/datatable/1203/databook_1203.pdf.
3. NSSO (2014), "Key Indicators of Situation of Agricultural Households in India, NSS 70th Round", January-December, Ministry of Statistics and Programme Implementation, Government of India, New Delhi.
4. Narayanamoorthy, A. (2007), "Deceleration in Agricultural Growth: Technology Fatigue and Policy Fatigue?", *Economic and Political Weekly*, Vol. XLII, No. 25, June 23-29, p. 2376.
5. Singh, S.P. (2007), "Pampering Corporates Pauperizing Masses, Alternative Economic Survey, 2006-07", Danish Books: New Delhi.
6. Shivay, Yashbir Singh and Anshu Rahul (2010), "Increasing Agricultural Production in India", *Kurukshetra,* A Journal of Rural Development, Publication Division, Ministry of I&B,

Government of India, New Delhi, Vol. 58, No. 9, July, p. 21.

7. Dwarkanath, H.D. (2010), "Emerging Agrarian Policies and Programme Implementation", *Kurukshetra,* A Journal of Rural Development, Publication Division, Ministry of I&B, Government of India, New Delhi, Vol. 58, No. 9, July, p. 17.
8. Hazra, C.R. (2001), "Crop Diversification in India", FAO Paper, Ministry of Agriculture and Cooperation, New Delhi.
9. Birthal, P.S., A.K. Jha., P.K. Joshi and D.K. Singh (2006), "Agriculture Diversification in North-Eastern Region of India: Implications for Growth and Equity", *Indian Journal of Agriculture Economics*, Vol. 61, No. 3, July-September, pp. 328-339.
10. Pratap, S. Birthal., P.K. Joshi, Sonia Chauhan and Harvinder Singh (2008), "Can Horticulture Revitalize Agricultural Growth?," *Indian Journal of Agriculture Economics*, Vol. 63, No. 3, July-September, p. 319.
11. Patel, Amrit (2010), "Strengthening Rural Banking Infrastructure," *Kurukshetra*, A Journal of Rural Development, Publication Division, Ministry of I&B, Government of India, New Delhi, Vol. 58, No. 6, April, p. 27.
12. Deshpandey, R.S., Pradeep Mehta and Khalil Shah (2007), "Crop Diversification and Agricultural Labour in India", *The Indian Journal of Labour Economics*, Vol. 50, No. 4, pp. 597-598.
13. Barghouti, S., S. Kane, K. Sorby and M. Ali (2004), "Agricultural Diversification for the Poor, Agricultural and Rural Development", Discussion Paper, No. 1, ARD Department, World Bank, Washington D.C.
14. Chand, Ramesh (1999), "Agriculture Diversification in India: Potentials and Prospects in Developed Region", Mittal Publications: New Delhi.
15. Jha, D. (1996), "Rapporteur's Report on Diversification of Agriculture and Food Security in the Context of New Economic Policy", *Indian Journal of Agricultural Economics*, 51(4), pp. 829-832.
16. Chand, Ramesh (1996), "Diversification through High-Value Crops in Western Himalayan Region: Evidence from Himachal Pradesh", *Indian Journal of Agriculture Economics,* 41(4), pp. 652-663.
17. Vyas, V.S. (1996), "Diversification in Agriculture: Concept,

Rationale and Approaches", *Indian Journal of Agricultural Economics*, 51(4), pp. 636-643.

18. Joshi, P.K., Ashok Gulati, P.S. Birthal and L. Tewari (2002), "Agricultural Diversification in South Asia", paper presented in a workshop on Agricultural Diversification in South Asia, November 21-23, Paro, Bhutan.
19. Joshi, P.K., A. Gulati, P.S. Birthal and L. Tiwari (2004), "Agriculture Diversification in South Asia: Pattern, Determinants and Policy Implications", *Economic and Political Weekly*, June 12.
20. Joshi, P.K., P.S. Birthal and N. Minto (2006), "Source of Agricultural Growth in India: Role of Diversification towards High Value Crops", MTID Discussion Paper No. 98, International Food Policy Research Institute, Washington D.C.
21. Weinberger, K. and T.A. Lumpkin (2007), "Diversification into Horticulture and Poverty Reduction: A Research Agenda", *World Development*, Vol. 35, No. 8, pp. 1464-1480.
22. Jorge, A. Quiroz and Alberto Valdes (1995), "Agricultural Diversification and Policy Reform," *Food Policy*, Vol. 20, No. 3, pp. 245-255.
23. Jana, B.L. (2006), "Concept of Crop Diversification in Agriculture", Agrotech Publishing Academy: Udaipur.
24. Srinivasan, G. (2010), "The Union Budget: Agriculture at Centre Stage", *Kurukshetra*, A Journal of Rural Development, Publication Division, Ministry of I&B, Government of India, New Delhi, Vol. 58, No. 6, April.
25. Shivay, Yashbir Singh and Anshu Rahul (2010), "Increasi g Agricultural Production in India", *Kurukshetra*, A Journal of Rural Development, Publication Division, Ministry of I&B, Government of India, New Delhi, Vol. 58, No. 9, July, p. 19.
26. Yadav, R.K., D.S. Yadav, N. Rai and K.K. Patel (2003), "Prospects of Horticulture in North-Eastern Region", Division of Horticulture, ICAR, Research Complex for North East Region, ENVIS Bulletin: Himalayan Ecology, 11(2), Meghalaya.
27. Basu, Ratan Lal (2008), "Diversification of Agriculture in Eastern India and the Poor", in Thakur, Anil Kumar and K.B. Padmado (eds.), 'Growth and Agriculture Diversification', Deep and Deep Publications: New Delhi.
28. Jana, B.L. (2006), "Diversification in Agriculture," Agrotech Publishing Academy: Udaipur.

29. Government of India (2015), Directorate of Economics and Statistics, Department of Agriculture and Farmers Welfare, New Delhi.
30. Population Reference Bureau (2015), "2015 World Population Data Sheet with a Special Focus on Women's Empowerment", available at:
http://www.prb.org/pdf15/2015-world-population-data-sheet_eng.pdf.
31. Punam (2008), "Growth and Diversification of Agriculture in Eastern India", in Thakur, Anil Kumar and K. B. Padmadeo (eds.), 'Growth and Diversification of Agriculture', Deep and Deep Publications: New Delhi.
32. Chand, Ramesh (1999), "Agricultural Diversification in India: Potential and Prospects in Developed Region", Mittal Publications: New Delhi.
33. Salve, W.N. (2008), "Crop Diversification and Food Security in Hilly Tribal Areas of Eastern India", in Thakur, Anil Kumar and K.B. Padmadeo (eds.), 'Growth and Diversification of Agriculture', Deep and Deep Publications: New Delhi.
34. Singh, S.P. (2005), "Agriculture in Alternative Economic Survey: 2004-05, Dis-equalising Growth", Daanish Books. New Delhi.
35. Government of India (2008), "Bihar's Agriculture Development: Opportunities and Challenges", A Report of The Special Task Force on Bihar, April, p. 28.
36. Kumar, P., Mruthyunjaya and P.S. Birthal (2003), "Changing Consumption Pattern in South Asia", paper Presented at FICCI-ICRISAT-IFPRI International Workshop on Agricultural Diversification and Vertical Integration in South Asia, New Delhi, November 5-6.
37. Aksoy, M.A. (2005), "The Evolution of Agricultural Trade Flows", in M.A. Aksoy and J.C. Beghim (eds.), 'Global Agricultural Trade and Developing Countries', The World Bank, Washington, D.C.
38. Kumar, Anjani, Pramod Kumar and Alakh N. Sharma (2012), "Crop Diversification in Eastern India: Status and Determinants", *Indian Journal of Agricultural Economics,* Vol. 67, No. 4, October-December.
39. Government of India (2014), "Economic Survey, 2013-14: Agriculture and Food Management", Ministry of Finance,

Government of India, New Delhi.

40. Government of India (2016), "Economic Survey, 2016-17", Ministry of Finance, Government of India, New Delhi.

8

Crop-wise Trends in Agricultural Diversification

8.1 Trends and Growth in Area, Production and Yield of Horticulture Crops

Having predominance in Indian agriculture, eastern region is considered as one of the major producers of horticultural crops, especially the vegetable production in the country. Nature has endowed eastern region with agro-climatic suitability, topographical and soil conditions, and abundant water availability which contribute to the immense potentiality and wide scope for promotion and development of agricultural diversification in favour of horticulture crops, including fruits, vegetables, floriculture, medicinal and aromatic plants, spices, bee-keeping, sericulture etc., which have been an important activity in eastern states (Rizvi, 2010) and is likely to resolve the problems of low productivity, low income, poverty and unemployment (Basu, 2008). [1]

Tiny land-man ratio coupled with low crop yields lead to lower average per capita annual incomes for farm households in the eastern region. Besides, this region is also extremely vulnerable to climate change and thus suffers from high inter-year crop yield variability, making agriculture vulnerable to climate extremes such as droughts and floods" (Financial Express, October 7, 2017).

8.1.1 Trends and Growth in Area, Production and Yield of Vegetables: Table 8.1 reveals that the major vegetables grown in the country are onion, potato, brinjal, cabbage, cauliflower, okra, peas and tomato. Area under cultivation of total vegetables in India continuously increased from 5.04 million hectares (Mha) during TE-1992-93 to 6.17 Mha in TE-2002-03 and further to 9.98 Mha during TE-2016-17.

It is important to note that as compared to 2000-01, eventually in comparison to 1990-91, there has been a remarkable increase in area under cultivation for all listed vegetables viz. brinjal, cabbage, cauliflower, potato, tomato, okra and onion, cultivation in India during the period TE- 2016-17.

Table 8.1: Triennium Average and CAGR (Percent) of Area, Production and Yield of Vegetables in India: 1990-91 to 2016-17

Crop	APY	Triennium Ending		
		TE-1993	TE-2003	TE-2017
Onion	Area	0.31	0.43	1.25
	Production	3.43	4.53	20.47
	Yield	10.95	10.53	16.32
Potato	Area	1.01	1.26	2.12
	Production	15.61	23.23	45.99
	Yield	15.53	18.48	21.71
Brinjal	Area	0.28	0.49	0.67
	Production	4.24	8.00	12.50
	Yield	14.96	16.19	18.71
Cabbage	Area	0.18	0.25	0.40
	Production	2.88	5.53	8.79
	Yield	16.06	22.50	22.21
Cauliflower	Area	0.21	0.26	0.43
	Production	3.16	4.68	8.17
	Yield	15.00	17.97	19.03
Okra	Area	0.25	0.34	0.51
	Production	2.15	3.31	5.90
	Yield	8.69	9.67	11.47
Peas	Area	0.18	0.31	0.51
	Production	1.05	2.37	4.97
	Yield	5.75	7.63	9.81
Tomato	Area	0.29	0.47	0.78
	Production	4.25	7.44	18.27
	Yield	14.65	15.98	23.30
Vegetable	Area	5.04	6.17	9.98
	Production	57.32	89.10	171.18
	Yield	11.36	14.45	17.15

contd...

Crop	APY	CAGR (percent)		
		Pre	Post	Overall
Onion	Area	5.29	8.18	6.09
	Production	4.24	11.65	8.38
	Yield	-1.00	3.21	2.15
Potato	Area	3.83	4.12	3.21
	Production	5.44	5.82	4.57
	Yield	1.55	1.64	1.32
Brinjal	Area	8.35	2.57	3.38
	Production	9.18	3.74	4.44
	Yield	0.77	1.14	1.02
Cabbage	Area	3.99	3.90	3.19
	Production	9.30	3.90	4.46
	Yield	5.11	0.01	1.23
Cauliflower	Area	2.93	4.13	3.28
	Production	5.59	4.57	4.53
	Yield	2.58	0.42	1.21
Okra	Area	4.72	3.39	2.77
	Production	6.64	4.91	3.91
	Yield	1.83	1.48	1.10
Peas	Area	6.35	3.97	3.87
	Production	14.68	6.20	4.98
	Yield	7.84	2.15	1.07
Tomato	Area	6.12	4.62	4.52
	Production	7.79	7.44	6.51
	Yield	1.58	2.69	1.90
Vegetable	Area	3.2*	3.1*	3.1*
	Production	5.6*	4.9*	4.7*
	Yield	2.4*	1.7*	1.6*

Source: Author's Estimation based EPW Research Foundation India Time Series Online Database (www.epwrfits.in) and Indian Horticulture at a Glance, 2017.
Note: Area in Million hectare and Production in (10^6) Million Metric Tonnes and Yield in Metric Tonne/Hectare; Pre: 1990-91 to 1999-00 and Post: 2000-01 to 2016-17 and Overall Period: 1990-91 to 2016-17.

A perusal of the data reveals that in terms of both the area and production of all the vegetables in India, an increasing trend was witnessed over a period of time. The main factor underlying the diversification in favour of fruits and vegetables has been higher returns relative to other crops (Chand et al., 2008). [2]

To examine the growth and performance of vegetables in terms of area expansion of individual vegetable in the country, the compounded annual growth rate was estimated for the overall period (1990-91 to 2016-17) including two sub-periods; pre-period (1990-91 to 1999-2000) and post-period (2000-01 to 2016-17). The statistics showed that except onion, cauliflower and potato, share of all the remaining vegetables decelerated in their area under vegetable cultivation during the post-period compared to the pre-period.

Moreover, total vegetables taken into account as a whole, registered a steady decline in their yields from 2.4 percent per annum during pre-period to 1.7 percent per annum during the post-period. It is because of a significant decline in growth rates of both the area and production of vegetables during the post-period against the pre-period.

A perusal of Table 8.1 demonstrates that the production of total vegetables in the country increased continuously from 57.32 MMT in TE-1992-93 to 89.10 MMT in TE-2002-03 and further to 171.18 MMT in TE-2016-17. Crop-wise analysis reveals that except onion, and potato, all the remaining vegetables, namely brinjal, cabbage, cauliflower, okra, pea and tomato registered deceleration in their production growth rates during the post-period compared with the pre-period. However, the production of total vegetables decelerated from 5.6 percent to 4.9 percent per annum during the post-period over the pre-period, while during the overall period it accounted for about 4.7 per cent per annum.

In conclusion, as the present analysis of the data explains, that among the vegetables, potato and onion were the most diversified vegetable crops during the post-period over the pre-period. It was mainly due to gradual shift of area from traditional crops such as rice and wheat during the post-period.

Similar to area and production, the yield of total vegetables increased from 11.36 metric tonne/hectare (mt/ha) to 14.45 mt/ha in 1990-91 and 2000-01 respectively; and further to 17.15 mt/ha during 2016-17. Moreover, table 8.1 also depicts that among the listed vegetables, onion accounted for the highest yield growth rates (3.21 percent per annum) followed by tomato (2.69 percent per annum), and peas (2.15 percent per annum) during the post-period as against the pre-period. Similarly, during the same period, cabbage accounted for the lowest or negligible yield growth rate i.e., 0.01 percent per annum. The growth rate in yields of total vegetables declined sharply from pre-period to the post-period and the most prominent reason for this decline was the sharp decline in the yield growth of peas, cabbage, cauliflower and okra during the post-period.

8.1.2 Trends and Growth in Area, Production and Yield of Fruits: Table 8.2 highlights the major fruits grown in India which includes banana, papaya, citrus, lemon, mosambi, orange, guava, litchi, mango, pineapple and sapota. The total area has continually increased under the fruits cultivation in the country from 2.9 million hectares (Mha) during TE-1992-93 to 3.9 Mha in TE-2002-03 and further to 6.3 Mha in TE-2016-17. Concurrently, except lemon/lime, all the fruit crops have shown an increasing trend in their acreage during the two comparable periods i.e. the post period (TE-2002-03 and TE-2016-17) and the overall period (TE-1990-91 and TE-2016-17). However, out of 10 major fruits, only four fruits such as guava, papaya, citrus, and mango got a boost in their area under cultivation during the overall period.

Table 8.2 also reveals that the compound annual growth rate in area under fruits like papaya (5.40 percent per annum), mosambi (4.70 percent per annum), banana (4.40 percent per annum), citrus (4.40 percent per annum), lemon (4.10 percent per annum) and guava (4 percent per annum) showed higher growth rates during the post-period. It is very surprising that compared to the earlier period, in the subsequent period, there was a considerable decline in the three fruits including papaya, lemon and guava, but despite this decline, their growth rate was quite appreciable. The growth rate of area under total fruits decreased steadily from 4.10 percent per annum to 3.8 percent per annum during the pre- and post-period respectively. The remaining fruits, namely litchi, sapota, pineapple and mango recorded the least growth rate during the same period.

Table 8.2: Triennium Average and CAGR (Percent) of Area, Production and Yield of Fruits in India: 1990-91 to 2016-17

Fruits	Year	Area and Production in Million Tonnes and Yield in MT/Ha.		
		TE-1992-93	TE-2002-03	TE-2016-17
Banana	Area	0.4	0.5	0.8
	Production	8.5	13.9	29.2
	Yield	22.2	29.5	34.7
Papaya	Area	0.0	0.1	0.1
	Production	0.7	2.2	5.6
	Yield	15.9	30.8	43.6
Citrus	Area	0.4	0.6	1.0
	Production	2.8	5.0	12.0
	Yield	7.5	8.9	11.9
Lemon/Lime	Area	0.1	0.2	0.3
	Production	0.8	1.4	2.7
	Yield	10.1	9.0	10.6
Mosambi	Area	0.1	0.1	0.2
	Production	0.7	1.1	3.7
	Yield	11.8	8.9	15.4
Guava	Area	0.1	0.2	0.3
	Production	1.1	1.7	3.9
	Yield	11.3	11.2	15.3
Litchi	Area	0.1	0.1	0.1
	Production	0.2	0.4	0.6
	Yield	4.9	7.5	6.3
Mango	Area	1.1	1.6	2.2
	Production	8.8	10.9	19.0
	Yield	8.1	7.0	8.6
Pineapple	Area	0.1	0.1	0.1
	Production	0.8	1.2	2.0
	Yield	13.8	15.2	17.1
Sapota	Area	0.0	0.1	0.1
	v	0.4	0.7	1.3
	Yield	14.4	10.8	12.2
Fruits	Area	2.9	3.9	6.3
	Production	29.7	43.8	89.9
	Yield	10.4	11.3	14.3

contd...

Fruits	Year	CAGR (percent)		
		Pre	Post	Overall
Banana	Area	2.8	4.4	3.6
	Production	8.6	5.9	5.2
	Yield	5.7	1.4	1.6
Papaya	Area	6.0	5.4	4.3
	Production	12.9	8.4	8.6
	Yield	6.6	2.8	4.1
Citrus	Area	4.0	4.4	4.6
	Production	6.7	6.4	5.9
	Yield	2.6	2.0	1.2
Lemon/Lime	Area	8.9	4.1	5.4
	Production	6.6	5.2	5.5
	Yield	-2.1	1.0	0.2
Mosambi	Area	2.1	4.7	7.5
	Production	3.5	7.3	7.6
	Yield	1.4	2.4	0.1
Guava	Area	6.4	4.0	3.7
	Production	6.3	6.4	4.7
	Yield	-0.1	2.3	0.9
Litchi	Area	1.4	3.7	2.5
	Production	8.1	2.7	2.8
	Yield	6.6	-1.0	0.4
Mango	Area	4.0	2.5	3.6
	Production	2.0	4.3	3.1
	Yield	-1.9	1.7	-0.4
Pineapple	Area	3.5	2.9	2.7
	Production	3.0	3.5	3.3
	Yield	-0.5	0.6	0.6
Sapota	Area	10.6	3.2	7.4
	Production	7.1	4.5	5.8
	Yield	-3.1	1.2	-1.5
Fruits	Area	4.1	3.8	3.9
	Prod	6.9	5.0	4.6
	Yield	2.7	1.0	0.6

Source: Author's Estimation based on Indian Horticulture Database (various years); Indian Horticulture at a Glance, 2017, Ministry of Agriculture and Farmers Welfare, Government of India, New Delhi and EPW Research Foundation India Time Series Online Database (www.epwrfits.in).

If we analyze the growth rate of area under total fruits for the whole period, it was found that orange was at the top of all listed fruits; thereafter, fruit like sapota took the second place followed by lemon, citrus, and papaya during the same period. Fruits like guava, banana, mango, pineapple, and litchi were placed at the bottom of ladder.

In terms of growth rate of fruit production, papaya topped the list by achieving about 8.6 percent per annum annual growth rate during the overall period. It was distantly followed by mosambi/orange (7.6 percent per annum), citrus (5.9 percent per annum), sapota (5.8 percent per annum), and lemon (5.5 percent per annum). Contrarily, litchi, mango, pineapple, guava and banana showed sluggish growth rates during the overall period.

Simultaneously, annual growth in yield of total fruits reached below the one percent mark i.e. 0.6 percent during the overall period. It was due to the gradual decline in the growth of area and production that the yield growth of total fruits declined significantly from 2.7 percent per annum in the pre-period to 1.0 percent per annum in the post-period (Table 8.2).

Amongst the fruits, papaya was placed among the highest yielding fruits in the country having about 4.1 percent growth per annum, distantly followed by banana (1.6 percent per annum), citrus (1.2 percent per annum), and guava (0.9 percent per annum).

The remaining fruits such as, mosambi, lemon, litchi and pineapple were found the least yielding fruits as they registered negligible growth rates: mosambi (0.1 percent per annum), and pineapple (0.6 percent per annum). However, during the same period, amongst the listed fruits, sapota (-1.5 percent per annum) and mango (-0.4 percent per annum) registered negative growth rates.

8.2 Share of Area and Production of Horticulture Crops

8.2.1 Share of Area and Production of Vegetables: Table 8.3 earmarks the vegetables grown in India and their percentage share. Potato topped the list (21 percent) followed by onion (12.34 percent), tomato (7.86 percent), brinjal (6.50 percent), peas (5.31 percent), okra (5.13 percent), and cauliflower (4.10 percent). Cabbage was listed at the bottom (3.96 percent) in the share of total area under vegetable cultivation in India during 2016-17.

Table 8.3: Share in Area and Production of Vegetables in India: 1990-91 to 2016-17

Crop	Area			Production		
	1990-91	2000-01	2016-17	1990-91	2000-01	2016-17
Potato	20.9	19.5	21.0	30.7	24.0	26.6
Onion	6.7	6.7	12.3	6.5	4.9	12.3
Tomato	6.1	7.4	7.9	8.0	7.7	11.3
Brinjal	6.1	7.6	6.5	8.2	8.2	7.1
Cabbage	3.8	3.9	4.0	5.3	5.9	5.1
Cauliflower	4.4	4.1	4.4	5.8	5.0	4.9
Okra	4.8	5.6	5.1	3.7	3.6	3.5
Peas	3.8	5.1	5.3	1.7	3.2	3.1
Vegetables	100.0	100.0	100.0	100.0	100.0	100.0

Source: Author's Estimation based on Indian Horticulture Database (various years), Ministry of Agriculture and Farmers Welfare, Government of India, New Delhi and EPW Research Foundation India Time Series Online Database (www.epwrfits.in).

It is discernible from Table 8.3 that remarkable progress was made in area under cultivation for onion during 2016-17 compared to 2000-01. This is the effect of a well-knit strategy to achieve multiple goals of increasing production of horticulture crops, enhancing income, and ensuring food security in terms of nutritional or calorie intake.

It is evident from the data that after the effective implementation of National Horticulture Mission in the country in 2005-06, the production of brinjal, okra, and cabbage decelerated due to remarkable shift of area under production in favour of potato, onion, and tomato.

These three items hold the largest share both in terms of area and production as regards the total vegetable production in India during 2016-17 in comparison to 2000-01. However, during the same period, it is very noticeable that even after comparative increase in the area of brinjal and peas; the share of their production declined during the same period.

On the other hand, it is evident from the data that due to the negligible increase in the share of area under cultivation for cauliflower, peas and cabbage, there was a sharp decline in their production share during the same period.

8.2.2 Share of Area and Production of Fruits: A perusal of Table 8.4 demonstrates that of all the listed fruits, the share of area under mango (34.9 percent) dominated, followed by citrus fruits (16.3 percent) and banana (13.2 percent) during 2016-17. But, it needs to be noted here that, despite having the highest area share in cultivation, the share of mango in production terms (21.2 percent) was at the second place rather than being at the first place.

This decline was mainly because of the shrink in the share of area under mango among the states, namely West Bengal, Jharkhand, Bihar, and Odisha, Uttarakhand, Andhra Pradesh, Karnataka, Maharashtra and Gujarat during the period 2014-15 to 2016-17 (Agriculture Statistics at a Glance, 2017).

Table 8.4: Share of Area and Production of Major Fruits in India: 1990-91 to 2016-17

Horticulture	Area			Production		
Crops	1990-91	2000-01	2016-17	1990-91	2000-01	2016-17
Banana	14.6	12.1	13.2	26.0	32.8	31.4
Mango	41.2	39.3	34.9	30.7	23.3	21.2
Citrus	14.7	12.8	16.3	9.7	10.2	13.7
Papaya	1.5	1.8	2.1	1.6	4.2	6.6
Guava	3.6	3.8	4.0	3.8	3.8	3.9
Mosambi	2.1	2.1	3.2	2.3	2.7	3.8
Lemon*	3.0	4.2	4.0	2.8	3.2	3.0
Pineapple	2.2	2.0	1.9	2.7	2.8	2.2
Sapota	1.0	1.9	1.7	1.3	1.7	1.4
Litchi	1.9	1.4	1.4	0.9	1.0	0.6
Fruits	100.0	100.0	100.0	100.0	100.0	100.0

Source: Author's Estimation based on Indian Horticulture Database (various years), Horticulture at a Glance, 2017, Ministry of Agriculture and Farmers Welfare, Government of India, New Delhi and EPW Research Foundation India Time Series Online Database (www.epwrfits.in).

*refers to lemon/lime

Alternatively, despite the lower share of area under bananas (13.2 percent and even after being at the third position, its share in production (31.4 percent) was the highest amongst all the fruits. Thus, it can be interpreted that due to higher demand of bananas, the growers showed a keen interest in producing more bananas, due to which, despite having a lesser share of area, its share in the production was the highest amongst all the fruits in the country. Hence, banana is the most important fruit crop in India and is favoured due to affordability, usefulness, taste, nutritive and medicinal value, and having a good export potential.

Banana is a popular and favourite fruit amongst all classes of people, due to which it is found throughout the year. Apart from these, the noticeable increase in the share of cultivated area under banana may be due to the adoption of advanced technologies and introduction of National Horticulture Mission (NHM) in 2005-06 including supporting policies regarding horticulture development.

On the other hand, pineapple, sapota and litchi received less importance both in terms of area and production and were listed at the bottom with their share decelerating over the period. Barring sapota, the share of area under pineapple and litchi continuously shrunk from 2.2 percent and 1.9 percent respectively in 1990-91 to 2 percent and 1.4 percent in 2000-01 and again to 1.9 percent and 1.4 percent respectively, during 2016-17.

Contrary to the highest change in cropping pattern in favour of citrus, mosambi and banana, the share of area under the cultivation of these crops increased gradually during 2016-17 as compared to the 1990-91 and especially after 2000-01. Besides these fruits, papaya and guava also received importance and the area under cultivation of these crops increased during the same period.

While summing up, despite a decline in area share and production share among various fruit crops, banana topped the list with a 31.4 percent share during 2016-17. Next to banana was mango (21.2 percent), the second largest fruit produced in India followed by citrus (13.7 percent) and papaya (6.6 percent) during 2016-17. In terms of area share, mango topped the list followed by citrus and banana during the same period.

8.3 Share of HVCs (High Value Crops) and Livestock vis-à-vis LVCs (Low Value Crops)

Comparative analysis of percentage share of cereals, pulses, horticulture and livestock in total value of output in agriculture and allied sector in India from 2004-05 to 2014-15 at 2004-05 prices reveals large variations in the share of cereals. Food grains over the years had the highest share of 19 percent recorded in 2008-09 but decelerated thereafter to reach 15.8 percent in 2014-15.

The reason behind this decrease was that a majority of Indian farmers shifted their cropping pattern from low valued or traditional crops, such as wheat, paddy, maize, ragi and bajra towards high valued crops, such as fruits, vegetables etc. over the period of time.

Likewise, a parallel pattern was seen in the share of horticulture and livestock to total value of output from agriculture and allied sector which increased from 15.2 percent and 24.2 percent in 2004-05 to 18.1 percent and 27.6 percent respectively in 2014-15.

Although, it showed a large fluctuation during the period 2004-05 and 2013-14, yet, it increased remarkably in 2014-15. However, the total share of pulses remained more or less uniform at 2.7 percent in 2004-05, at 2.9 percent in 2013-14, but decelerated to 2.6 percent during 2014-15.

Thus, it can be concluded from the present analysis that in total value of output from agriculture and allied sector, the highest share was observed in livestock sector that accounted for 27.6 percent, followed by horticulture (18.1 percent), and cereals (15.8 percent) during 2014-15.

This increase may be due to agricultural diversification that has been identified as a tool in making agriculture a more profitable venture through efficient land use, optimum utilization of natural resources i.e., soil, water, and environment and creating skill employment for rural masses especially women folk (Planning Commission of India, 2001).

Similar to horticulture, diversification in favour of livestock has also been accorded a special significance during the recent years. This is so because, it is known to be the main source of farm income in India, especially during the failure of crops caused by occurrence of natural calamities such as droughts and floods. Besides these, livestock also plays an important role in rural transportation.

Moreover, in the form of milk, meat and dung etc., it is recognised as productive assets for augmenting farm income in rural areas in the country, particularly in the eastern states of India.

The study also reveals that among the eastern states "more than 75 percent of the rural households of Bihar have been maintaining livestock, especially cattle, buffaloes, and goat with a view to meet their domestic needs in the form of milk and relate by-products" (Kumar and Sinha, 2008). Finally, as per the present analysis, diversification in agriculture, in favour of horticulture and livestock, has emerged as a tool to augment farm income and generate additional employment in rural areas.

In the present study, we also estimated the compound annual growth rate (CAGR) using Simpson Diversification Index (SID) for measuring the speed of diversification across the regions vis-à-vis India for the two sub-periods, including pre- (1990-91 to 1999-00), post -(2000-01 to 2013-14) and overall period (1990-91 to 2013-14). As per Table 8.5, the annual growth of SID in favour of horticulture crops negatively declined among the eastern and northern regions during post as well as overall period at 10 percent and 1 percent level of significance, respectively.

However, the southern and the western region achieved positive growth rates during the same period and this growth rate showed some improvements in agricultural diversification in favour of horticulture crops.

But, if we look at it comparatively during the post-period, we find that, except northern and western region, eastern and southern regions recovered in their SID growth rates which were estimated between -0.18 percent and -0.04 percent in eastern region; and from 0.01 percent to 0.07 percent per annum in southern region during the pre- and post-period, respectively.

As a result, improvement in the SID growth in India was achieved only because of recovery in SID growth rates made by southern and eastern region during the same period.

Thus, the present analysis expounds about the meagre existence of diversification in favour of horticulture crops during the post-period. However, the people of the country have still partially shown their interest in the specialization for growing of traditional crops like wheat, rice, maize and coarse cereals including sugarcane and commercial crops etc., during the post-period.

It is also evident from Table 8.5 that the highest deterioration was estimated in the northern region i.e., from (-) 0.15 percent during the pre-period to (-) 0.17 percent per annum during the post-period at 1 percent level of significance.

On the other hand, in terms of SID, the highest deceleration was observed in the northern region from 0.817 in 1990-91 to 0.789 in 2000-01 and further to 0.783 in 2013-14.

However, despite the abundance of natural resources and favourable climatic conditions, in terms of agriculture diversification, the eastern region was the most backward region in the country. The main reason for this is erratic weather conditions and economic constraints which come out as major hindrances in diversification towards high valued crops (HVCs).

Table 8.5: Region Wise CAGR (Percent) by Using Dummy Technique of Simpson Diversification Index (SID): 1990-91 to 2013-14

Year	Eastern	Northern	Western	Southern	All-India
Pre	-0.18	-0.15*	0.02	0.01	-0.01
Post	-0.04***	-0.17*	0.01	0.07*	0.01
Overall	-0.01***	-0.18*	0.01	0.08*	0.01

Source: Computed by author.

Note: * denotes at 1 percent, ** at 5 percent and *** at 10 percent level of significance.

Hence, as per the above analysis, we can conclude that in terms of agricultural diversification, the southern region was found as the most diversified region in favour of horticulture. This is only because this region gradually diversified in favour of floriculture during the post- as well as overall period, followed by western and the northern region.

At the same time, the eastern region was found as the least diversified region in the country (Figure 8.1).

Figure 8.1: Region-wise Simpson Diversification Index (SID) in India: 1990-91 to 2013-14

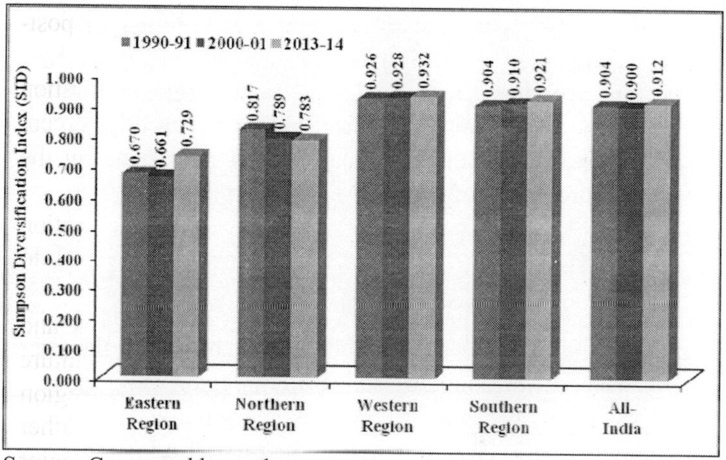

Source: Computed by author.

Thus, diversification of Indian agriculture in favour of horticulture and livestock picked up movement especially after 2000-01. Except the northern region, agricultural diversification in favour of horticulture in southern and western regions has increased handsomely since 1990-91.

The eastern region, with various ups and downs, has also improved in its SID growth rate from -0.18 percent to -0.04 percent during the pre- and post- period respectively. While in terms of SID, a similar trend was witnessed in the eastern region, its diversification index slightly increased from 0.661 in 2000-01 to 0.729 in 2013-14.

Thus, the paltry growth in SID in the eastern region was

mainly due to economic constraints, erratic weather conditions coupled with the partitions of states of Bihar and Jharkhand in 2000.

In addition to this, these states were also suffering from a high incidence of poverty, poor road network, poor market access, price volatility and lack of cold storage facilities and low per capita income which led to lower demand for horticulture products and since these commodities are perishable in nature, the farmers of this region were not inclined towards growing these crops.

Similarly, the share of livestock sector in the total value of agriculture and allied sector in India continuously increased from 24.2 percent, with many ups and downs, to 26.9 percent in 2014-15. Despite the measly increase in its share, yet, it accounted the highest share among all the horticulture crops, pulses and cereals during the entire period of study.

8.4 Summary

From the above analysis, it can be concluded that agriculture sector in India has been gradually picking up steam in favour of horticulture and livestock especially after the year 2000-01. Except for southern and eastern region, SID growth rates in northern and western regions marginally decelerated during the post-period as compared to the pre-period.

By and large, if we glance at the analytical results, it is manifest that in almost all the regions, growth rate in agricultural diversification was almost stagnant during the post-period as against the pre-period under study.

Moreover, the areas under horticulture crops like fruits, vegetables and flowers were not uniformly distributed amongst the regions. In terms of flower production too, southern and western region were considered as the highest flower producing regions in the country over the period of time.

The share of livestock in the total value of agriculture and allied sector output has gradually picked up in India over the years and its share has increased from 24.2 percent in 2004-05, with many ups and downs, to 26.9 percent in 2014-15. Despite this measly increase in its share, it accounted for amongst the highest share among all the horticulture crops, pulses and cereals during the entire period of time.

Endnotes

1. Basu, Ratan Lal (2008), "Diversification of Agriculture in Eastern India and the Poor", in Thakur, Anil Kumar and K.B. Padmadeo, (eds.), Growth and Diversification of Agriculture', Deep and Deep Publications, New Delhi, p. 20.
2. Chand, Ramesh, S.S. Raju and L.M. Pandey (2008), "Progress and Potential of Horticulture in India", *Indian Journal of Agricultural Economics,* Vol. 63, No. 3, July-September, p. 301.

9

Problems of Agricultural Diversification

India's rising population coupled with shrinking per capita availability of cultivable land is a serious threat to food security of the country. This is so because of the limited scope of increasing additional production through subsistence farming. Thus, this situation calls for agriculture diversification in favour of horticulture i.e., fruits, vegetables and flower farming and their proper integration with the local and global markets (GoI, 2001 [1] and 2007; [2] CSD, 2010). [3]

However, with the continuous decline of land-man ratio, especially after the economic reforms, India is facing a number of socio-economic constraints i.e., tiny land-man ratio, climate change, low level of literacy, and low production which have largely bypassed the self-sufficiency during the Green Revolution. Consequently, it has lost its leading position in the yield of food grains after the Green Revolution. The model of Green Revolution was mostly successful in some pockets in the north-western region and it has not widely covered the other regions, especially the eastern region.

A study by Deshpande (2007) [4] reveals that among the Indian regions, western and southern region have been found to be largely diversified in favour of fruits, vegetables, oilseeds and pulses, but the situation is totally different for the eastern region as it is still dependant on cultivation of rice because of numerous socio-economic constraints, namely higher population density, low per capita income, high poverty ratio, low literacy rate, tiny and fragmented land holdings, poor infrastructural development (i.e., poor road network, poor power supply, poor irrigation facilities and poor extension services etc.).

Apart from this, the institutional, organizational and technological constraints like low inputs, low productivity, low risk technology, erratic weather conditions, poor adoption of technology and traditional methods of farming, low irrigation coverage, deviation in rainfall, and high dependency on mono-cropping (mainly concentrating on rice production) has pushed this region towards backwardness, and these factors have compelled farmers to stick to subsistence farming.

Eastern region is characterized by abundant natural resources like, diverse agro-climatic conditions, varied soil type and abundance of rainfall which has immense scope for growing number of varieties of horticulture crops (Basu, 2008). [5] Despite this, eastern region is the least diversified region in the country.

Thus, this situation calls for a change in cropping pattern from low value subsistence farming to high value multi-cropping pattern. Past studies (Jorge and Valdes, 1995; [6] Chand, 1999; [7] Chand, 1996; [8] Joshi et al., 2004; [9] and Jana, 2006) [10] have also suggested that agricultural diversification may be a means for rapid agricultural development in the country in order to solve the existing economic ills.

On the basis of previous studies done on this topic, it can be considered that the production of high value crops is comparatively more risky rather than the traditional crops.

However, a majority of farmers in the eastern region fall under the small and marginal category and they commonly face the problem of resource constraints and risk-aversing. Besides, the "marketable surplus for small farmers is low since the local rural markets are fragile and emaciated and selling in distant urban markets is costlier. All these problems pose as major obstructions in the diversification of agriculture towards high valued crops in the eastern states of India.

9.1 Institutional Constraints

9.1.1 Issues Related to Land Holdings: India is predominatly a rural economy and agriculture-oriented. In addition, while taking stock of the total agricultural holdings, about 85 percent of them belong to small and marginal farmers. Also, the per capita land availability for agriculture declined from 0.19 hectare in 1990 to 0.16 hectare in 2000, and further to 0.13 hectare in 2012-13 (GoI, 2013) [11] and is projected to slide further to 0.20 hectares by 2035 (State of Indian Agriculture, 2015-16). "Such tiny holdings by a large majority of farmers is neither viable nor sustainable for a country with a billion plus mouths to feed and the continuous decline in the average size of land holdings creates a serious problem for future" (Kumar, 2010). [12]

The average size of land holdings in India has declined from 1.55 hectare in 1990-91 to 1.33 hectare in 2000-01, and further to 1.15 hectares in 2010-11 (CMIE, 2015). [13] This is due to the continuous increase in population as well as the number of operation holdings, thereby reducing the average size of holdings and making them non-viable.

In addition to this, fragmentation of land holdings, lack of off-farm occupations, and inheritance laws of an equal division of property among heirs, has led to the division of land into small blocks. Such small holdings are often over-manned, resulting in disguised unemployment and low productivity of labour. Moreover, there are several tenancy restrictions in many states.

These restrictions range from a complete ban in some states to complete freedom of leasing in some states. There is a growing consensus about the need to have a re-evaluation of current tenancy legislations, which sometimes restricts participation of private sector in agriculture. However, under the Indian Constitution, land administration falls within the jurisdiction of state governments; hence, there are large variations across states (Sharma, 2008). [14] Furthermore, skewness in land distribution continues to be serious in these states.

At the all-India level, small and marginal land holdings (below 2 hectares of land) taken together witnessed a marginal increase and constituted about 85.01 percent during 2010-11 as compared to 83.29 percent during 2005-06. Similarly, the area under operation was 41.14 percent during 2005-06 which reached the level of 44.58 percent during 2010-11 (CMIE, 2015). On the other hand, the number of operational holdings increased from 1,066.37 lakh in 1990-91 to 1,383.48 lakh in 2010-11, thereby reducing the size of holdings from 1,655.07 lakh hectares in 1990-91 to 1,595.92 lakh hectares in 2010-11, making them operationally non-viable.

Among all the regions, the eastern region is the only region which has displayed the lowest percentage share of area under operations, number of land holdings and average size of land holdings amongst small, semi-marginal, medium and large farm programmes, while the western region has been found just opposite compared to the eastern region during 2010-11.

On the other hand, in terms of percentage share of total area operated, the eastern region consists of the highest share of marginal and small farmers while the western region has the highest share of large and medium farm programmes. Thus, in eastern region, the situation is more vital since 94 percent operational holdings consist of small and marginal farmers as against the national average of 84.9 percent in 2010-11.

The findings portray eastern region as a backward region in terms of percentage share of area operated, number of land holdings and average size of land holdings for the period 2010-11. Further in-depth analysis reveals that among the eastern region, in Bihar, about 97 percent of operational holdings consisted of small and marginal farmers followed by West Bengal (96 percent), Odisha (91.85 percent), Assam (85.56 percent) and Jharkhand (84.06 percent) during 2010-11.

However, these small and marginal farmers have a poor economic base and consequently it has an adverse impact on diversification in favour of high value crops. This is so because average cost of cultivation of horticulture crops per hectare on tiny land holdings was higher as compared to the cultivation of low value crops (Singh and Bodra, 2008). [15]

However, the small and marginal farmers are more efficient compared to the medium size farmers while producing quantities of vegetables per hectare. This could be attributed to the reason that small and marginal farmers prefer growing more vegetables due to surplus labour and quick returns. Whereas, big farmers are more efficient in producing fruits as compared to small and marginal farmers due to economic constraints as well as due to long gestation period (Mysore, 2008). [16]

Finally, it can be summarized as per the findings, that in the eastern region, about 94 percent of the total number of holdings belonged to small and marginal farmers during the year 2010-11. In addition, it is also important to highlight that in all the major eastern states except Assam, the size of operational holdings of small and marginal farmers remarkably increased due to shift in the area under cultivation of semi-marginal, medium, and large size farmers during 2010-11 as compared to 2005-06.

However, as per Agricultural Census 2011, in case of Odisha and Bihar, the total number of holdings increased from 37.5 lakh and 141.2 lakh respectively in 2005-06 to 42.9lakh and 156.9 lakh respectively in 2010-11. Additionally, the total size of operational holdings of these states viz., Odisha and Bihar also increased respectively by 17 percent and 7 percent from 29.3 lakh hectares and 45.4 lakh hectares to 34.2 lakh hectares and 48.6 lakh hectares in 2005-06 and 2010-11 due to shift in the area of large, medium and semi-medium farms towards small and marginal farm sizes.

Thus, this high fragmentation of land restricted and hindered dissemination of modern technology in the agriculture sector. Despite tiny land holdings, there was a continuous decline in barren, grazing, waste and fallow land for cultivation in Assam, Bihar and West Bengal in 2013-14 as compared to 2004-05.

As a result, the area under barren, grazing and fallow land was shifted and brought under cultivation in Assam, Bihar and West Bengal during the same period. Concurrently, Odisha and Jharkhand reported an increase in area only under fallow land during the same period. Despite small land holdings in the eastern region, especially in Bihar, high incidence of tenancy cultivation was dominated largely by absentee landlords which further choked the growth prospects since much of the land remained out of investment domain.

9.1.2 Problems of Agricultural Credit: Credit is a major stimulus for each sector of the economy. Moreover, it is one of the vital prerequisites for the farmers that enables them to increase crops yields and also facilitates in meeting investment as well working capital requirements.

Poor credit facilities for investment are hindrances in the expansion of area under HYVs and the use of optimal measured quantity of inputs like fertilizers, pesticides, etc. Like other sectors, availability of credit for the agriculture sector must be easy, adequate, and timely. Despite a large network of rural financial institutions (RFIs), a large portion of the society, especially low-income group is having little access to the formal and semi-formal sources of finance in India (GoI, 2014). [17].

This is so because only about 13 bank branches were available for access per lakh population. It is quite unfortunate that a majority of low-income households depend on moneylenders for financial requirements (The Hindu, December 22, 2017).

On the other hand, inflexible credit flows and security-based lending system is widespread in formal Indian banking sector; consequently, a majority of the people are dependent on their own or informal source of finance. It has been estimated by NSSO (2014) [18] that about 40 percent of the funds sourced by farmers still come from the informal sources. Besides this, about 26 percent of the total agricultural credit comes from local money lenders which is generally at unreasonably high interest rates.

Besides, "long gestation period, lack of trained technical staff to identify potential activity in this field, poor eligibility and security problems are some of the reasons behind insufficient credit flow to the agriculture sector" (Kumari et al., 2008). [19] This needs to be rectified for speedy and easy flow of credit to the agriculture sector.

The reason for poor agricultural performance in the eastern region can also be attributed to the commercial and regional rural banks (RRBs) in the region who are often reluctant to extend agricultural credit. Also, the limited existence of co-operative banks in eastern states, especially in Bihar, also seems to have triggered less flow of agricultural credit in all the districts of Bihar.

Besides, their achievements against the targets also have been lowest among all the three sources in all the districts of Bihar where they are present" (GoB, 2014). [20] It is evident from the fact that most of the agro-machines are costlier, which is beyond the purchasing power of the farmers in eastern states. This is primarily because 94 percent of the farmers fall in small and marginal farmers' category and on an average about one-third of them are living in abject poverty (GoI, 2014). [21]

Hence, Bihar on this front, requires friendly and advanced treatment from commercial banks (CBs) and RRBs and there is an urgent need to establish cooperative banks in the remaining districts of the state to boost agricultural activities.

9.1.3 Infrastructural Constraints: Agricultural growth performance depends highly on the use of farm power derived from modern farm implements and their judicious utilization. On the other hand, availability of tractors, pumpsets, cold storage facilities, adequate supply of power, good rural-urban road network, efficient transportation and developed agriculture marketing and other technological advancements maximize benefits for the farmers.

However, the availability of these inputs is highly inadequate in the country, and large inter-state disparities exist in the use of modern inputs which has led to dismal agriculture performance in India.

9.1.4 Farm Mechanization: As we know that due to the

erratic rainfall and unpredictable weather conditions, a large section of the Indian farmers depend on diesel run electric pumps for irrigating their crops.

Since, the performance of agriculture in India is largely based on the availability of irrigation facilities, the agriculture sector has become a big consumer of electricity and diesel. Equipments like threshers, power tillers, and drillers etc., are fuelled by diesel power, while digging, clod breaking, sowing, harvesting, threshing, cleaning, and grading are performed by human power using traditional tools and implements (Singh, 2006). [22]

Since inception, human and animal power had played a vital role in agriculture, and it was traditionally used for various farm activities. But during the recent past, it is evident from the statistics, that due to efficient adoption of modern technologies in agriculture, the share of agricultural workers and animals in total power (kilowatt per hectare (kW/Ha) has declined, which is a good sign for agriculture development in India.

Similarly, the share of tractors, power tillers and electric motors have showed an increasing trend. Use of tractor power and electric motors increased from 30.3 percent and 20.9 percent respectively in 1991-92 to 45.8 percent and 26.8 percent in 2012-13, respectively. Thus, the evident data suggests that the agriculture sector is gradually shifting from traditional farming methods towards mechanized farming during the recent past. It is because of the continuous increase in per hectare consumption of mechanical energy (kW/Ha) in agriculture.

9.1.5 Transportation Infrastructure: Infrastructure is the ba kbone and a basic requisite for economic development. The marketable products of varied nature and their value addition are deeply influenced by the nature of infrastructural support. Availability of good quality physical infrastructure also helps in improving the investment climate both internally and externally. There is an extensive and well-developed rail system passing through eastern India and a substantial potential exists for development and utilization of inland waterways. Rapid development and strengthening of the road network will provide momentum for accelerating the process of economic development in the region.

Undoubtedly, continuous increase in the GDP has turned India into one of the fastest growing economies in the Asian region vis-à-vis world. This economic advancement is a sign of development for 700 million rural population living in six lakh villages, as they are largely dependant on the agriculture for their livelihhod (Rao and Sekhar, 2010). [23]

Hence, infrastructure is significant for the economic development of the rural economy. Rural infrastructure like road connectivity and transport facilities is one of the most crucial mechanism, which has a close link with employment generation, poverty reduction, reduced transportation costs, market expansion, and improved agricultural productivity and competitiveness in the country. "Rural infrastructure and support services play a key role in promoting rural development, particularly in enhancing the agricultural production. They influence the quality, quantity, diversity, affordability, distribution, and stability of food supply from rural areas" (Yadav, 2010). [24]

The lack of development of agricultural diversification in favour of horticultural crops is presently characterized by absence of good quality infrastructure and thus any development of the sector has to be underpinned by provision of good infrastructure, both physical and social. In this regard, proper connectivity and transport links for delivery of services, transaction of commerce, connection with growth centres, and development of tourism are considered to be the most critical and have far-reaching implications on the social and economic life in the country.

Compounded annual growth rate of rural road network in the eastern region increased from 2.97 percent per annum in pre-period to 6.07 percent per annum in the post-period which was far better than the northern region's which stood at 5.5 percent in post-period up from 4.33 percent per annum in the pre-period. However, among all the regions, the western region performed on a slow wicket with CAGR of 3.69 percent per annum during the post-period.

However, in terms of rural road connectivity (in kilometres), the northern vis-à-vis eastern region exhibited a poor show leading to huge wastage of horticultural produce and the consequent price volatility. It may be said that this is one of the foremost causes of low agricultural diversification in the states of these regions.

Therefore, in order to reduce such wastages, major attention has to be given to improve rural infrastructure, especially post-harvest technologies, marketing infrastructure, and connectivity with major business hubs. In this regard, according to India Rural Infrastructure Report, the funds for rural infrastructural development were raised to ₹ 12,000 crore from ₹ 10,000 crore (Rao and Sekhar, 2010). [25]

9.1.6 Agriculture Marketing: Agriculture marketing is a key instrument for the development of the agriculture sector. Agricultural marketing includes movement of agricultural produce from farms where it is produced to the consumers or manufacturers. It also includes marketing of production inputs like fertilizers, pesticides and other agricultural chemicals, livestock feed, farm machinery, tools and equipment and services to the farmers (Patnaik, 2003) [26] and plays a major role in accelerating the process of economic development by stimulating production and consumption (COA, 2015) [27]

The basic feature of an efficient agricultural marketing system is not only to provide goods to the consumers but also to provide incentives to farmers to produce more, encourage true competition among the traders and abolish exploitation of farmers, particularly small and marginal farmers. In a market system, farmers sell their agricultural and horticultural produce directly or indirectly to the consumers as well as to the rural associations. India's agriculture marketing system is classified into three broad categories, namely:

- Rural primary markets.
- Secondary/assembly markets.
- Wholesale markets.

The rural primary markets cater to the local demand and are located in nearby villages as *haats* (they are also called *petas* or *angadis* in Telgu, *hatwaras* in Rajasthan, *shandies or chindies* in Kerala, and *painths* in Uttar Pradesh).

Secondary markets are located nearby the centres of wholesale markets which cater to distant demands, whereby, the wholesale markets accumulate large quantity of agricultural produce from different sources, and take care of small assortments to meet the needs of retailers in the country.

According to the Tenth Plan document, "the current market system is dominated by traders. Appropriate and effective linkages between the producers and sellers continue to be weak. The absence of rural road connectivity and other infrastructure combined with improper management, lack of market intelligence, and inadequate credit support has resulted in a system that is unfavourable to the farmers.

The adverse impact of all these is more pronounced in the case of small and marginal farmers who constitute about 78 percent of the entire farming community. The primary rural markets are the first contact point for the rural producers and sellers. There are over 27 thousand primary rural markets, scattered across the country.

These are, however, not equipped with basic facilities, such as platforms for sale and auction, electricity, drinking water, link roads, traders premises, facilities for post-harvest management, etc. The private sector and joint ventures for setting up markets need to be encouraged with suitable policies and incentives for free and competitive trade" (Chakraborty, 2003). [28]

Unfortunately, among the eastern states, agriculture marketing seems to be inefficient. Due to high input cost, poor marketing facilities as well as poor marketing network, farmers are not able to produce horticultural commodities. Besides, this region is also considered to have ample potential in animal husbandry. However, it is incapable to exploit this potential due to lack of marketing network.

However, there is an excellent demand for these products in the region. In spite of this, farmers are not willing to produce these crops because of the unfair or lesser remuneration (Rizvi, 2010). [29]

Among all the regions, policies and programmes for growing horticultural commodities and its marketing deserve special attention, as for small farmers, vegetable cultivation is the most profitable venture. However, in the case of eastern region, especially in Bihar, because of poor marketing infrastructure and due to perishable nature of horticulture produce, farmers sell their produce immediately after harvest which before reaching the final consumers passes through various types of intermediaries. This large chain of intermediaries is the main cause of market disabilities for horticulture produce, leading to high marketing costs and margins (Prasad, 2008). [30]

9.2 Technological Constraints

9.2.1 Use of HYV Seeds: Under the new agricultural approach, special emphasis has been made on the development and widespread adoption of high-yielding varieties of seeds. There is a mismatch between demand and availability of HYV seeds in major regions of India.

In southern region, the demand of HYV seeds was the highest, i.e. 35.4 lakh quintals with supply of 48.2 lakh quintals during 2006-2007, leading to surplus of 12.9 lakh quintals. While, during 2013-14, the demand for HYV seeds remarkably increased to 73.4 lakh quintals with supply of 83.3 lakh quintals, leading to surplus of 9.9 lakh quintals in the southern region.

However, in the eastern region, the demand of HYV seeds was the lowest i.e., 23.5 lakh quintals with supply of 23.3 lakh quintals during 2006-2007, leading to deficiency of (-) 0.2 lakh quintals. However, during 2013-14, the total demand of HYV seeds increased to 70.1 lakh quintals with supply of about 70.8 lakh quintal, leading to gradual improvement and reaching a surplus level of 0.7 lakh quintal during the same period.

In case of CAGR, the highest demand for and supply of HYV seeds was observed in the eastern region i.e., 21.4 percent and 23.3 percent per annum respectively followed by western region (16.7 percent and 16.8 percent), and northern region (14.9 percent 12.8 percent) during 2006-07 to 2013-14. Contrarily, the southern region accounted for the least growth in demand for and supply of HYV seeds i.e., 11.1 percent and 9.8 percent respectively during the same period, which was lower than the national average.

It is also important to note that on an all-India level, the availability of HYV seeds stood at 347.3 lakh quintal in relation to demand of 335.3 lakh quintals, showing a surplus of 12.1 lakh quintals during the period 2013-14.

However, northern region and eastern region respectively presented a miserable picture with a deficiency of 3.9 lakh quintals and 0.7 lakh quintals in totality. This is mainly because of the seed replacement rate for most of the crops in the state which is very poor among these regions.

However, introduction of such HYV seeds depends on the availability of adequate irrigation, fertilizers, pesticides and insecticides. Therefore, they have to be launched in the form of a 'package programme'.

It may be underlined that the HYV seeds technology continues to escape very important section of the farming economy such as pulses, oilseeds, fruits and vegetables; and hence, there is an urgent need to incorporate these crops too.

9.2.2 Use of Fertilizers: Optimal use of fertilizers and manures can reduce the deficiency of nitrogen and phosphorus, leading to an increase in the total factor of productivity of the soil in the country.

The consumption of fertilizers in India increased from 69.8 kg/ha in 1991-92 to 128.3 kg/ha in 2012-13 with an overall compounded annual growth rate of 3.8 percent per annum. Coming to the regional level analysis, it was found that there existed wide inter-regional disparities over the period of time. The highest consumption of fertilizers was observed in the northern region at 153 kg/ha followed by southern region (144 kg/ha) and eastern region (138 kg/ha), while western region was recorded as the least fertilizer consuming region in India during 2012-13.

However, the CAGR of fertilizer consumption in western region was observed at the highest level during the post-period. Thus, the highest growth rate in fertilizer consumption was observed in the western region (6.7 percent) followed by eastern region (5.9 percent), southern region (4.4 percent) and northern region, showing the least CAGR of 3.4 percent per annum during the post-period.

However, during the same period, regarding the use of fertilizers, two regions, namely southern and northern region not only lagged behind the eastern region but also at all-India level. However, in the consumption of fertilizers, eastern region and western region fared better than the all-India level. It is a fact that despite being economically backward, eastern region displayed the highest level of fertilizer consumption.

9.2.3 Use of Pesticides/Chemicals: Pesticides is a mixture of substances which helps in preventing and controlling unwanted species on plants. It is evident that consumption of pesticides in southern and western region showed remarkable improvement with positive changes by 24.4 percent and 4.4 percent respectively, while the remaining two regions viz., eastern and northern region registered remarkable deceleration with negative changes of (-) 8.94 percent and (-) 0.54 percent respectively between the two periods i.e. from 2000-01 till 2012-13.

However, at the all-India level, the total consumption of pesticides increased from 43.58 thousand metric tonnes (TMT) to 45.39 TMT with 10.7 percent of coefficient of variation and 0.94 percent per annum of annual growth rate from 2000-01 till 2012-13.

Furthermore, it is also important to highlight that the consumption of pesticides among the regions was much less than that of all-India average in both the periods.

Among those, eastern region presented a skimpy picture in the consumption of pesticides as compared to the remaining regions like northern, southern and western. It may be attributed to less awareness among farmers in the eastern states of India.

9.3 Socio-economic Constraints

9.3.1 Region-wise Population of India: In India, as per Census, 2011, more than 377.1 million people lived in urban areas and 833.5 million people in rural areas out of the total population of 1210.6 million.

Similarly, in the western states, about 120 million people lived in urban areas which is the highest urban population amongst the regions as against 120 million in rural areas out of the total population of 340 million. Alternatively, the eastern region registered the highest rural population among the regions i.e., about 241 million people living in rural areas as against 60.2 million in urban areas out of the total population of 302 million.

As per the Census 2011, among the regions, western region was the most populated region and eastern region, the second most populous region in the country. Southern region was considered the least populated region of India.

All the sample regions under the study actually witnessed an increase in urbanization due to continuous decrease in rural population which is gradually moving towards urban areas for better education, jobs and livelihoods. Among the regions, as per Census 2011, eastern region was the only region which was categorized as the least urbanized region in the country.

One of the major reasons for this decline was the bifurcation of the states e.g., Bihar and Jharkhand in this region. But the fact remains that due to economic stagnation, urban growth in eastern region has been dismal. The level of urbanization in this state is very low and accounted for 20 percent which is much lesser than the all-India figure of 31.1 percent.

9.3.2 Low Literacy Rate: Education plays an important role in the socio-economic development of a country. It is a vital component of human capital and has greater impact in the growth and development of the economy and makes possible to change people's attitude by creating awareness to accept new and modern technologies.

Without education, the thought of and growth and development is not effectively possible. In an agrarian society, education plays a key role in the sense that utilization of appropriate proportion of different agro-inputs like fertilizers, HYV seeds, uses of insecticides and pesticides not only increase production and productivities of crops but also minimize environmental degradation.

Literacy rate has been rising in the country and increased from 64.7 percent in 2001 to 73.0 percent in 2011. The improvement has been noticed both in male and female literacy rates. In 2001, only 53.7 percent females were literate compared to 75.3 percent males. While in 2011, the rate increased to 64.6 percent and 80.9 percent respectively.

However, among the regions, eastern and northern regions continued to occupy the lowest ranks in terms of both male and female literacy rates. The literacy rates (in both males, females as well as in total) in eastern region was the lowest among all the regions as well as in the country. It accounted for an overall literacy rate of 69.5 percent, with male literacy rate at 77.2 percent and female literacy rate at 61.3 percent.

Similarly, the literacy rate (in the males, females as well as in total) in rural areas in the eastern region was observed not only to be the lowest among the regions, but it was far below at the national average also.

Thus, the highest rural literary rate was observed at 69.7 percent in the southern region and lowest was in eastern region at 65.9 percent. However, the highest male literacy rate in rural areas was found at 79.3 percent in western region, while lowest was observed in the eastern region at 74.4 percent.

Rural female literacy rate was as low as 56.2 percent and 56.8 percent in northern and eastern region respectively.

However, the highest female rural literacy was found at 61.8 percent in the southern states. An overwhelming majority of females in rural areas in eastern and northern regions are still illiterate.

An important feature of the literacy profile in the eastern region, as also in remaining sampled region, is the pronounced disparity between urban and rural areas in case of both male and female literates.

Various studies suggest that education creates awareness among the people to take advantage from the changing market situations by adopting agricultural diversification and minimizing risk of crop failures. After the post-reforms period, especially after Census 2001, the literacy rate of eastern region has increased but still about one-third of the population is illiterate.

9.3.3 Poverty in India: Poverty is a major obstacle in the economic development of India, particularly in eastern states. Due to low purchasing power of the people, they are unable to purchase adequate and appropriate amount of agricultural inputs at the time of cultivation, which causes low productivity of food grains.

People are unable to meet their minimum basic needs because of poverty, which adversely affects the consumption pattern and the standard of living of the people in the regions particularly in the eastern region. There are various factors, such as rapid rise of population, poor literacy rate, unemployment, agricultural backwardness, lack of industries, infrastructural facilities, unfavourable social environment, recurrence of the floods and droughts, skewed distribution of land, corruption and lastly lack of commitment towards development among the leaders who are responsible for the rise in poverty in the states.

At the all-India level, the poverty ratio declined in rural areas by 25.7 percent in 2011-12 from 41.8 percent in 2004-05, while in urban areas it declined by 13.7 percent from 25.7 percent during the same period.

Whereas, the eastern region had the largest poverty ratio in both rural (33.4 percent) and urban (21.7 percent) areas, the southern region had the lowest poverty ratio at 15.1 percent and 8.2 percent respectively during the year 2011-12. After the eastern region, the western region had the second largest poverty ratio in both rural (28.4 percent) and urban (15.1 percent) areas during the same period.

Endnotes

1. Government of India (2001), "Report of the Working Group on Horticulture Development (Fruits, Vegetables, Tuber Crops, Floriculture, Medicinal and Aromatic Plants, Spices, Plantation Crops Including Tea, Coffee and Rubber) for The Tenth Five Year Plan (Main Report)", Planning Commission, June.
2. Government of India (2007), Planning Commission of India, "Report of the Working Group on Horticulture, Plantation Crops and Organic Farming for the Eleventh Five Year Plan (2007-12)", January, available at: http://planningcommission.nic.in/aboutus/committee/wrkgrp11/wg11_aghorti.pdf.
3. Council for Social Development (2010), "Constraints and Potentials of Diversified Agricultural Development in Eastern India", December, Project Sponsored by Planning Commission, Government of India, New Delhi.
4. Deshpandey, R.S., Pradeep Mehta and Khalil Shah (2007), "Crop Diversification and Agricultural Labour in India", *The Indian Journal of Labour Economics*, Vol. 50, No. 4. Pp. 597-610.
5. Basu, Ratan Lal (2008), "Diversification of Agriculture in Eastern India and the Poor", in Thakur, Anil Kumar and K.B. Padmadeo (eds.), 'Growth and Diversification of Agriculture', Deep and Deep Publications, New Delhi, p. 19.
6. Jorge, A. Quiroz and Alberto Valdes (1995), "Agricultural Diversification and Policy Reform," *Food Policy*, Vol. 20, No. 3, pp. 245-255.
7. Chand, Ramesh (1999), "Agriculture Diversification in India: Potentials and Prospects in Developed Region", Mittal Publications, New Delhi.

8. Chand, Ramesh (1996), "Diversification through High-Value Crops in Western Himalayan Region: Evidence from Himachal Pradesh", *Indian Journal of Agriculture Economics,* 41(4), pp. 652-663.
9. Joshi, P.K., A. Gulati, P.S. Birthal and L. Tiwari (2004), "Agriculture Diversification in South Asia: Pattern, Determinants and Policy Implications", *Economic and Political Weekly*, June 12.
10. Jana, B.L. (2006), "Concept of Crop Diversification in Agriculture", Agro-Tech Publishing Academy, Udaipur, p. 16.
11. Government of India (2013), paper presented on "Utilization of Land Resources for Agriculture Sector in India: Present Practices and Polices", in two days seminar (September 18-19) on 'Draft National Land Utilisation Policy 2013' by Pandey, C.M., Ministry of Agriculture and Farmers Welfare, New Delhi.
12. Kumar, Praveen (2010), "Food Security: The Challenge Ahead", *Yojana,* A Development Monthly, Ministry of Information and Broadcasting, New Delhi, p. 28.
13. Centre for Monitoring Indian Economy (2015), online database.
14. Sharma, Vijay Paul (2008), "India's Agrarian Crisis and Smallholder Producers' Participation in New Farm Supply Chain Initiatives: A Case Study of Contract Farming", IIM-Ahmedabad, Working Paper No. 2007-08-01, August.
15. Singh, R.P and Seema Bodra (2008), "Economic Analysis of Crop Diversification: A Comparative Study of Foodgrains and Vegetable Crops", *Indian Journal of Agriculture Economics*, Vol. 63, No. 3, July-September, p. 363.
16. Mysore, Sudha (2008), "Triggering Agricultural Development through Horticultural Crops", Rapporteur's Report, *Indian Journal of Agricultural Economics*, Vol. 63, No. 3, July-September, p. 546.
17. Reserve Bank of India (2014), "Financial Inclusion", September 4, available at: https://rbi.org.in/scripts/publicationsview.aspx?id=10494.
18. NSSO (2014), "Key Indicators of Situation of Agricultural Households in India, NSS-70th Round", January-December, Ministry of Statistics and Programme Implementation, Government of India, New Delhi.
19. Kumari, Mridula and R.C. Choudhary (2008), "An Economic Analysis of MAP Cultivation in Bihar", in Thakur, Anil Kumar

and K.B. Padmadeo (eds.), 'Growth and Diversification of Agriculture', Deep and Deep Publications, New Delhi, p. 293.

20. Government of Bihar (2014), "Economic Survey: 2013-14", Ministry of Finance, Patna, available at: http://finance.bih.nic.in/Documents/Reports/Economic-Survey-2014-EN.pdf.
21. Government of India (2014), "Databook Compiled for Use of Planning Commission", December 22, available at: http://planningcommission.gov.in/data/datatable/data_2312/comp_data2312.pdf.
22. Singh Gyanendra (2006), "Agricultural Machinery Industry in India", in 'Status of Farm Mechanization in India', IARI, March.
23. Rao, K. Srinivasa and K. Chandra Sekhar (2010), "Rural Infrastructure: A Vital Ingredient for Double Digit Growth", *Kurukshetra,* A Journal of Rural Development, Ministry of I&B, Government of India, Vol. 58, No. 10, August, p. 4.
24. Yadav, Krishan. K. (2010), "Road Connectivity as a Stimulant for Rural Poverty Reduction", *Kurukshetra,* A Journal of Rural Development, Ministry of I&B, Government of India, August, Vol. 58, No. 10, pp. 12-13.
25. Rao, K. Srinivasa and K. Chandra Sekhar (2010), "Rural Infrastructure: A Vital Ingredient for Double Digit Growth", *Kurukshetra,* A Journal of Rural Development, Ministry of I&B, Government of India, August, Vol. 58, No. 10, p. 5.
26. Patnaik, Gokul (2003), "Marketing, Storage, and Extension Services: State of Agriculture in India", in Debroy, Bibek and Amir Ullah Khan (eds.), 'Enabling Agricultural Markets for the Small Indian Farmer', Bookwell Publications, New Delhi, pp. 81-100
27. College of Agriculture (2015), Palampur, September, available at: http://www.hillagric.ac.in/edu/coa/AgriEcoExtEduRSocio/lectures/AgEcon244.PDF.
28. Chakraborty, Debashis (2003), "Enabling Agricultural Markets for the Small Indian Farmers", in Debroy, Bibek and Amir Ullah Khan (eds.), 'Enabling Agricultural Markets for the Small Indian Farmer', Bookwell Publications, New Delhi, p. 189.
29. Rizvi, Halima Sadia (2010), "Agricultural Diversification in Eastern Region of India: Problems and Prospects", in Roy, Pashupati, Kumar and Shiv Pershan Sharma (eds.),

'Globalization and Agricultural Diversification of India', Deep and Deep Publications, New Delhi, pp. 37-38.

30. Prasad, Anajali (2008), "Pattern of Agricultural Diversification and Vegetable production in Bihar", in Thakur, Anil Kumar and K.B. Padmadeo (eds.), 'Agriculture Diversification in India', Deep and Deep Publications, New Delhi, pp. 459-460.

10

Prospects of Agricultural Diversification

10.1 Agricultural Diversification and Employment

Generating additional employment in rural areas is a very decisive step required in the near future. The question arises as how to create additional employment opportunities for the rural people of India. In this regard, information has been gathered regards the labour used in the production of different crops in order to make a comparative analysis. Various studies reveal that crop diversification can generate additional farm employment. Hence, labour use in the production of high value crops like fruits, vegetables, flowers and commercial crops is substantially higher than that of cereal crops like wheat, paddy, pulses etc. (Rao, et al., 2008). [1] This is so because high value crops are more labour intensive as compared to low value crops during the entire process of production. Labour requirement for per unit output of vegetables, fruits, and flowers was found to be higher than that of cereal crops (Joshi, et al., 2003; [2] Deshingkar, et al., 2003). [3]

For instance, horticultural crops during the winter season employ more than double the human labour than what is used in wheat cropping. However, summer vegetables offer more than double the employment in paddy cultivation. Among the landless-based activities, there is tremendous scope for raising employment by substituting area of wheat-paddy in favour of fodder crops. Unemployed people in the farm sectors can be absorbed in India especially in the eastern region by promoting agriculture-based industries. Milk and milk products industry, sugarcane industry, and horticulture processing food industries, can provide gainful employment to the poor and landless labourers in the state.

Rao, et al. also discussed in their study about the labour absorption in the entire process of production of high value crops versus low value crops under rainfed vis-à-vis irrigated area in four districts of Andhra Pradesh. They found that the labour requirement for vegetables is high as it accounted for 156 mandays/hectare followed by flowers, cotton and oilseeds. However, for area under irrigated land, highest amount of labour was required for the production of flowers, i.e. 264 mandays/hectare followed by vegetables, paddy, cotton and oilseeds. Hence, it can be said that in the entire process of production, labour requirement is much higher for vegetables, flowers and fruits as compared to paddy and oilseeds etc.

Joshi, et al. (2004), [4] in their paper advocated that roughly 1 hectare shift in area from wheat to potato would generate additional employment opportunities i.e., close to 145 mandays in rural areas. Similarly, 1 hectare area shift from coarse cereals to onion would generate additional employment opportunities to the tune of 70 mandays. Also, shift in area from coarse cereals like sorghum and millet to vegetables like cabbage, cauliflower, eggplant, tomato and lady finger would generate additional 70 mandays per hectare.

Hence, as per the above study, it can be concluded that a marginal shift in area under cereals and coarse cereal crops towards high value crops i.e., fruits, vegetables and flowers etc., could result in significant generation of additional employment opportunities.

10.2 Agricultural Diversification and Income Growth

Prospects of large-scale agriculture diversification towards horticulture crops like fruits, vegetables and flowers are some of the alternatives, which are more profitable than traditional crops like wheat and paddy. Ultimately, they lead to generation of additional income for the farmers and labourers in the regions as well as the country. Thus, agricultural diversification has emerged as an important mechanism to increase farm income and augment employment opportunities for the growers. This fact is statistically verified by study of Chand (1999). [5] He established a significant association between growth of agricultural income

(NSDP) and agricultural diversification.

Various studies also support the fact that agricultural diversification is a tool to increase farm income, generate additional employment opportunities, alleviate poverty especially rural poverty (Michler and Josephson, 2017) and conserve natural resources like soil and water (Joshi, et al., 2004). This fact also has been found in the study by Rao, et al. (2008), [6] in their study which reveals the cost of production and net return per unit of high value crops vis-à-vis low value crops. According to their study, high value crops i.e., vegetables are more profitable as compared to the low value crops like pulses, cotton and oilseeds in Kurnool district under rainfed and irrigated areas in Andhra Pradesh.

10.3 Diversification through Dairying

Dairy co-operatives enhanced farm incomes along with generation of additional employment opportunities for approximately 13.4 million farm families and 1.33 lakh village-level dairy cooperative societies, spread over 265 districts in the country (Dhanasekaran and Srinivasan, 2010).[7]

In case of milk production, India holds the first place and accounted for about 18.5 percent of the total milk production in the world (Economic Survey, 2016) and is still the largest producer of milk in the world (GoI, 2017). Milk production in the country increased from 53.9 million metric tonnes (Mt) in 1990-91 to 80.6 Mt in 2000-01 which further increased to 132.41 Mt during 2016-17. As a result, per capita consumption of milk increased from 176 grams per day in 1990-91 to 217 grams per day in 2000-01 and to 351 grams per day in 2016-17 (GoI, 2014 [8]; GoI, 2017 [9]). Increase in the growth rate of milk production in India by 4.33 percent per annum was higher than that of the increase in the growth rate of population by 1.99 percent per annum during the pre-period i.e., 1990-91 to 2000-01. However, during the post-period (2000-01 to 2016-17), the growth rate of milk production increased at a constant/negligible rate of 4.52 percent per annum), while population growth rate declined sharply to 1.48 percent from 1.99 percent per annum.

Similar case also prevailed in the production and availability of eggs during the same period. The available figures clearly depict that the India had a surplus milk and egg production during the study period. In India, animal husbandry is characterized by small and marginal farmers. Unfortunately, scattered production, inefficient marketing system, lack of modern inputs and poor infrastructural facilities have adversely affected the development of livestock and dairy farming in the eastern states of India.

Thus, the view is that if appropriate marketing infrastructure is developed for purchasing the surplus produce in the states, the producers of the states will benefit from it. Poverty, which is a major obstacle to economic development in the country, especially among the eastern states, can be alleviated through diversification in favour of horticulture and animal husbandry by generating additional employment opportunities and income of the people in rural areas in these states. India's dairy product exports increased from 87.82 TMT, valued at ₹ 1,412.10 crore in 2012-13 to 159.23 TMT with the value of ₹ 3,318.60 crore in 2013-14 (GoI, 2015). Diversification of agricultural sector has promoted export of various non-traditional items such as vegetables, floriculture, and animal husbandry, which has picked up during the post-period.

10.4 Provision of Food Security

Food security is a major issue in respect of diversification of agriculture at the state, region and national level. Continuous rise in population, degradation of natural resources, and producing additional food is a major challenge before the country. Crop substitution has been taking place gradually by diverting the area under cultivation in favour of horticulture. Production trends reveal that the per capita daily availability of food grains decreased from 472.6 grams per day in 1991 to 416.2 grams per day in 2001. However, after 2000, it has increased with various ups and down and ultimately reached 510.8 grams per day during 2016-17 (Economic

Survey, 2016-17).

The consumption pattern of the people has shifted from cereal to non-cereal commodities in both rural and urban areas. But in rural areas, consumption of cereal crops has declined while that of vegetables and fruits has increased significantly (NSSO, 2010; [10] NSSO, 2014). [11] Thus, inclination of the people in both urban and rural areas confirms that diversification of agricultural crops will provide not only food security but would also help in employment generation, augmentation of farm income, eradication of poverty, sustainable development of agriculture, and promotion of agricultural exports. The present analysis shows that agricultural diversification of crops had a positive impact on consumption patterns and an increase in the production of non-cereal commodities consequently leading to increase in farm incomes in the study regions vis-à-vis India.

10.5 Agricultural Diversification and Resource Utilization

Among the regions in India, eastern region is endowed with vast land resources that are highly suitable for agricultural crops. It is one of the regions of India where water supply is abundant. However, it is unfortunate that due to lack of efficient water management, vast water resources are a bane rather than a boon for these states. Recurring floods destroy agricultural crops, lives of people and their properties worth thousands of crores of rupees and render thousands of poor people homeless every year. An effective and comprehensive water management programme has to be formulated and implemented to channelise the excess water from water surplus areas to water deficit areas. It should also be aimed at increasing the gross irrigated area as percentage of total cropped area that can lead to a higher crop diversification (Mandal, Raju and M.P. Bezbaruah, 2013; [12] Gupta, R.P. and S.K. Tewari, 1985). [13]

The present study finds a strong case in favour of crop diversification in the eastern states of India to take them out of agricultural backwardness, poverty, unemployment, and low economic growth. But for successful diversification of agriculture in these states, rural basic infrastructure like power, irrigation, road, and transportation, marketing facilities etc. are pre-conditions which would make crop diversification economically attractive. The prospects of agricultural diversification can be seen clearly in Figure 10.1.

Figure 10.1: Prospects of Agriculture Diversification

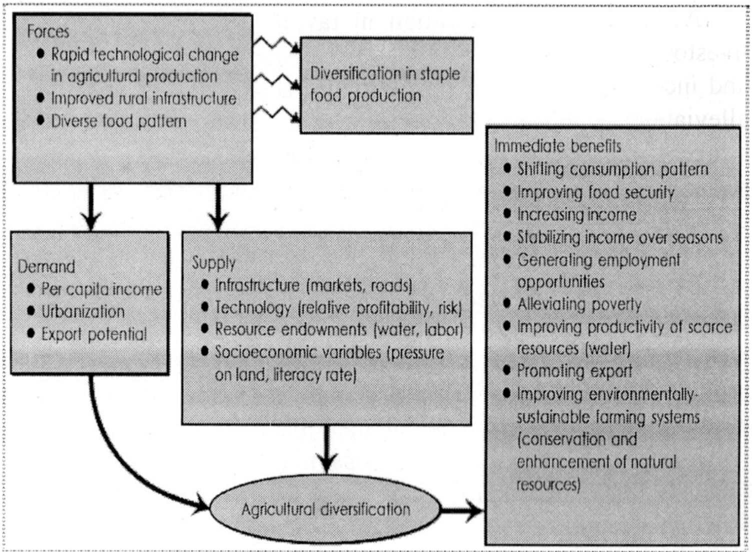

Source: Adopted from Joshi et al. (2002) [14]

10.6 Summary

The present study reveals that there are several factors which are responsible for the setback of agriculture and allied sector in the country as well as the states after the era of economic reforms. The factors include a long list of reasons, such as rapid rise of population, poor literacy rate, unemployment, high incidence of poverty, agricultural backwardness, lack of industries, poor agricultural credit, decline of investment in agriculture, high input cost, inadequate supply of HYV seeds, low seed replacement rate, lack of farm mechanization, decline in the overall net sown area, sluggish growth in cropping intensity especially after the post-period (2000-01), lack of irrigation facilities, low consumption of fertilizers and pesticides, lack of storage and cold storage facilities, poor marketing facilities as well as poor marketing network, unfavourable social environment, gamble of monsoons, recurrence of floods and droughts, skewed distribution of land, corruption and lack of commitment towards development among the leaders.

Agricultural diversification in favour of horticulture and livestock products is desirable to increase farm employment and income, reduce income disparities across space and time, alleviate poverty, improve food security and productivity of scarce resources (e.g., water) and improve environmentally sustainable farming systems through conservation and enhancement of natural resources, check degradation of natural resources and enhance exports.

In order to promote agricultural diversification along with agriculture market reforms, the Government of India has launched various programmes and models from time to time, such as National Horticulture Mission (NHM), establishment of terminal markets, Agriculture Technology Management Agency (ATMA), contract farming, and establishment of rural business hubs (RBHs). It has been observed that these programmes and schemes are not functioning properly, particularly in the eastern states of India. This is mainly due to lack of proper information, whereby farmers in the eastern region are still unaware about most of these schemes. But during the recent years, it cannot be denied that, in view of the current problems of the agricultural sector, the Indian government has initiated a number of effective plans, such as National Agriculture Market (e-NAM), Modified National Agricultural Insurance Scheme (MNAIS), and Weather Based Crop Insurance Scheme(WBCIS).

We can conclude that in spite of various Government schemes and programmes, agriculture and allied sector disparity remains widespread among the regions, which is clearly visible in the eastern states of India. As a result, agricultural diversification in favour of horticulture crops in eastern states is very poor. Most of the Government programmes have not been implemented in a proper manner which is a major hindrance towards the growth and development of agriculture diversification in eastern states of India as compared to other regions, namely northern, western, and southern regions. Thus, it is the need of the hour that schemes should be introduced at a greater level so that a large number of farmers can take benefits out of them.

Endnotes

1. Rao, P. Parthasarathy, P.K. Joshi, Shravan Kumar and Kavery Ganguly (2008), "Agricultural Diversification in Andhra Pradesh, India: Patterns, Determinants and Implications", International Food Policy Research Institute, International Crops Research Institute for the Semi Arid Tropics (ICRISTAT), New Delhi, December.
2. Joshi P.K., A. Gulati, L. Tewari and P.S. Birthal (2003), "Agricultural diversification in South Asia: Patterns, Determinants and Policy Implications", Markets, Trade and Institutions Division, Discussion Paper No. 57, Washington D.C: International Food Policy Research Institute, February.
3. Deshingkar P., Usha Kulkarni., Laxman Rao and Srinivas Rao (2003), "Changing Food Systems in India: Resource Sharing and Marketing Arrangements for Vegetable Production in Andhra Pradesh", *Development Policy Review*, 21 (5-6), pp. 627-639.
4. Joshi, P.K., Ashok Gulati, P.S. Birthal and Laxmi Tewari (2004), "Agriculture Diversification in South Asia: Patterns, Determinants and Policy Implications", *Economic and Political Weekly,* Vol. 39, No. 24, June 12-18, pp. 2457-2467.
5. Chand, Ramesh (1999), "Agricultural Diversification in India: Potential and Prospects in Developed Regions", Mittal Publications: New Delhi.
6. Rao, P. Parthasarathy, P.K. Joshi., Shravan Kumar and Kavery Ganguly (2008), "Agriculture Diversification in Andhra Pradesh, India: Pattern, Determinants and Implications," International Crops Research Institute for the Semi-Arid Tropics, Research (Published jointly with the International Food Policy Research Institute, IFPRI), Report No. 2. Patancheru, Andhra Pradesh.
7. Dhanasekaran, K. and R. Srinivasan, (2010), "Milk Production: Future Prospects in India", *Kurukshetra,* A Journal of Rural

Development, Ministry of Information and Broadcasting (I&B), Government of India, New Delhi, Vol. 58, No. 10, August, p. 34.

8. Ministry of Agriculture, (2014), "Agriculture Statistics at a Glance, 2014", Government of India, New Delhi.
9. Government of India (2017), Press Information Bureau, November 26.
10. NSSO (2010), "Household Consumer Expenditure in India: 2007-08", Ministry of Statistics and Programme Implementation, Government of India, March, 64th Round, Report No. 530, pp. A22-23.
11. NSSO (2014), "Report No. 555", Government of India, February.
12. Mandal, Raju and M.P. Bezbaruah (2013), "Diversification of Cropping Pattern: Its Determinants and Role in Flood Affected Agriculture of Assam Plains", *Indian Journal of Agriculture Economics*, Vol. 68, No. 2, April-June.
13. Gupta, R.P. and S.K. Tewari (1985), "Factors Affecting Crop Diversification: An Empirical Analysis", *Indian Journal of Agricultural Economics*, 40(3), pp. 304-311.
14. Joshi, P.K, G. Ashok, P.S. Birthal and T. Laxmi (2002), "Nature and Speed of Agricultural Diversification in South Asian Countries", paper presented at the ICRIER-ICAR-IFPRI Conference on 'Economic Reforms and Food Security: The Role of Trade and Technology', April 24-25, New Delhi.

11

Conclusions, Findings and Suggestions

Agriculture sector in India faced two major structural breaks from 1990-91 to 2015-16. Its share declined continuously from 29.5 percent in 1990-91 to reach 11.7 percent during 2015-16 and the sector contributed approximately 12.55 percent and 11.7 percent to India's total exports during 2015-16 and 2016-17 respectively. Despite this decline, agriculture sector still occupies a key position and plays a major role in the growth and development of the Indian economy. The role of agriculture remains critical as it provides employment to around 49 percent of the workforce in the country. Moreover, various studies reveal that India has been facing problems of low productivity, low profitability, and low employment in the agriculture sector. This is mainly caused by drastic fall in real investment in irrigation, poor water management, low quality of research and extension services, and inadequate infrastructure. The growth rate of agriculture has decelerated, and it accounted for the lowest rate of growth of 3.1 percent per annum as compared to industry (7.2 percent per annum) and services (8.8 percent per annum) sectors in India over the entire period of time from 1990-91 to 2015-16.

In this backdrop, the study has tried to make in depth analysis of growth and diversification of agriculture among four major regions of India, namely southern, western, northern, and eastern with special reference to the eastern states. The study has tried to show the importance of agriculture in India vis-à-vis regions, particularly the eastern region by considering various economic parameters like growth and share in GSDP, employment generation, imports and exports including issues related to food security in India during the reference period. The study has also tried to find the growth and pattern of area, production and yield of food grains versus non-food grains, highlighting the importance of diversification in agriculture in favour of high value crops, namely fruits, vegetables and flowers including livestock from the point of view of value addition. For this, diversification index was calculated for pre- (i.e., 1990-91 to 1999-00) and post- (i.e., 2000-01 to 2013-14) period to draw an economic conclusion. The conclusions of the study are summarized as under.

11.1 Growth and Share of Agriculture in GSDP

The agrarian situation in India vis-à-vis regional states may be seen from GSDP (at 2004-05 constant prices) growth rate. Study reveals that at the national level, agriculture sector grew at the rate of 3.1 percent per annum during 1990-91 to 2015-16. However, as per the region-wise analysis, the highest growth rate in agriculture and allied sector was achieved by the western region i.e., 3.5 percent per annum followed by southern region (2.9 per cent), and eastern region (2.7 percent), while the northern India achieved the lowest growth rate of 2.4 percent per annum over the period 1990-91 to 2015-16. In the western region, the highest growth rate was observed in agriculture by Gujarat (4.1 percent), followed by Rajasthan (3.8 percent), Maharashtra (3.5 percent), and Madhya Pradesh (3.5 percent) during the same period. After the western region, the second highest growth rate in agriculture and allied sector was observed in southern region with major growth rates achieved by Andhra Pradesh (including Telangana) (4 per cent per annum), followed by Tamil Nadu (2.4 percent per annum) and Karnataka (2.1 percent per annum) during the post- as well as the overall period. The eastern region accounted for the second least annual growth rate in agriculture and allied sector during the same period. In the eastern region, the highest growth rates was achieved by Jharkhand (5.4 percent per annum) followed by West Bengal (2.9 percent), Bihar (2.7 percent), Odisha (2.3 percent), and Assam (1.5 percent) during the overall period (1990-91-2015-16).

Thus, it can be observed from the present analysis that except the western region, miserable growth rates in agriculture and allied sector were observed in the remaining three regions viz., northern, southern and eastern.

On the other hand, the share of agriculture in GSDP of India declined by more than 60 percent between 1990-91 and 2015-16. However, as per the region-wise analysis, the highest decline in the share of agriculture and allied sector was observed in western region and lowest in northern and eastern region. However, among the eastern states, the share of agriculture in all the states sharply declined in 2015-16 in comparison to 1990-91. Amongst the eastern states, Odisha registered the highest decline by 61.6 percent followed by Bihar (57.7 percent), West Bengal (54.3 percent) and Assam (44.9 percent) during the same period of time.

While glancing state-wise annual growth rates, for comparative analysis, the study also revealed that the state of Jharkhand scored a remarkable rate of growth in agriculture and allied sector i.e., 5.4 percent per annum during the overall period. It is surprising to note that the annual growth of industrial sector of Jharkhand during the overall period was about 3.5 percent per annum which is lower than that of the agriculture as well as the services sector. It is very surprising that even though Jharkhand is a major industrial state, yet, the agricultural sector has grown rapidly in the state. Thus, the results clearly indicate that people of Jharkhand are attracted more towards agriculture and allied sector for livelihood options compared to the industrial sector. Similarly, agriculture sector in West Bengal accounted for a moderate rate of growth i.e., about 2.9 percent per annum, but it was remarkably low compared to the services (8.2 percent per annum) and industrial (6.3 percent per annum) sectors during 1990-91 to 2015-16. Like West Bengal, a similar growth trend in services and industrial sector was observed in Bihar and Odisha also.

It is clearly depicted from the present results that, barring Bihar, all the remaining states of the eastern region achieved higher annual growth rates in services sector in comparison to the industrial sector during the overall period. The highest growth rates in services sector was mainly because of significant contribution of construction and communication sector during the recent past. Thus, we can conclude that, except the western region, the performance of agriculture amongst all the regions under this study seems to be very poor. The remaining 3 regions witnessed annual growth rates of nearly 3 percent which is below the national standard and even this growth rate was lower than that of the services and industrial sector.

11.2 Agriculture and Employment Generation

According to 50th, 61st and 66th rounds of NSSO, the share of employment in non-agriculture sector in India increased by more than 45 percent i.e., from 35.2 percent to 51.1 percent respectively during 1993-94 to 2011-12. Conversely, the share of employment in agriculture sector decelerated by 24.5 percent, from 64.8 percent in 1993-94 to 48.9 percent in 2011-12. The reason behind this declining share is the sluggishness of agriculture sector. Similarly, the share of employment in the services and industrial sector showed an increasing trend from 20.5 percent and 14.7 percent respectively to 26.7 percent and 24.4 percent respectively, during the two NSSO rounds i.e. 1993-94 and 2011-12. Furthermore, the share of rural employment in agriculture sector of India increased slightly by 32.1 percent from 21.7 percent during 1993-94 to 2009-10. But the rate of growth of employment in rural non-farm sector witnessed a moderate growth rate i.e. 3.2 percent per annum during 1993-94 and 2009-10.

Amongst the regions, higher rural non-farm employment growth rates were observed among the eastern states in Bihar, Jharkhand and Odisha; in northern states in Jammu and Kashmir, Uttarakhand and Himachal Pradesh; in western states in Rajasthan and Madhya Pradesh and in southern states in Kerala and Andhra Pradesh during the two NSSO rounds. Hence, it can be concluded that the growth rate of rural farm employment has declined over the period of time. This is due to decline in the share of agriculture coupled with decline in the real farm wages and purchasing power of the wage earners.

11.3 Growth and Share of Agriculture in India's Exports

In India, high valued crops such as fruits, vegetables and spices registered the maximum export growth rate of about 23.4 percent and 20.9 percent per annum respectively during the post-period. Although, during the same period, the export growth rate of rice stood at 20 percent per annum. Therefore, as per the statistics, it may be concluded that during the post-period, the export growth of high valued crops like fruits, vegetables, and spices in India witnessed remarkable growth rates in comparison to rice as well as other allied products.

11.4 Area, Production and Yield of Food Grains versus Non-food Grains

Indian agriculture sector has meagrely diversified towards high value crops over a period of time. There has been a moderate change in cropping pattern during TE-1993 to TE-2008. The real scenario derived from the data depicts a remarkable decline in the share of gross cropped area under coarse cereals (from 18.6 percent to 15.5 percent) and food grains (from 68.9 percent to 63.8 percent). The area under high value crops, namely spices (0.9 percent to 1.0 percent), and fruits and vegetables (9.6 percent to 13.6 percent) has increased because of changes in relative prices during 1990-93 to 2005-08.

Moreover, it is important to underline that despite a decline in the area, food grains still occupy more than 63.8 percent of total cropped area due to traditional cropping pattern as well as traditional food habits. It can be said that following a change in cropping pattern in India, there was a significant shift from coarse cereals (i.e., jowar, barley, ragi and small millets) and pulses to non-food grains such as fruits and vegetables, and spices during

TE-2008. Finally, it can be summarized that India has diversified its agriculture in favour of horticulture and commercial crops but this growth was observed at a very slow rate during the post-period i.e., TE-2008.

11.5 Trend of Consumption Expenditure

In general, it is observed that with increasing incomes, food basket of people also tend to change. People replace inferior food items with superior ones in their food consumption baskets. This substitution of inferior food items by more qualitative one in consumption bowls of people is known as the Engel's law, which states that as the income increases, expenditure on food items decline.

Therefore, it can be stated that the dietary patterns of Indians have been changing over the years and has seen a shift towards fruits, vegetables and the rich-calorie diets. Evidently, the share of pulses, milk, edible oil, eggs, meat, fish, vegetables and fruits in total food consumption in India grew by 54.1 percent in rural areas and 54.8 percent in urban areas from 45.4 percent in rural areas and 52.7 percent in urban areas during 1993-94 and 2011-12, respectively. Similarly, the share of food in the total consumption decelerated by 48.6 percent and 38.5 percent from 63.20 percent and 54.7 percent in rural and urban areas respectively during the same period. While summing up, the share of non-food grains, especially horticulture products, in total consumption expenditure in the country was comparatively higher than the food grains during the two NSSO rounds.

11.6 Growth and Pattern of Area, Production and Yield of Horticulture Crops

The nature of diversification towards horticulture varies across regions due to wide disparity in agro-climatic and socio-economic conditions. The study shows that the area under horticulture crops in India increased from 116.2 lakh hectares to 249 lakh hectares during 1990-91 and 2016-17. Over the last 27 years, area under horticulture crops significantly grew up by 3.0 percent per annum, while production and yield of horticulture grew by 4.6 percent and 1.50 percent per annum, respectively. It is also evident from the analysis of the data that the annual growth rate of production of horticulture was much higher than that of area and even the yield during the same period. Further, in absolute terms, production and yield of horticulture crops increased from 863.90 lakh metric tonnes (lmt) and 7.40 mt/ha in 1990-91 to 2,951.6 lmt and 11.8 mt/ha in 2016-17, respectively.

11.6.1 Area, Production and Yield of Vegetables:

A. Growth and Trend of Area and Production of Vegetables: The total area under vegetable cultivation in India increased from 5 million hectares (mha) during TE-1993 to 6.2 mha in TE-2003 and further increased to 10.3 mha during TE-2017. The major vegetables grown in the country are onion, potato, brinjal, cabbage, cauliflower, okra, peas and tomato. Out of these, onion, potato and tomato showed remarkable increase in their acreage during TE-2017 compared to TE-2003 and even in TE-1993 also. Perusal of data also reveals that the area and production of vegetables in India showed an increasing trend over the period of time. The main factor underlying diversification in favour of fruits and vegetables has been the higher returns relative to other crop groups (Chand et al., 2008). [1]

The results reveal that among the vegetables, area under brinjal, cabbage, okr.., peas and tomato have fallen, while for onion, potato, and cauliflower it grew up during the post-period (1990-91 to 1999-00) compared to the pre-period (2000-01 to 2016-17). However, the expansion of area under total vegetables increased from 2.38 percent per annum during the pre-period to 3.61 percent per annum during the post-period. This is only because of the remarkable increase in the growth of area under cultivation of onion, potato, and cauliflower.

However, in terms of production, except onion and potato, remaining all the vegetables, namely brinjal, cabbage, cauliflower, okra and pea and tomato registered a deceleration in their production during the post-period over the pre-period. The growth rate of production of total vegetable decelerated from 5.84 percent to 5.06 percent per annum during the later period over the earlier period. During the overall period, (from 1990-91 to 2016-17), it accounted for 4.75 percent per annum. Thus, it is clear from the present analysis, that among the listed vegetables, only onion and potato registered acceleration in their production growth during the post-period as compared to the pre-period. Finally, the data explains that among the vegetables, potato and onion were the most diversified vegetable crops during the post- as well as overall period under study. It was mainly due to gradual shift of area from low value coarse cereal crops like jowar, ragi, bajra etc. to high value crops like fruits, vegetables and flowers etc. Furthermore, the yield growth of vegetable crops declined from 3.38 per cent per annum and reached 1.4 percent per annum during the same period of time. In absolute terms, yield of total vegetables increased from 11.3 metric tonne per hectare (mt/ha) in 1990-91 to 14.45 mt/ha in 2000-01 and to 17.1 mt/ha during 2016-17.

B. Share of Area and Production of Vegetables in India: In India, large numbers of vegetable are cultivated, out of which, in terms of percentage share, potato (21 percent) tops the list followed by onion (12.3 percent), tomato (7.9 percent), brinjal (6.5 percent), peas (5.3 percent), okra (5.1 percent), and cauliflower (4.4 percent) while cabbage was listed at the bottom (4.0 percent) in the total area under vegetable cultivation during 2016-17. In terms of change in the area share between two comparable periods (2000-01 and 2016-17), remarkable progress was observed only in two vegetables such as onion and potato, which was largely caused by shift of area under okra, and brinjal, in favour of potato and onion cultivation during the recent period. This is the effect of a well-knit strategy to achieve multiple goals of increasing production of horticulture sector, enhancing income, and ensuring food security in terms of nutritional or calorie intake.

Similar to the area, in terms of production share too, potato (26.6 percent) topped the list followed by onion (12.3 percent), tomato (11.3 percent), brinjal (7.1 percent), cabbage (5.9 percent) and cauliflower (4.9 percent) during 2016-17. While during the same period, amongst the listed vegetables, the production share of peas and okra laddered at the bottom i.e., 3.1 percent and 3.5 percent, respectively.

11.6.2 Area, Production and Yield of Fruits

A. Growth and Trend of Area and Production of Fruits: The major fruits grown in India include banana, papaya, citrus, lemon, mosambi, orange, guava, litchi, mango, pineapple and sapota. The total area under cultivation for fruits in India increased from 2.9 million hectares (mha) during TE-1992-93 to 6.3 mha during TE-2016-17. However, fruits such as citrus, mosambi, and banana, accounted for a measly increase in their acreage during TE-2016-17 in comparison to TE-2002-03. The compounded annual growth rate in area under fruits like mosambi, citrus, banana, and litchi sharply increased during the post-period as compared to the pre-period. However, growth rate of the remaining fruits, such as lemon, guava, sapota, pineapple and mango declined rapidly during the same period of time. The growth rate of area under fruits declined from 4.10 percent per annum to 3.7 percent per annum during the pre- and post-period, respectively.

Further, in terms of annual growth rate of area under fruits, papaya topped the list (5.40 percent per annum) followed by mosambi (4.70 percent pa), banana (4.40 percent pa), citrus (4.40 percent pa), lemon (4.10 percent pa), and guava (4 percent pa). The remaining fruits, namely litchi (3.70 percent pa), sapota (3.20 percent pa), pineapple (2.90 percent pa), and mango (2.50 percent pa) recorded the least growth rates during the post-period as against the previous period. On the other hand, during the overall period, mosambi, sapota, lemon, citrus, papaya, guava, banana and mango showed higher annual growth rates. Fruits like litchi and pineapple were placed at the bottom of the list during the same period.

During the post-period, the growth rate of production of total fruits fell by 5 percent from 6.9 percent per annum in the post-period compared to the pre-period, respectively. It is important to highlight that the annual growth in yield of total fruits reached 1 percent, which decelerated to 1.0 percent per annum in the post-period from 2.7 percent per annum in the pre-period. However, during the overall period, the growth rate of production showed a moderate growth of 4.6 percent per annum. Similarly, the growth rate of yield showed a stagnant trend of 0.6 percent per annum during the overall period.

While undertaking analysis of fruits in absolute terms, the total fruit production in India increased from 29.7 million metric tonne (mmt) in TE-1992-93 to 43.8 mmt in TE-2002-03, and considerably increased to 89.9 mmt in TE-2016-17. However, if we look at the fruit-wise analysis, amongst the listed fruits, only few fruit crops like papaya, guava, mango and pineapple registered increasing growth rates in both the production and yield during the post-period as against the pre-period. On the other hand, despite declining production growth rates, the annual growth rate in yields of litchi and citrus fruits grew remarkably during the post-period, which was largely caused by the expansion of area under these crops during the same period of time.

B. Share of Area and Production of Fruits: Out of the ten fruits, in terms of area share, mango dominated the list followed by citrus and banana. Alternatively, in terms of production of fruits, banana topped the list followed by mango and citrus during 2016-17. It is noticeable that despite a lower share of area under bananas (13.2 percent), even after being in the third position, its production share (31.4 percent) was the highest amongst all fruits i.e., it stood at the first rank in India during the recent period. This is mainly because of higher demand for banana due to its nutritional values. As a result, despite having lesser share of area, its share in the production was the highest amongst all the major fruits in the country.

More than 41.2 percent of the total fruits area in the

country was devoted to mango cultivation in 1990-91, which declined to 34.9 percent in 2016-17. However, its production share has declined almost amongst all the regions of India. Therefore, states like Bihar, West Bengal, Odisha, Uttar Pradesh, Karnataka and Andhra Pradesh reported a decline in the share of mango production during 2012-13 and 2016-17, respectively. Among the regions, only the western region showed an increasing trend with major contributions from Gujarat and Maharashtra during the same period of time (GoI, 2015). [2]

Alternatively, fruits like litchi, sapota and pineapple are receiving less importance, both in terms of share of area and production are therefore listed at the bottom and their share has decelerated over the period of time. Contrary to the highest change in cropping pattern, it was observed that area under citrus, mosambi and banana increased remarkably in 2016-17 as compared to 2000-01 and 1990-91. Besides, citrus, mosambi and banana, remaining fruits such as papaya and guava also received some importance and the area under these crops increased with lower share during the same period. The share of area under cultivation of mango, lemon, sapota and pineapple declined sharply during the same period.

The production of mango has declined sharply due to contraction in its area under cultivation during 2016-17 over 2000-01. In terms of production share, banana (31.4 percent) topped the list followed by mango (21.2 percent), citrus (13.7 percent) and papaya (6.6 percent) during 2016-17.

11.7 Region and State-wise Share of Area and Production of Horticulture Crops

Region and state-wise analysis reveals that increase in the share of area under fruits and vegetables were not uniformly distributed across the regions as well as states of India. Among the regions, southern region had the major contribution towards area under fruit cultivation followed by western, northern and eastern region in 2016-17. In case of production of fruits too, southern region occupied the first place with a share of about 34 percent followed by the western region (30.1 percent), northern region (17.8 percent) and eastern region (14.9 percent) during 2016-17. Thus, it may be summarized that amongst all the regions, eastern region was found as the least fruit growing region in the country. It was lagging behind not only in least area under fruit cultivation but also with respect to least share in production too during 2016-17.

11.7.1 Region and State-wise Share of Area and Production of Vegetables: Area under vegetable crops in India increased from 45 lakh hectares in 1990-91 to 102.9 lakh hectares in 2016-17. During this period, in terms of share of area under production of vegetables, eastern region was a major contributor and constituted about 33.7 percent of the total vegetable area under cultivation followed by western (28.8 percent), northern (22.4 percent) and southern (12.3 percent) regions during 2016-17.

During 1991-92, among the eastern region, Bihar was the only state that was registered as a major contributor and constituted about 15.1 percent of the total area under vegetable cultivation. However, during 2016-17, Bihar observed a slackened growth with a share of 8.2 percent and was placed second. Resultantly, West Bengal emerged as the major contributor and constituted about 13.5 percent of the area under vegetable production. Further, besides Bihar, the shares of Odisha and Assam also reportedly declined during the same period of time. Amongst the eastern states, only West Bengal was observed to have improved its share in the country's total area under vegetables. On the other hand, the share of area under vegetables by Odisha, Bihar and Assam declined sharply between 1991-92 and 2016-17.

Moreover, in case of vegetable production too, West Bengal topped the list by having about 14.6 percent share in total production during 2016-17. It was distantly followed by Bihar (8.1 percent) and Odisha (5 percent). These three states from eastern India together contributed about 28 percent of the total vegetable production during 2016-17.

11.7.2 Region and State-wise Share of Area and Production of Fruits: Following a state-wise analysis, during 2016-17, southern region was found to be the major fruit growing region in the country with major contributions from Andhra Pradesh (including Telangana), Karnataka, Tamil Nadu and Kerala. The western region was found as the second major cultivator of fruits with major contributions by Maharashtra, Gujarat, Madhya Pradesh, Chhattisgarh and Rajasthan. The northern region emerged as the third most fruit growing region in the country with major contributions from Uttar Pradesh followed by Jammu and Kashmir, Himachal Pradesh and Uttarakhand during the same period. It is surprising to highlight that the most agriculture dominant states such as Punjab and Haryana accounted for the least share of area under fruit cultivation in India during the study period.

Among the regions, eastern region lagged behind among all the regions and had the least share regards the total area under production of fruits in India during the study period. However, in terms of area share, three eastern states, namely Bihar, Odisha and West Bengal were the major contributors in fruit cultivation during 1991-92, but their share in both the area and production decelerated dramatically. In 1991-92, among the eastern states, Bihar was the only state which had about 9.3 percent of the total area under fruit cultivation followed by Odisha which had a share of 4.7 percent and West Bengal whose share stood at 3.9 percent.

Similarly, in case of production share too, Bihar occupied the first rank with a share of about 4.6 percent followed by West Bengal (4 percent) and Odisha and Assam (2.6 percent and 2.6 percnt respectively). Jharkhand accounted for the least share during the same period of time.

11.7.3 Region and State-wise Share of Area and Production of Flowers: During 2016-17, southern region dominated as the largest flower growing region in India followed by northern and western region. However, the eastern region was found to be the least flower producing region in the country during the same period. Thus, it is depicted from the present analysis that the western and eastern region was found as the least diversified regions in favour of floriculture in India during 2016-17. It is also evident from our study that area under floriculture in eastern region decelerated by 5 percent from 17.5 percent to 12.5 percent during 2003-04 to 2013-14, yet, its production share increased by 12.8 percent. On the contrary, in spite of increase in the share of area in the northern region by 15.5 percent, its production share decelerated by (-) 0.2 percent between the two comparable periods (2003-04 and 2016-17).

11.8 Region and State-wise Share of Livestock and Horticulture to Total Value of Agricultural Output

It is obvious from the present study that in 2004-05, the contribution of livestock sector in the total value of agricultural (agriculture and allied sector) output was the highest in northern region (26.0 percent) followed by southern region (24.8 percent) and western region (24.0 percent) region. However, among the regions, livestock contribution was recorded the lowest in the eastern region at 20.8 percent during 2004-05. Hence, while comparing the data between 2004-05 and 2014-15, we can easily notice that in terms of absolute percentage change, the contribution of livestock sector in total value of agriculture of output in southern region sharply increased by 5.1 percent followed by northern (4.8 percent), western (2.4 percent) and eastern region (2.4 per cent) between the two comparable periods i.e., 2004-05 to 2014-15.

Similarly, during 2014-15, the highest share in livestock was observed in northern region (31.1 percent) followed by southern region (29.9 percent), western region (26.4 percent) and eastern region (23.2 percent) in 2014-15. The present study also reveals that among the regions, along with the low performance in fruit production, eastern region was lagging behind in livestock too. If we look at the combined share of horticulture and livestock sector in the total agricultural income in 2014-15, we find that the percentage share ranges from 39.7 percent (lowest) in western region to 51.3 percent (highest) in the eastern region during the same period. Thus, eastern region recorded the highest combined share of horticulture and livestock in total agricultural income during 2014-15. This was also due to major contribution in the share of vegetable production. Besides this, it is important to highlight that among the eastern states, only in Bihar, the share of these two sectors i.e., horticulture and livestock was approximately 62.6 percent in the total value of agricultural and allied sector's output. It is only because of the recurrence of floods that most of the gross cropped area (GCA) was ruined during the *kharif* season. For the compensation of these losses, people of eastern region, particularly in Bihar, utilized the livestock option for their livelihood. However, the remaining states of this region viz. West Bengal, Jharkhand, Odisha and Assam observed lower share in horticulture and livestock to total value of output of agriculture and allied sector during 2014-15.

11.9 Share of HVCs (High Value Crops) vis-à-vis LVCs (Low Value Crops) in Total Value of Output from Agriculture and Allied Sector

The present study presents a comparative analysis of growth rate and percentage share of food grains i.e. cereals, pulses, horticulture and livestock in total value of output from agriculture and allied sector in India from 2004-5 to 2014-15. It is evident from the analysis that there exist large variations in the share of food grains over the years. The highest share of 18.8 percent was recorded in 2004-05 and it constantly decreased to 15.8 percent in 2014-15. The reason behind this decrease is that the Indian farmers gradually shifted their cropping pattern from low valued or traditional crops, such as wheat, paddy, maize, ragi and bajra towards the high value crops such as fruits, vegetables and spices over the period of time.

Conversely, the total share of horticulture and livestock to total value of output from agriculture and allied sector increased in a parallel pattern from 15.2 percent and 24.2 percent in 2004-05 to 18.1 percent and 27.6 percent in 2014-15, respectively. Although, it showed a meagre fluctuation between 2007-08 and 2010-11, but after this period, it registered a continuous increase till 2012-13. Thereafter, the share of both the horticulture and livestock sectors has been steadily rising, with a slight upturn, till the year 2014-15.

Hence, it can be concluded that the livestock sector commands a special significance in the country since it is known as the main source of income during crop failure in the event of droughts and floods. Apart from these, it also plays a vital role in rural transportation and ploughing. In continuation, products made from livestock such as milk, meat, dung etc., are known as productive assets in rural parts of India, especially in eastern states, namely Bihar, Jharkhand, West Bengal, Odisha and Assam. More than 75 percent of the rural households of Bihar have been maintaining livestock, especially cattle, buffaloes, and goat with a view to meet their domestic needs in the form of milk and its by products (Kumar and Sinha, 2008). [3]

11.10 Estimation of Simpson Index of Diversity (SID)

11.10.1 Region and State-Wise Trend of Simpson Diversification Index: It is general fact that the degree of crop diversification varies from one location to another due to variation in resource endowment, infrastructure level and market accessibility. We tried to estimate the crop diversification index for the major regions of India for the period 1990-91 to 2013-14. Actually, the value of SID ranges between zero (complete specializations) to one (higher diversification). If the value of SID increases towards one, it denotes shifting of resources which is generally used for the production of traditional crops towards diversification in favour of horticulture. The Simpson Index of Diversity (SID) for India was estimated at 0.900 in 2000-01 which was less than 0.904 observed in 1990-91. However, during 2013-14, it increased to 0.912 which was marginally higher as compared to the year 1990-91.

Following a region-wise analysis, agricultural diversification in western region was found to be the highest at 0.932 followed by the southern region (0.921) and the northern region (0.783). The eastern region (0.729) lagged behind the remaining three regions as well as compared to the national average not only during 2013-14 but also during 1990-91 and 2000-01.

Similarly, it was also observed that the western region is remarkably diversifying its crops in favour of horticulture i.e., fruits and vegetables due to major contribution from Maharashtra, Gujarat, Rajasthan and Madhya Pradesh on account of favourable climatic conditions, high urbanization and per capita income and larger average size of land holdings (Birthal, et al., 2013). [4] Contrary to this, the eastern region appeared as the least diversified region in the country during 2013-14. This is primarily because of the fact that the eastern region is not only an agriculturally less developed region but is also marred by other poor economic indicators viz., poor road conditions, transportation problems, low literacy rate, burgeoning population, low urbanization, highest poverty ratio, low per capita income and poor employment (Birthal et al., 2007; [5] CSD, 2010; [6] Anjani, 2012; [7] Lakshmana, 2014). [8]

Apart from this, poor accessibility of proper irrigation facilities is also one of the major hindrances in the development of agriculture, and thus resulting from this, majority of the people of this region largely rely on erratic rainfall. Furthermore, due to low per capita income, there is low demand for HVCs and their traditional consumption patterns force the farmers to cultivate rice-wheat dominant combination crops leading to low agricultural diversification in eastern states, namely Bihar, Odisha, West Bengal and Assam. It is evident from the data that whatever is the participation of eastern region, it is mainly due to states like Jharkhand and Bihar as they registered the highest degree of diversification during 2013-14. The SID for Jharkhand and Bihar correspondingly increased from 0.473 and 0.711 in 2000-01 to 0.818 and 0.794 in 2013-14 respectively followed by Odisha and West Bengal. However, the SID of Assam (0.571 to 0.590) was listed as the lowest during 2013-14 compared to 2000-01, due to continuous decline of SID over the period of time. Yet, in spite of acceleration of SID, the eastern region still lagged behind all the other regions, namely, western, southern and northern during 2013-14.

11.10.2 Region and State-Wise Growth of Simpson Diversification Index (SID): In the present study, we also estimated the compounded annual growth rate of diversification index for two sub-periods i.e., pre- (1990-91 to 1999-00), post- (2000-01 to 2013-14) and overall period (1990-91 to 2013-14) to compare the four major regions with national average. The CAGR of SID in favour of horticulture crops was found having a negative value among the eastern and northern regions during the post-period as compared to the pre-period. These results advocate that the least annual growth rate of diversification (SID) in favour of high value crops was observed in eastern and western region during the recent past (2013-14). It may be due to lack of proper policy support and consequently seems slant towards the divergence in diversification during the post-period. Thus, on the basis of the present analysis, it can be said that the famers in the country especially in eastern states have shown interest in specialization towards growing of traditional crops as earlier including wheat, rice, maize and coarse cereals including sugarcane and commercial crops etc., during the post-period.

As per the data, it was found that the highest deterioration was estimated in the northern region i.e., (-) 0.17 percent per annum during the 2013-14. However, during the same period, the eastern region showed marginal improvement in its growth rates (-) 0.18 percent to (-) 0.04 percent per annum during the pre- and post-period, respectively. It is only because of the abundance of natural resources and favourable climatic conditions, that there is an interest to grow horticultural crops. On the other hand, in spite of having abundance of these natural resources, economic constraints prove to be a major hindrance in diversification towards high value crops (HVCs) in the eastern region. The western region accounted for negligible growth rate of 0.01 percent per annum during the post-period. Although, southern region is the only region which showed a positive growth rate (0.07 percent pa), but it may also be considered as negligible or stagnant growth rate during the same period of time.

During this period, among all the regions, only southern and eastern region showed some improvements in their CAGR of SID which was estimated per annum during the post-period. Similarly, northern region showed rapid deterioration in its growth rates during the post-period. The compounded annual growth rate of SID at the national level showed a positive trend (-) 0.01 percent per annum in pre-period to (+) 0.01 percent per annum in the post-period that recovered their situation and reached the neutral level. This recovery in the SID growth in India has been achieved only because of the recovery in SID growth made by southern and eastern regions.

11.11 Findings of the Study

Major findings of the study may be summarized as follows:

1. Although, horticulture sector emerged as the most important component of the crops sub-sector to absorb agricultural labour in all regions of India, yet it has been losing its importance during the recent period i.e., 2013-14. There has been gradual shift of cropping pattern towards specialization especially after the period 2000-01 due to poor cold storage facilities, gamble of monsoons, and lack of minimum support price for horticultural produce.
2. The compounded annual growth rate of agricultural exports grew at a rate of 17 percent per annum which was found

lower than that of horticultural crops such as fruits and vegetables. However, during the period, rice witnessed a significant decline from 29.2 percent per annum to 20.0 percent per annum.

3. The agriculture GSDP growth rate was significantly high among the western region (5.2 percent pa) followed by southern region (3.3 percent pa), and eastern region (3.1 percent pa), while northern region stood at the bottom i.e., 2.4 percent per annum during the post-period (i.e., from 2000-01 to 2015-16).
4. Among eastern states, the highest GSDP growth rate in agriculture was achieved by Jharkhand (6.7 percent pa) followed by Odisha (3.6 percent pa), Bihar (3.1 percent pa), Assam (2.9 percent pa) and West Bengal (2.2 percent pa) during the post-period as against the pre-period.
5. The agriculture GSDP growth rate of India was remarkably lower (3.1 percent pa) than that of the growth rate of services (8.8 percent pa) and industrial (7.2 percent pa) sectors during the overall period.
6. Regards the share of GSDP in agriculture, among the regions, northern region (17.3 percent) registered the highest share followed by eastern region (15.5 percent), southern region (11.5 percent) and western region (11.2 percent) during 2015-16.
7. There was a continuous increase in area (from 116.20 lakh hectare to 249.3 lakh hectare), production [from 863.90 lakh metric tonnes (lmt) to 2951.6 lmt] and yield [from 7.4 metric tonnes/hectare (mt/ha) to 11.80 mt/ha] of horticultural crops during 1990-91 to 2016-17.
8. The production of horticultural crops in India registered the highest average annual growth rate (4.2 percent pa) as compared to food grains (by 2.0 percent per annum) during the post-period (2000-01 to 2016-17).
9. In terms of share of fruits, southern region was a major contributor to the area under fruits (29.1 percent) followed by western region (27 percent), northern region (20.2

percent) and eastern region (18 percent) region in 2016-17. In case of production of fruits too, southern region occupied the first place with a share of about 34 percent followed by western region (30.1 percent), northern region (17.8 percent) and eastern region (14.9 percent) during the same period.

10. From 1991-92 to 2016-17, in terms of share of area under production of vegetables, eastern region was the major contributor, and constituted about 33.7 percent and 32 percent of the total vegetable area under cultivation and production thereto followed by western region (28.8 percent and 28.0 percent), northern region (22.4 percent and 24 percent) and southern region (12.3 percent and 14.2 percent).
11. The contribution of livestock in the total value of agricultural (agriculture and allied sector) output was the highest in northern region (31.1 percent) followed by southern region (29.9 percent), and western region (26.4 percent). Among the regions, livestock contribution was recorded the lowest in the eastern region (23.2 percent) during the year 2014-15.
12. Diversification of agriculture was witnessed the highest in western region at 0.932 followed by southern region (0.921) and northern region (0.783), while eastern region (0.729) lagged behind the other three regions as well as the national average (0.912) not only during the 2013-14 but also during 1990-91 and 2000-01.
13. In terms of area under fruits, mango (34.9 percent) topped the list followed by citrus (16.3 percent), banana (13.2 percent), guava (4 percent), lemon (4 percent), and mosambi (3.2 percent), while litchi (1.4 percent), sapota (1.75 percent), pineapple (1.9 percent) and papaya (2.1 percent) were at the bottom during 2016-17.
14. Production of various fruits in India indicates that the share of banana topped the list (31.4 percent) followed by mango (21.2 percent), citrus (13.7 percent), papaya (6.6 percent), guava (3.9 percent), mosambi (4.6 percent), and lemon (3

percent), while pineapple (2.2 percent), sapota (1.4 percent) and litchi (0.6 percent) were listed at the bottom during 2016-17.

15. Area under vegetables in India indicates that the share of potato topped the list (21 percent) followed by onion (12.3 percent), tomato (7.9 percent), brinjal (6.5 percent), peas (5.3 percent), okra (5.1 percent), and cauliflower (4.4 percent), while cabbage (4 percent) was listed at the bottom during 2016-17.
16. The production of vegetables in India highlights that the share of potato (26.6 percent) topped the list followed by onion (12.3 percent), tomato (11.3 percent), brinjal (7.1 percent), cabbage (5.1 percent), and cauliflower (4.9 percent), while okra (3.5 percent) and peas (3.1 percent) were at the bottom rung during 2016-17.
17. The average size of land holding was the lowest in eastern region (0.63 hectare), and was observed the highest in western region (1.95 ha), followed by southern region (0.96 ha), and northern region (0.95 ha) during 2010-11.
18. The lowest share of agriculture credit to total agriculture credit in India was observed in eastern region (8.32 percent), followed by northern region (11.45 percent), and southern region (27.32 percent), while the highest share was observed in the western region (37.67 percent) during 2013-14.
19. The lowest per capita consumption of electricity was found among the eastern states during 2010-11. While, among the northern states, Haryana, Punjab; in western region, Gujarat and Rajasthan; in southern region, Andhra Pradesh, Karnataka, and Tamil Nadu availed the highest per capita consumption (PCC) of electricity during the same period. It is surprising to underline that among the western region, all the sample states accounted for remarkable PCC of electricity during 2010-11.
20. In terms of irrigation ratio (percent of gross irrigated area to total gross cropped area), northern region (79.3 percent) topped the list followed by eastern region (45.1 percent),

southern region (43.6 percent), and western region (33.3 percent) during 2011-12, while at the national level, this ratio stood at 47 percent during the same period.

21. The highest growth rate in irrigation ratio was found higher among the eastern region (2.1 percent pa), followed by western region (2 percent pa), southern region (1.1 percent pa) and northern region (0.8 percent pa) over the period 1990-91 to 2011-12.
22. The growth rate in cropping intensity (CI) was witnessed high among the western region (0.6 percent pa), followed by northern region (0.3 percent pa), southern region (0.2 percent pa) and eastern region (0.1 percent pa). However, despite the highest irrigation expansion, eastern region still accounted for the lowest CI growth during the overall period.
23. In terms of the capacity of cold storages, the highest share was registered in the northern region (49.03 percent), followed by eastern (30.18 percent), western (13.45 percent) and southern (6.56 percent) regions during the year 2009-10.
24. In terms of availability of cold storage for horticultural produce, northern region had the highest cold storage facilities at about 22.5 percent for the total horticultural produce in India followed by eastern region (10 percent), and western region (2.4 percent), while the southern region (0.1 percent) stood at the bottom during 2009-10.
25. In terms of length of rural roads, all the regions of India witnessed a remarkable growth rate during the post-period in comparison to the pre-period. The highest growth in rural road network was recorded in eastern region (6.07 percent pa), followed by northern region (5.5 percent pa), southern region (3.81 percent pa) and western region (3.69 percent pa) region during the post-period over pre-period (1990-91 to 2011-12).
26. In terms of the share of total rural roads in India, except eastern region, all the regions witnessed a declining share during the period (1990-91 to 2011-12).

27. Delving upon region-wise analysis, the growth rate in demand and supply of seeds accounted for the highest among the eastern region followed by western region, northern region and southern region during 2006-07 to 2013-14.
28. The growth rate in the use of fertilizers was highest among the western region (6.7 percent pa), followed by eastern region (5.9 percent pa), southern region (4.4 percent pa) and northern region (3.4 percent pa) during the post-period over the pre-period.
29. The consumption of pesticides was observed high in southern region (2.3 percent pa), followed by western region (1.26 percent pa), and northern region (0.7 percent pa). The eastern region showed a negative CAGR of (-) 1.76 percent pa during the post-period (2000-01 to 2012-13).
30. Percentage share of the total urban population was the highest among the southern region (40.9 percent), followed by western region (35.2 percent), northern region (25.1 percent) and eastern region (20 percent) during 2011.
31. The highest rural literacy was found in southern region (69.7 percent), followed by western region (68.5 percent), and northern region (67.2 percent), while the eastern region accounted for the lowest literacy rate of 65.9 percent during 2011.
32. In terms of below poverty line (BPL) population, the highest poverty ratio was recorded among the eastern region (31.1 percent), followed by western region (24 percent), northern region (13.1 percent) and southern region (12.1 percent) region during 2011-12.
33. The highest rural poverty was also found in eastern region (33.4 percent), followed by western region (28.41 percent), southern region (15.1 percent) and northern region (13.6 percent) during 2011-12.

11.12 Suggestions

Based on the findings of our study, the following strategies may help in achieving the desired results in the field of agriculture:

1. Special efforts are required in socially and economically backward regions like the eastern region in providing basic facilities to farmers and promoting agricultural diversification.
2. There is a great need to develop rural infrastructure including electricity, irrigation facilities, road network, and rural markets for horticultural produce particularly in agriculturally backward region i.e. the eastern region of India.
3. Cold storage facilities should be widely provided for horticultural produce in every panchayat at subsidized rates, especially in eastern, western and southern regions of India. Minimum support prices should be announced especially for horticultural commodities.
4. Per capita consumption of electricity should be increased in the eastern region. Majority of the villages in this region are still un-electrified.
5. HYV as well as quality seeds should be provided at the time of sowing in adequate amount at low cost.
6. Crop insurance should be explored efficiently in eastern states. For this purpose, Government should take initiatives to spread awareness among farmers regarding crop insurance especially for horticultural produce.
7. Government should pass a legislative law regarding absentee land holders for increasing area under cultivation, particularly for horticultural crops.
8. Government should provide innovative techniques to the farmers at subsidized rates.
9. Government should provide training facilities to farmers regarding the use of new method of production of agriculture in every panchayat as well as village at the time of sowing of crops.
10. On the basis of agro-climatic zones, especially for the eastern zone, Government should setup a farm community radio station for broadcasting the news and information regarding

agriculture and allied services for the farmers in the state on a regular basis.

11. Daily market updates regarding prices of inputs as well as agriculture produce especially horticultural produce should be displayed in every panchayat bhawan in the villages.
12. Farmers' *mela* should be arranged in every district as well as panchayats in the states particularly in eastern states for displaying new farm machineries, farm inputs, and new initiatives of the Government on a quarterly basis.
13. Public transport facilities should be provided for perishable products like fruits and vegetables in every panchayat to the farmers at low prices/concessional rates.
14. Season-wise wage rate should be fixed following collaboration with farmers and Government departments according to crops as well as areas.
15. Mobile soil testing laboratories should be setup in every panchayat in the states.
16. Land records and agriculture database should be updated and uploaded on regular basis for better research and extension services as well as for policy decisions.
17. A holistic approach should be adopted to integrate production and post-harvest infrastructure.
18. The need of the hour is to establish competitive seed markets at attractive prices along with enhancing availability of agricultural credit to farmers in all panchayats of the state.

Endnotes

1. Chand, Ramesh, S.S. Raju and L.M. Pandey (2008), "Progress and Potential of Horticulture in India", *Indian Journal of Agricultural Economics*, Vol. 63, No. 3, July-September, p. 301.
2. "Indian Horticulture Data Base, 2015", Ministry of Agriculture and Farmers Welfare, Government of India.
3. Kumar, Amalendu and Rajiv Kumar Sinha (2008), "A Micro Level Study on Diversification of Agricultural Enterprises Through Livestock Processing Activities: Possibilities in Eastern Bihar", in Thakur, Anil Kurmar and K.B. Padmadeo (eds.), 'Growth and Diversification of Agriculture', Deep and Deep Publications, New Delhi, p. 185.

4. Birthal, Pratap S., P.K. Joshi, Digvijay S. Negi and Shaily Agarwal, (2013), "Changing Sources of Growth in Indian Agriculture: Implications for Regional Priorities for Accelerating Agricultural Growth", IFPRI Discussion Paper December 2013, New Delhi.
5. Birthal, P.S, P.K. Joshi and Devesh Roy, (2007), "Diversification in Indian Agriculture towards High-Value Crops: The Role of Smallholders", IFPRI Discussion Paper 00727, November, p. 13.
6. Council for Social Development (2010), "Constraints and Potentials of Diversified Agricultural Development in Eastern India".
7. Kumar, Anjani, Pramod Kumar, and Alakh N. Sharma (2012), "Crop Diversification in Eastern India: Status and Determinants", *Indian Journal of Agricultural Economics*, Vol. 67, No. 4, October-December.
8. Lakshmana, C.M. (2014), "Population, Development, and Environment in India", *Chinese Journal of Population Resources and Environment*, Vol. 11, No. 4, pp. 367-374.

Bibliography

Bibliography

Acharya, S.S. (1998), "Agricultural Price Policy and Development: Some Facts and Emerging Issues", *Indian Journal of Agricultural Economics*, Vol. 52, No. 1.

—(2001), "Domestic Agricultural Marketing Policies, Incentives and Integration", in S.S. Acharya and D.P. Chaudhri (eds.), 'Indian Agricultural Policy at the Crossroads', Rawat Publications, Jaipur and New Delhi.

Acharya, Shankar (2006), "India's Growth: Past Performance and Future Prospects", paper for presentation at Tokyo Club Macro Economy Conference on 'India and China Rising', December 6-7, Tokyo.

Ahluwalia, M.S. (1996), "New Economic Policy and Agriculture: Some Reflections", *Indian Journal of Agricultural Economics*, Vol. 51, No. 3.

Ahluwalia, M.S. (2000), "Economic Performance of States in Post-Reforms Period", *Economic and Political Weekly*, 35(19).

Ahuja, Astha (2006), "Agriculture and Rural Development in India: Post Liberalization Initiatives", New Century Publications, New Delhi.

Akhoury, Rashmi (2008), "An Economic Analysis of Agricultural Diversification in Eastern India with Special Reference to Bihar", in Thakur, Anil Kumar and K.B. Padmadeo (eds.), 'Growth and Diversification of Agriculture', Deep and Deep Publications, New Delhi.

Aksoy, M.A. (2005), "The Evolution of Agricultural Trade Flows", in M.A. Aksoy and J.C. Beghim (eds.), 'Global Agricultural Trade and Developing Countries', The World Bank, Washington D.C.

Alagh, Y.K. and P.S. Sharma (1980), "Growth of Crop Production: 1960-61 to 1978-79: Is it Decelerating?", *Indian Journal of Agricultural Economics,* 35(2).

Ballabh, Anand and Kameshwar Choudhary (2002), "Groundwater Development and Agriculture Production: A Comparative Study of Eastern Uttar Pradesh, Bihar and West Bengal", Draft Discussion Paper Presented in 2nd IWMI-Tata Annual Partners' Meet, January 27-29.

Ballabh, Vishwa and B.M. Sharma (1992), "HYV Adoption, Productivity Gaps and Production Adjustment Mechanisms in Flood-prone Areas of Uttar Pradesh: A Synthesis", Research Report

5, IRMA.

Ballabh, Vishwa and Sushil Pandey (1999), "Transitions in Rice Production Systems in Eastern India: Evidence from Two Villages in Uttar Pradesh", *Economic and Political Weekly*, 34(13).

Ballabh, Vishwa and T.S. Walker (1992), "Land Fragmentation and Consolidation in Dry Semi-arid Tropics of India", *Arth Vijnana*, 34(4).

Barghouti, S., K. Sorby and M. Ali (2004), "Agricultural Diversification for the Poor, Agricultural and Rural Development", Discussion Paper No. 1, ARD Department, World Bank, Washington D.C.

Barghouti, S., S. Kane and K. Sorby (2003), "Poverty and Agricultural Diversification in Developing Countries", The World Bank (Memio), Washington, DC, USA.

Bastine, C.L. and K.P. Palanisami (1994), "An Analysis of Growth Trends in Principal Crops in Kerala", *Agricultural Situation in India,* 48(12).

Bhal, S.K. (1997), "Diversification of Indian Agriculture: Issues and Perspectives", *Indian Journal of Economics,* 78(308), pp. 101-111.

Bhalla and Singh (1997), "Recent Development in Indian Agriculture: A State Level Analysis", *Economic and Political Weekly*, March 29.

Bhalla, G.S. and Gurmail Singh (2001), "Indian Agriculture: Four Decades of Development", Sage Publications, New Delhi.

—(2010), "Economic Liberalization and Indian Agriculture: A State-wise Analysis", *Economic and Political Weekly*, Vol. XLIV, No. 52, January.

Bhalla, G.S. (2002), "Globalization and Agricultural Liberalization in India", A Study Sponsored by Ministry of Agriculture, Government of India, CSRD, Jawaharlal Nehru University, New Delhi.

Bhanumurthy, N.R. and Sapna Sinha (2004), "Industrial Recovery: Can It Be Sustained", *Economic and Political Weekly,* Vol. 39, No. 5, January 31-February 6.

Bhat, G.M. and Manzoor Ahmad Wani (2010), "Growth and Diversification of Agriculture in North Eastern India", in Roy, Pashupati Kumar and Shiw Pershan Sharma (eds.), 'Globalization and Diversification in India, Deep and Deep Publications, New Delhi.

Bhatia, J. and S.K. Tewari (1990), "Diversification, Growth and Stability of Agricultural Economy in Uttar Pradesh", *Agricultural Situation in India*, 45(6).

Bhatia, M.S. (1979), "Changing Pattern of Resource Structure and

Demand for Inputs in Indian Agriculture", *Agricultural Situation in India,* 34(7).

Bhide, Shashanka and Ric Shand (2000), "Inequalities in Income Growth in India: Before and After Reforms", *South Asian Economic Journal*, Vol. 1 No. 1, March.

Birthal, P.S., P.K. Joshi and A. Gulati (2005), "Vertical Coordination and High-Value Commodities: Implications for Smallholders", MTID, International Food Policy Research Institute, Washington, D.C.

Birthal, P.S. (2007), "Diversification in Indian Agriculture towards High-Value Crops: The Role of Smallholders", IFPRI Discussion Paper 00727, USA: International Food Policy Research Institute.

Centre for Monitoring Indian Economy (2009), "Report on Agriculture", Economic Intelligent Service, January, Mumbai.

Chadha, G.K. (2004), "State of the Indian Farmer: A Millennium Study", Ministry of Agriculture: Department of Agriculture and Cooperation, Academic Foundation, New Delhi, Vol. 2.

Chadha, G.K. (1993), "Non-farm Employment for Rural Households in India: Evidence and Prognosis", *Indian Journal of Agricultural Economics*, 36(3).

Chadha, G.K. and P.P. Sahu (2002), "Post-reform Setbacks in Employment: Issues that Need Further Scrutiny", *Economic and Political Weekly,* 37(21).

Chadha, R. (1999), "Trade and Balance of Payments", National Council of Applied Economic Research, New Delhi.

Chakraborty, Debashis (2003), "Corporate Participation in Marketing Activities: Scope and Challenges to Indian Agriculture", in Debroy, Bibek and Amir Ullah Khand (eds.), 'Enabling Agricultural Markets for the Small Indian Farmers', Bookwell, New Delhi.

Chand, K.P., R. Singh and M.L. Sharma (1986), "Diversification of Agriculture in Himachal Pradesh: A Spatio-temporal Analysis", *Agricultural Situation in India,* 41(5).

Chand, R. and P.S. Birthal (1997), "Pesticide Use in Indian Agriculture in Relation to Growth in Area and Production and Technological Change", *Indian Journal of Agricultural Economics,* 52(3).

Chand, Raju (1996), "Diversification through High Value Crops in Western Himalayan Region: Evidence from Himachal Pradesh", Seminar Paper, Indian Society of Agricultural Economics, October-December.

Chand, Ramesh, S.S. Raju and L.M. Pandey (2008), "Progress and

Potential of Horticulture in India", *Indian Journal of Agricultural Economics*, Vol. 63, No. 3, July-September.

Chand, Ramesh (1999), "Agriculture Diversification in India: Potentials and Prospects in Developed Region", Mittal Publications, New Delhi.

—(2001), "Emerging Trends and Issues in Public and Private Investments in Indian Agriculture: A State-wise Analysis", *Indian Journal of Agricultural Economics*, April-June, Vol. 56, No. 2.

—(2008), "The State of Indian Agriculture and Prospects for the Future", in Kanchan Chopra and C.H. Hanumantha Rao (eds), Growth, Equity, Environment and Population', Sage Publications, New Delhi.

Chand, Ramesh and S.S. Raju (2008), "Instability in Andhra Pradesh Agriculture: A Disaggregate Analysis", *Agricultural Economics Research Review,* Vol. 21, No. 2, July-December, pp. 283-288.

—(2009), "Instability in Indian Agriculture during Different Phases of Technology and Policy", *Indian Journal of Agricultural Economics,* Vol. 64, No. 2, April-June, pp. 283-288.

Chandrakar, M.R. and A.K. Koshta (1997), "Contribution of Relative Factors in the Growth of Productivity and Production of Crops in Chattisgarh Plains: A Component Analysis", *Indian Journal of Agricultural Economics*, 52(3).

Chaplin, Hannah (2007), "Impediments to the Diversification of Rural Economics in Central and Eastern Europe: Evidence from Small-Scale Farms in Poland", *Regional Studies*, 41(3).

Chengappa, P.A. and Sudha Mysore (2005), "Changing Pattern of Comparative Advantage of Horticultural Crops in India under Post-WTO Regime", SAARC Seminar Paper.

Chengappa, P.G., L. Achoth, A. Mukherjee, B.M. Ramachandra Reddy and P.C. Ravi (2003), "Evolution of Food Retail Chains in India", paper presented in a joint FICCI-ICRISAT-IFPRI International Workshop on Agricultural Diversification and Vertical Integration in South Asia, November 5-6, New Delhi.

Daftari, Irshad (2006), "Contract Farming Lures India Inc Biggies", *Times New Network*, May 8, available at: http://economictimes.indiatimes.com/articleshow/1519650.cms.

Dandekar, V. (1980), "Introduction, Seminar on Data and Methodology for the Study of Growth Rates in Agriculture", *Indian Journal of Agricultural Economics,* 35(2).

Das, Saudamini (2009), "Addressing Coastal Vulnerability at the Village

Level: The Role of Socio-economic and Physical Factors", IEG Working Paper Series No. E/295/2009, Institute of Economic Growth, New Delhi.

De, Utpal K. (2000), "Diversification of Crop in West Bengal: A Spatio-Temporal Analysis", *Artha Vijnana*, XLII(2).

——(2005), "Economics of Crop Diversification: An Analysis of Land Allocation towards Different Crops", *Assam Economic Review*.

Desai, Bhupat and N.V. Namvoodiri (1998), "Determinants of Total Factor Productivity in Indian Agriculture", *Economic and Political Weekly*, Vol. 32.

Desai, M. (1999), "What Should be India's Economic Priorities in a Globalized World?", Indian Council for Research on International Economic Relations, New Delhi.

Deshingkar, P. K., Usha, R. Laxman and R. Srinivas (2003), "Changing Food Systems in India: Resource-Sharing and Marketing Arrangements for Vegetable Production in Andhra Pradesh", *Development Policy Review*, Vol. 21, Nos. 5-6.

Dev, Mahendra, S. (1990), 'Non-Agricultural Employment in Rural India; Evidence at Disaggregate Level", *Economic and Political Weekly*, July 14.

——(1996), "Agricultural Policy Framework for Maharashtra: Issues and Options", Proceeding/Project Report No. 21, July, Indira Gandhi Institute of Development Research, Mumbai.

Deshpandey, R.S., Pradeep Mehta and Khalil Shah (2007), "Crop Diversification and Agricultural Labour in India", *The Indian Journal of Labour Economics*, Vol. 50, No. 4.

Dhanasekaran, K. and R. Srinivasan (2010), "Milk Production: Future Prospects in India", *Kurukshetra,* A Journal of Rural Development, Ministry of Information and Broadcasting (I&B), Government of India, New Delhi, Vol. 58, No. 10, August.

Dholkia, R.H. and Dholkia, B.H. (1993), "Growth of Total Factor Productivity in Indian Agriculture", *Indian Economic Review*, 33(1).

Diwakar, D.M. (2009), "WTO and Myths of Level Playing Gift-Perspective of Food Sovereignty of India", in Rais Ahmad (ed.), 'WTO and Indian Agriculture', Mittal Publications, New Delhi.

Dorjee, K., S. Broca, and P. Pingali (2002), "Diversification in South Asian Agriculture: Trends and Constraints", in International Workshop on Agricultural Diversification in South Asia, MoB-NCAP-IFPRI, Paro.

Dwarkanath, H.D. (2010), "Emerging Agrarian Policies and Programme Implementation", *Kurukshetra,* A Journal of Rural Development, Publication Division, Ministry of I&B, Government of India, New Delhi, Vol. 58, No. 9, July.

Ellis, Frank (1998), "Household Strategies and Rural Livelihood Diversification", *Journal of Development Studies,* 35(1).

Emani, Ashok (1997), "Economic and Ecological Aspects of Land and Water Use Diversification: A Case Study of the Agriculture: Aquaculture Interface in Two Coastal Villages of Andhra Pradesh", Centre for Development Studies, New Delhi.

Escobal, Javier (2001), "Determinants of Non-farm Income Diversification in Rural Peru", *World Development*, 29(3).

Fraser, R.W. (1991), "Production Risk, Product Complementarily and Product Diversification", *Journal of Agricultural Economics*, 43(1).

Gellynck, Xavier (2002), "Market-Oriented Positioning of On-Farm Processed Foods as a Condition for Successful Farm Diversification", *Journal of Agricultural Economics*, 53(3).

Ghose, Rinku (2006), "Growth and Diversification of Agriculture in Eastern States wi'h Special Reference to Bihar", Economic Association of Bihar, March 26-28.

Ghosh, Nilabja (2005), "Trade Liberalization and Diversification in Indian Agriculture", *Foreign Trade Review*, 40(2).

Gill, Kanwaijit Kaur (2001), "Diversification of Agriculture and Women Employment in Punjab", *Indian Journal of Labour Economics,* 44(2).

Government of India (1991), "Census of India, 1991", available at: http://www.censusindia.gov.in.

—(1998), "Agricultural Statistics at a Glance", Directorate of Economics and Statistics, Ministry of Agriculture, Government of India, New Delhi.

—(2001), "Report of the Special Group on Targeting Ten Million Employment Opportunities Per Year", Planning Commission, New Delhi.

—(2001), "Census of India, 2001", available at: http://www.censusindia.gov.in.

—(2008), "Bihar's Agriculture Development: Opportunities and Challenges: A Report of the Special Task Force on Bihar", New Delhi.

—(2001), "Report of the Working Group on Agricultural Development in Eastern and North-Eastern India for the Formulation of the Tenth

Five Year Plan", Planning Commission, August.

—(2005), "Situation Assessment Survey of Farmers: Some Aspects of Farming", NSS 59th Round (January-December), Report No. 496 (59/33/3), Ministry of Statistics and Programme Implementation, New Delhi.

—(2006), CSO, "Report of the Technical Group on Population Projections", Constituted by the National Commission on Population, May, Office of the Registrar General and Census Commissioner, India, New Delhi.

—(2007), "Report of the Steering Committee on Agriculture and Allied Sectors for Formulations of the Eleventh Five Year Plan (2007-12)", Planning Commission, New Delhi.

—(2008), "Bihar's Agriculture Development: Opportunities and Challenges; A Report of the Special Task Force on Bihar", New Delhi, April.

—(2008), "Eleventh Five Year Plan, 2007-12", Planning Commission, New Delhi, Volume III.

—(2008), "Agricultural Statistics at a Glance", Directorate of Economics and Statistics, Ministry of Agriculture, New Delhi.

—(2008), "National Accounts Statistics", Central Statistical Organization, Ministry of Statistics and Programme Implementation, New Delhi.

—(2008), "National Accounts Statistics: Back Series 1950-51 to 1999-2000", Central Statistical Organization, Ministry of Statistics and Programme Implementation, New Delhi.

—(2008), "State Domestic Products", Central Statistical Organization, Ministry of Statistics and Programme Implementation, New Delhi.

—(2009), Central Electricity Authority, New Delhi, available at: www.agricoop.nic.in.

—(2009), "Agricultural Statistics at a Glance", Ministry of Agriculture and Cooperation, New Delhi.

—(2009), "Economic Survey", Ministry of Finance, New Delhi.

—(2009), "Indian Horticulture Database", Ministry of Agriculture, New Delhi.

—(2010), "Planning Commission Annual Report", available at: www.planningcommissionofindia.nic.in.

Government of India (n.d.), "Estimation Loss of Horticulture Produce due to Non-Availability of Post-Harvest and Food Processing Facilities in Bihar and Uttar Pradesh: Socio Economic Research", Planning Commission, ASET, New Delhi.

Government of Bihar (2010), "Bihar Economic Survey", Ministry of Finance, Patna.

Goswami, Padma Sharma and Rabin Jyoti Khataniar (2009), "Irrigation Development in Assam", *Yojana,* Ministry of I&B, Government of India, December.

Goswami, S.N. (2006), "Crop Concentration and Diversification in India: A Spatio-Temporal Analysis", *Geographical Review of India,* 66(1).

Gulati, A. and A.N. Sharma (1995), "Subsidy Syndrome in Indian Agriculture", *Economic and Political Weekly*, September 30.

Gulati, Ashok and Seema Bathla (2001), "Capital Formation in Indian Agriculture", *Economic and Political Weekly,* Vol. 36, No. 20, May 19-25.

Gulati, Ashok and Tim Kelly (1999), "Trade Liberalization and Indian Agriculture", Oxford University Press, New Delhi.

Gupta, B.S. and P.K. Saraswat (1997), "Growth of Rapeseed and Mustard in Western Rajasthan", *Agricultural Situation in India,* 54(5), pp. 261-263.

Gupta, R.P. and S.K. Tewari (1985), "Factors Affecting Crop Diversification: An Empirical Analysis", *Indian Journal of Agricultural Economics,* 40(3).

Haque, T. (1985), "Regional Trends and Patterns of Diversification of the Rural Economy in India", *Indian Journal of Agriculture. Economics,* Vol XL, No. 3, July-September.

——(1995) (ed.), "Small Farm Diversification: Problems and Prospects", NCAP, New Delhi.

Hazra, C.R (2001), "Crop Diversification in Indian", *FAO Paper,* Ministry of Agriculture and Co-operation, New Delhi.

Hegde, B. and R. Pradeep (2002), "End-to-End Integration in Agriculture Sector: A Banking Perspective", paper presented in an International Workshop on Agricultural Diversification in South Asia, Jointly Organized by MoA, Bhutan, NCAP and IFPRI, Paro, Bhutan, November 21-23.

Ilbery, Brian (1996), "Agricultural Adjustment and Business Diversification by Farm Households", *Geography*, 81(353).

Jamal, H. and A. Zaman (1992), "Decomposition of Growth Trend in Agriculture: Another Approach", *Indian Journal of Agricultural Economics,* 47(4).

Jana, B.L. (2006), "Concept of Crop Diversification in Agriculture", Agro-Tech Publishing Academy, Udaipur, Rajasthan.

Jha, B., A. Tripathy and B. Mohanty (2009), "Drivers of Agricultural Diversification in India", IEG Working Paper Series No.E/-/2009, Institute of Economic Growth, New Delhi.

Jha, B. and D. Jha (1995), "Farmers Attitude towards Risk in the Greenbelt of India", *Journal of Rural Development*, 14(3), pp. 231-240.

Jha, B. (1995), "Growth and Instability in Agriculture Associated with New Technology: District Level Evidences" *Agricultural Situation in India,* 49(7).

——(1996), "Farm-level Diversification: Some Disconcerting Evidences from the Green Belt of India", *Agricultural Economics Research Review,* 9(1), pp. 49-56.

——(2000), "Implications of Intensive Agriculture on Soil and Groundwater Resources", *Indian Journal of Agricultural Economics*, 55(2), pp. 182-193.

——(2004), "Towards Measuring Sustainability of Indian Greenbelt", IEG Discussion Paper Series No. 88/2004, Institute of Economic Growth, New Delhi.

——(2006), "Employment Wages and Productivity in Indian Agriculture", IEG Working Paper Series No.E/266/2006, Institute of Economic Growth, New Delhi.

——(2009), "Evaluating Agricultural Policy in a Farming System Framework: A Case Study from North West India", IEG Working Paper Series No.E/299/2009, Institute of Economic Growth, New Delhi.

Jha, Dayanatha (1996), "Report on Diversification of Agriculture and Food Security in the Context of New Economic Policy", *Indian Journal of Agricultural Economics*, 51(4).

——(1997), "Diversification of Agriculture and Food Security in the Context of New Economic Policy", *Indian Journal of Agricultural Economics*, 52(1).

Johnston, B.F. and J.W. Mellor (1961), "The Role of Agriculture in Economic Development", *American Economic Review,* 51(4).

Jorge, A. Quiroz and Alberto Valdes (1995), "Agricultural Diversification and Policy Reform", *Food Policy*, Vol. 20, No. 3.

Joshi P.K., A. Gulati and Ralph Cummings Jr. (eds.) (2007), "Agricultural Diversification and Smallholders in South Asia", Academic Foundation, New Delhi.

Joshi, P.K., M. Asokan, K.K. Datta and P. Kumar (2000), "Socio-Economic Constraints to Legumes Production in Rice-Wheat

Cropping Systems in India", in Johansen, C., J.M. Duxbury, S.M. Virmani, C.L.L Gowda, S. Pande, and P.K. Joshi (eds.), 'Legumes in Rice and Wheat Cropping Systems of the Indo-Gangetic Plain', Patancheru, India, International Crops Research Institute for the Semi-Arid Tropics, and Ithica, New York, USA.

Joshi, P.K., Ashok Gulati, P.S. Birthal and T. Laxmi (2002), "Nature and Speed of Agricultural Diversification in South Asian Countries", Paper Presented at the ICRIER-ICAR-IFPRI Conference on Economic Reforms and Food Security: The Role of Trade and Technology, April 24-25, New Delhi.

Joshi, P.K., A. Gulati, P.S. Birthal, and L. Tiwari (2004), "Agriculture Diversification in South Asia: Pattern Determinants and Policy Implications", *Economic Political Weekly*, June 12.

Joshi, P.K., A. Gulati, P.S. Birthal and P. Parthasarthy Rao (2005), "Agricultural Diversification and Vertical Integration in India: Will Smallholders Participate?", MTID, International Food Policy Research Institute, Washington D.C.

Joshi, P.K., P.S. Birthal, and N. Minto (2006), "Source of Agricultural Growth in India: Role of Diversification towards High Value Crops," MTID Discussion Paper No. 98, International Food Policy Research Institute, Washington D.C.

Joshi, P.K., S.S Acharya, Ramesh Chand and Anjani Kumar (2009), "Agricultural Sector: Status and Performance", in 'State of Indian Agriculture', National Academy of Agricultural Sciences, New Delhi.

Kaul, J.L. and R.K. Sondhi (1971), "Growth of Agriculture in Punjab: An Analysis by Component Elements", *Indian Journal of Agricultural Economics*, 26(6).

Kaushik, K.K. (1993), "Growth and Instability of Oilseeds Production", *Indian Journal of Agricultural Economics,* 48(3).

Khan, Jamal (1996), "Agricultural Diversification Project", *Journal of Rural Development and Administration,* 28(2).

Khare, M.P. (1995), "Impact of the National Pulses Development Programme on Small Cultivators in Maharashtra", Gokhale Institute Mimeograph Series No. 40, Gokhale Institute of Politics and Economics, Pune.

Kijima, Yoko (2005), "Economic Diversification and Poverty in Rural India", *Indian Journal of Labour Economics*, 48(2).

Kumar, P. (2002), "Agricultural Performance and Productivity", in Acharya, S.S. and D.P. Chaudhri (eds.), 'Indian Agricultural Policy at the Crossroads', Rawat Publications, Jaipur.

Kumar, Anjani (2008), "Rural Employment Diversification in Eastern India: Trends and Determinants", Working Paper No. 11, National Centre for Agricultural Economics and Policy Research, New Delhi.

Kumar, Anjani (2009), "Rural Employment Diversification in Eastern India: Trends and Determinants", *Agricultural Economics Research Review,* 22(1).

Kumar, Anjani (2010), "Exports of Livestock Products from India: Performance, Competitiveness and Determinants", *Agricultural Economics Research Review,* 23.

Kumar, Anjani and K. Elumalai (2007), "Agricultural Growth and Productivity in India: An Inter-State Variations", in Papola, T.S. and Alakh N. Sharma (eds.), 'Economic Growth and Regional Balance: Recent Experiences and Implications in India', Institute for Human Development, New Delhi.

Kumar, Ashok (2002), "Profitability, Risk and Diversification in Mountain Agriculture: Some Policy Issues for Slow Growth Crops", *Indian Journal of Agricultural Economics,* 57(3).

Kumar, P. and V.S. Mathur (1996), "Structural Changes in the Demand for Food in India", *Indian Journal of Agricultural Economics,* 51(4).

Kumar, P., P.K. Joshi, C. Johansen and M. Asokan (1998), "Sustainability of Rice-Wheat Based Cropping Systems in India", *Economic and Political Weekly*, September 26.

Kumar, P., L. Mruthyunjaya and P.S. Birthal (2003), "Changing Consumption Pattern in South Asia" Paper Presented at FICCI-ICRISAT-IFPRI International Workshop on Agricultural Diversification and Vertical Integration in South Asia, November 5-6, New Delhi.

Kumar, Praveen (2010), "Food Security: The Challenge Ahead", *Yojana,* A Development Monthly, Ministry of Information and Broadcasting, New Delhi.

Kumari, Mridula and R.C. Choudhary (2008), "An Economic Analysis of MAP Cultivation in Bihar", in Thakur, Anil Kumar and K.B. Padmadeo (eds.), 'Growth and Diversification of Agriculture', Deep and Deep Publications, New Delhi.

Kurulkar, R.P. (1998), "Agricultural Development of Maharashtra State: District Level Estimation of Agriculture Efficiency Index", in S.G. Bhanushali and A.G. Pujari (eds.), 'Changing Perspectives in Indian

Agriculture', Kolhapur.

Lakshmi, K.R. and T.K. Pal (1988), "Growth of Crop Output in Kerala", *Agricultural Situation in India,* 43(9).

Le Coq, Jean-Francois (2005), "Impact of Economic Liberalization on Rice Intensification, Agricultural Diversification and Rural Livelihoods in the Mekong Delta, Vietnam", *Southeast Asian Studies*, 42(4).

Swaminathan, M.S. (2004), "Atlas of the Sustainability of Food Security in India", National Food Security Summit, February 5.

Madhuri, S. and YV. Ramanaiah (2007), "Land Use Intensification and Diversification for Sustainable Agriculture: A Case Study of Rayalseema Region, Andhra Pradesh, India", *Indian Journal of Regional Science,* XXXIX(1).

Mahadevan, R. and K.P. Kalirajan (1999), "On Measuring Total Factor Productivity Growth in Singapore's Manufacturing Industries", *Applied Economics Letters*, Vol. 6.

Mellor, J.W. (2004), "Agricultural Growth and Poverty Reduction: The Rapid Increasing Role of Smallholder Livestock", in V. Ahuja (ed.), 'Livestock and Livelihoods: Challenges and Opportunities for Asia in the Emerging Market Environment', NDDB, Anand, India and FAO, Rome, Italy.

Mishra, Chaturanan (2007), "Diversion of Crops and Small Farmers", *Mainstream*, 45(22).

Miyata, Sachiko (2007), "Impact of Contact Farming on Income", IFPRI Discussion Paper 00742, International Food Policy Research Institute, USA.

Mohanty, B.K. (2010), "Agriculture Growth: It is Time for Gene Revolution", *Kurukshetra,* A Journal of Rural Development, Publication Division, Ministry of I&B, Government of India, New Delhi, Vol. 58, No. 9, July.

Mujumdar, N.A. (2002). "Rural Development: New Perceptions", *Economic and Political Weekly*, Vol. 37, No. 39, September 28.

Mukhopadhyay, Abhiroop and Indira Rajaraman (2007), "Rural Unemployment 1999-2005: Who Gained, Who Lost?", *Economic and Political Weekly,* 42(30).

Mundinamani, S.M., K.N.R. Sastry and T.N.V. Murthy (1995), "Growth Performance of Oilseeds in Karnataka", *Agricultural Situation in India*, 50(7).

Narain, Dharm (1965), "Impact of Price Movements on Areas under Selected Crops in India: 1900-1939", Cambridge University Press,

New Delhi.

Narayanamoorthy, A. (2007), "Deceleration in Agricultural Growth: Technology Fatigue and Policy Fatigue?", *Economic Political Weekly*, Vol XLII, No. 25, June 23-29.

Narender, I., G.M. Swamy and P.B. Parthasarathy (1989), "District-wise Measurement and Decomposition of the Growth of Agricultural Output in Andhra Pradesh", *Agricultural Situation in India,* 44(1).

Negi, J.P. (2002), "Horticulture development in India: An Aids to Rural Economy", in Souvenir, 62nd Annual conference of Indian Society of Agriculture Economics, December 19-21, IARI, New Delhi.

Pandey, V.K. and K.C. Sharma (1996), "Crop Diversification and Self-Sufficiency in Foodgrains", *Indian Journal of Agricultural Economics*, 51(4).

Pandya, H.R. (1998), "Diversification of Agriculture in Gujarat: A Spatio-Temporal Analysis", *Indian Journal of Agricultural Economics*, 53(4).

Patel, Amrit (2010), "Strengthening Rural Banking Infrastructure" *Kurukshetra,* A Journal of Rural Development, Publication Division, Ministry of I&B, Government of India, New Delhi, Vol. 58, No. 6, April.

Patnaik, Gokul (2003), "Marketing, Storage, and Extension Services: State of Agriculture in India", in Debroy, Bibek and Amir Ullah Khan, (eds.), 'Enabling Agricultural Markets for the Small Indian Farmer', Bookwell, New Delhi.

Pingali, P.L. and M.W. Rosegrant (1995), "Agricultural Commercialization and Diversification: Processes and Policies", *Food Policy,* 20(3).

Pokam, Jacques (2002), "Economic Crisis and Forest Cover Change in Cameroon: The Roles of Migration, Crop Diversification, and Gender Division of Labour", *Economic Development and Cultural Change*, 50(3).

Ponnusamy, K. and Jancy Gupta (2005), "Village Development through Crop Diversification in a Peri Urban Setting", *IASSI Quarterly,* 23(4), pp. 58-65.

Prasad, Anajali (2008), "Pattern of Agricultural Diversification and Vegetable Production in Bihar", in Thakur, Anil Kumar and K.B. Padmadeo (eds.), 'Agriculture Diversification in India', Deep and Deep Publications, New Delhi.

Punam, A. (2008), "Growth and Diversification of Agriculture in Eastern India", in Thakur, Anil Kumar and K.B. Padmadeo (eds.),

'Growth and Diversification of Agriculture', Deep and Deep Publications, New Delhi.

Radhakrishna, K. and C. Ravi (1990), "Food Demand Projections for India", Centre for Economic and Social Studies, Hyderabad.

Raju, V.T. and V.S. Darsi Rao (1988), "Agricultural Growth and Instability in Andhra Pradesh", *Agricultural Situation in India,* 43(2).

Ranade, C.G. (1980), "Impact of Cropping Pattern on Agricultural Production", *Indian Journal of Agricultural Economics,* 35(2).

Rani, Sanjeeta (2010), "Agriculture Diversification in Bihar", in Roy, Pashupati Kumar and Shiw Pershan Sharma (eds.), 'Globalization and Diversification in India', Deep and Deep Publications, New Delhi.

Rao, C. H. Hanumantha (2005), "Agriculture, Food Security, Poverty and Environment", Oxford University Press, New Delhi.

Rao, K. Srinivasa and K. Chandra Sekhar (2010) "Rural Infrastructure: A Vital Ingredient for Double Digit Growth", *Kurukshetra,* A Journal of Rural Development, Ministry of I&B, Government of India, New Delhi, Vol. 58, No. 10, August.

Rao, Parthasarthy P. (2006), "Diversification towards High Value Agriculture: Role of Urbanization and Infrastructure", *Economic and Political Weekly*, 41(26).

Ravallion, M. and G. Data (1996), "How Important to India's Poor is the Sectoral Composition of Growth in India", *World Bank Economic Review*, Vol. 10.

Ray, P.K. (2009), "Horticulture Production and Research in Bihar", *Jai Bihar*, Patna, available at:
http://jaibihar.com/horticultural-production-and-research-in-bihar/2212.

Reserve Bank of India (2001), "Indian Agriculture and Reform: Concerns, Issues and Agenda", *RBI Bulletin,* May, New Delhi.

Rizvi, Halima Sadia (2010), "Agricultural Diversification in Eastern Region of India: Problems and Prospects", in Roy, Pashupati, Kumar and Shiv Pershan Sharma (eds.), 'Globalization and Agricultural Diversification of India', Deep & Deep Publications, New Delhi.

Rola, A.C. and Pingali, P.L. (1993), "Pesticides, Rice Productivity, and Farmers' Health: An Economic Assessment", International Rice Research Institute, Washington, USA.

Ryan, J.G. and D.C. Spencer (2001), "Future Challenges and

Opportunities for Agricultural R&D in the Semi-Arid Tropics", Patancheru 502 324, International Crops Research Institute for the Semi-Arid Tropics, Andhra Pradesh, India.

Sah, D.C. (2006), "Shocks, Livelihood and Debt-Trap: Credit and Indebtedness in South-western Tribal Madhya Pradesh", *Madhya Pradesh Journal of Social Sciences*, 11(2).

Saleth, R. Maria (1997), "Diversification Strategy for Small Farmers and Landless: Some Evidence from Tamil Nadu", *Indian Journal of Agricultural Economics*, 52(1).

Salve, W.N. (2008), "Crop Diversification and Food Security in Hilly Tribal Areas of Eastern India", in Thakur, Anil Kumar and K.B. Padmadeo (eds.), 'Growth and Diversification of Agriculture', Deep and Deep Publications, New Delhi.

Satyasai, K.J.S. and K.U. Viswanathan (1999), "Dynamics of Agriculture-Industry Linkages", *Indian Journal of Agricultural Economics*, Vol. 54, No. 3.

Sau, Sachinandan and Sarat Pathak (2007), "Diversification of Agriculture: Rationale and Determinants: A Study with Special Reference to West Bengal", *Indian Journal of Regional Science,* XXXIX(1).

Sawant S.D., B.N. Kulkarni, C.V. Achuthan and K.J.S. Satyasai (1999), "Agricultural Development in Maharashtra: Problems and Prospects", Occasional Paper No. 7, National Bank for Agricultural and Rural Development, Mumbai.

Schumacher, Jr. A. (2000), "International Agricultural Trade at a Crossroads", *Economic Perspectives, An Electronic Journal of the US Department of State,* March.

Sen, Abhijit and M.S. Bhatia (2004), "State of the Indian Farmer: A Millennium Study", Ministry of Agriculture, Department of Agriculture and Cooperation, Academic Foundation, New Delhi, Vol. 14.

Sen, Sucharita and Raju Saraswati (2006), "Globalisation and Expanding Markets For Cut-Flowers: Who Benefits?", *Economic and Political Weekly*, 41(26),pp. 2725-2730.

Shah, Tushar, Avinash Kishore and P. Hemant (2009), "Will the Impact of the 2009 Drought be Different from 2002", *Economic and Political Weekly*, Vol. 44, No. 37.

Shand, R. (1997), "The Agriculture Manufacturing Nexus and Sequencing in India's Reform Process", Discussion Paper No. 4, Australia-South Asia Research Centre, Australian National

University.

Shand, Ric and S. Bhide (2000), "Sources of Growth in the Indian Economy before and With Reforms", *South Asia*, Vol. XX"I, Special Issue.

Sharma, H.R. (2005), "Agricultural Development and Crop Diversification in Himachal Pradesh: Understanding the Patterns, Process, Determinants and Lessons", *Indian Journal of Agricultural Economics*, 60(1).

Shenngen Fan, Peter Hazell and T. Haque (1999) "Impact of Public Investments in Agricultural Research and Infrastructure on Growth and Poverty Reduction in Rural India", Discussion Paper IFPRI, Washington D.C.

Shivay, Yashbir Singh and Anshu Rahul (2010), "Increasing Agricultural Production in India", *Kurukshetra,* A Journal of Rural Development, Publication Division, Ministry of I&B, Government of India, New Delhi, Vol. 58, No. 9, July.

Shiyani R.L. and H.R. Pandya (1998), "Diversification of Agriculture in Gujarat: A Spatiotemporal Analysis" *Indian Journal of Agricultural Economics*, 53(4).

Shiyani, R.L. and H.R. Pandya (1998), "Diversification of Agriculture in Gujarat: A Spatio-temporal Analysis", *Indian Journal of Agricultural Economics*, 53(4).

Sidhu, H.S. (2002), 'Crisis in Agrarian Economy in Punjab: Some Urgent Steps", *Economic and Political Weekly*, Vol. 37, (30), July 27.

Sidhu, M.S. (2008), "Diversification of Agriculture in East India-Some Issues", in Thakur, Anil Kumar and K. B. Padmadeo (eds.), 'Growth and Diversification of Agriculture', Deep and Deep Publications, New Delhi.

Sidhu, R.S. (2004), "Factors in Declining Crop Diversification: Case Study of Punjab", *Economic and Political Weekly*, 39(52).

Siju, T. and S. Kombairaju (2001), "Rice Production in Tamil Nadu: A Trend and Decomposition Analysis", *Agricultural Situation in India*, 58(4).

Sikka, B.K. and C.S. Vaidya (1985), "Growth Rates and Cropping Pattern Changes in Agriculture in Himachal Pradesh", *Agricultural Situation in India*, 39(11).

Singh, S.P. (2006), "Diversification of Rural Economy of Uttar Pradesh: Determinants, Regional, Social and Gender Concerns", in R.R. Prasad and G. Rajanikanth (eds.), 'Rural Development and Social

Change', Foundation Day Series, NIRD, Hyderabad, Discovery Publishing House, New Delhi, Volume I.

——(2006), "Rural Non-Farm Employment in Uttar Pradesh: Determinants, Dimensions and Regional Pattern", *Indian Journal of Labour Economics*, Vol. 49(4).

——(2005), "Agriculture, in Disequalising Growth: Alternative Economic Survey", India Rainbow Publishers New Delhi.

Singh, S.P and Bimal Kishore Sahoo (2007), "Diversification of Agricultural Economy toward Horticulture Livestock: Regional Variations, Convergence, and Determinants", *The Indian Journal of Labour Economics,* A Quarterly Journal of the Indian Society of Labour Economics.

Singh, Sukhpal (2004), "Crisis and Diversification in Punjab Agriculture: Role of State and Agribusiness", *Economic and Political Weekly*, 39(52).

——(2001), "Labour under Contract Farming in India: Issues of Gender and Child Labour", *Indian Journal of Labour Economics*, 44(4).

——(2000), "Contract Farming for Agricultural Diversification in the Indian Punjab: A Study of Performance and Problems", *Indian Journal of Agricultural Economics*, 55(3).

——(2004), "Crisis and Diversification in Punjab Agriculture: Role of State and Agribusiness; *Economic and Political Weekly*, Vol. 39, (52), December 25.

Singh, A.J., K.K. Jain and Inder Sain (1985), "Diversification of Punjab Agriculture: An Econometric Analysis", *Indian Journal of Agricultural Economics,* Vol. XL, No. 3.

Singh, A.K., R. Singh, and Balishter (1991), "Impact of Bank Finance on Cropping Pattern and Income on Small Farms: A Comparative Study", *Indian Co-operative Review*, Vol. 28, No. 4.

Singh, Ajit Kumar (2003), "Change Workforce Structure in India, 1981-2001: An Interstate Study", *The Indian Journal of Labour Economics,* Vol. 46, No. 4, Manohar Publishers and Distributors, New Delhi.

Singh, Bikrama (2008), "Agricultural Diversification: A Key to the Development of Agri-Business in East India", in Thakur, Anil Kumar and K. B. Padmadeo (eds.), 'Growth and Diversification of Agriculture', Deep and Deep Publications, New Delhi.

Singh, Joginder and R.S. Sidhu (2004), "Factors in Declining Crop Diversification: Case Study of Punjab", *Economic and Political Weekly*, Vol. 39, (52), December 26.

Singh, L. and S. Singh (2002), "Deceleration in Economic Growth in Punjab: Evidence, Explanation and a Way Out", *Economic and Political Weekly*, Vol. 37, (6), February 9.

Singh, Mahesh Pratap (2005), "Shifting Pattern of Agriculture Space: Evolution of Contract Farming in Punjab", *Social Change*, 35(4).

Singh, R.P. and Seema Bodra (2008), "Economic Analysis of Crop Diversification: A Comparative Study of Foodgrains and Vegetable Crops", *Indian Journal of Agriculture Economics*, Vol. 63, No. 3, July-September.

—(2004), "Agriculture, in Magnifying Mal-development: Alternative Economic Survey", India Rainbow Publishers, New Delhi and Zed Books Ltd., London.

—(2007), "Corporatization of Agriculture, Alternative Economic Survey, India, 2006-07: Pampering Corporates, Pauperizing Masses", Daanish Books, New Delhi.

Sivakumar, S.D., R. Balasubramaniam and N. Srinivasan (1999), "Growth Linkage Effects of Agro-Industrialization", Indian *Journal of Agricultural Economics*, Vol. 54, No. 3.

Srinivasan, G. (2010), "Need for Rural Infrastructure Development", *Kurukshetra*, A Journal of Rural Development, Ministry of I&B, Government of India, Vol. 58, August 10.

Tewari, L, Elumalai, K. Birthal, S. Pratap and P.K. Joshi (2001), "Implications of Globalization on Small Farm Holders: A SWOT Analysis" in the Annual Conference of the Agricultural Economics Research Association, November 21-22, Indian Agricultural Research Institute, New Delhi.

Thakur, D.S, M. Kapila and T.V. Moorti (1985), "Vegetable Production for Diversification of Farm Economy", *Indian Journal of Agricultural Economics,* Vol. XL, No. 3.

Thakur, N.K. (2006), "Growth and Diversification of Agriculture in Eastern India", National Seminar, Indian Economic Association of Bihar, March 26-28.

Tripathy, K.K. (2010), "Budget 2010-11 and Inclusive Growth: A Feel Good Factor for Rural India?", *Kurukshetra,* A Journal of Rural Development, Publication Division, Ministry of I&B, Government. of India, New Delhi, Vol. 58, No. 6, April.

Unni, Jeemol (1996), "Diversification of Economic Activities and Non-Agricultural Employment in Rural Gujarat", *Economic and Political Weekly*, 31(33).

Unni, Jeemol (1991), "Regional Variation in Rural Non-Agricultural

Employment: An Explanatory Analysis", *Economic and Political Weekly*, January 19.

Vidyanathan, A. (1986), "Labour Use in Rural India: A Case Study of Spatial and Temporal Variation", *Economic and Political Weekly*, December 27.

Visaria, P. (1995), "Rural Non-farm Employment in India: Trends and Issues for Research", *Indian Journal of Agricultural Economics*, 50(3).

Vyas, V.S. (1996), "Diversification in Agriculture: Concept, Rationale and Approaches", *Indian Journal of Agricultural Economics*, 51(4).

Walker, T.S., R.P. Singh and N. S. Jodha (1983). "Dimensions of Farm Level Diversification in the Semi-arid Tropics of Rural South India." Economic Programme Progress Report 51, ICRISAT, Hyderabad.

Warr, P.G. (2003), "Poverty and Economic Growth in India", in Kalirajann, K. and U. Sankar (eds), 'Economic Reforms and Liberalization of the Indian Economy', Edward Elgar, Cheltenham, UK and Northampton, MA, USA.

Weinberger, K. and A.T. Lumpkin (2007), "Diversification into Horticulture and Poverty Reduction: A Research Agenda, "*World Development*, Vol. 35, No. 8.

Yadav, Krishan. K. (2010), "Road Connectivity as a Stimulant for Rural Poverty Reduction", *Kurukshetra,* A Journal of Rural Development, Ministry of I&B, Government of India, Vol. 58, No. 10, August.

Yadav, R.K., D.S. Yadav, N. Rai and K.K. Patel (2003), "Prospects of Horticulture in North-Eastern Region", Division of Horticulture, ICAR, Research Complex for North East Region, Umroi Road, Umiam, Meghalaya.

Yao, Shujie (1997), "Comparative Advantages and Crop Diversification: A Policy Analysis Matrix for Thai Agriculture", *Journal of Agricultural Economics*, 48(2).

Yugandhar, B.N. and K.Gopal Iyer (eds.) (1993), "Land Reforms in India, Bihar: Institutional Constraints", Vol.1, Sage Publications, New Delhi.

Zohir, Sajjad (1993), "Problems and Prospects of Crop Diversification in Bangladesh", *Bangladesh Development Studies*, XXI(3).

Index

Index